Nicole Wilde, CPDT

Help for Your
Fearful Dog

**A Step-by-Step Guide
to Helping Your Dog
Conquer His Fears**

Phantom

Publishing

Help for Your Fearful Dog: A Step-by-Step Guide
to Helping Your Dog Conquer His Fears
by Nicole Wilde, CPDT

Copyright © 2006 by Nicole Wilde

Published by:
Phantom Publishing
P.O. Box 2814
Santa Clarita, CA 91386
www.phantompub.com

First Edition

Library of Congress Control Number: 2006902373

ISBN 0-9667726-7-9

Illustrations pp. 174, 194, 343, 361, and 366 by C.C. Wilde.

Photo credits:
p. 21 (photo 2) Lisa Harness
p. 22 (photo 3) Katie Hiett
p. 23 (photo 1) Katie Hiett
p. 23 (photo 2) Gerd Kohler
p. 25 Monty Sloan
p. 27 (photo 2) Mitzi Mandel
p. 81 C.C. Wilde
p. 87 courtesy of Premier Pet Products
p. 88 (photo 2) courtesy of Halti

p. 108 Brian Stemmler, Brian Stemmler
     Photography
p. 145 C.C. Wilde
p. 147 Laura Bourhenne
p. 307 C.C. Wilde
p. 364 Mychelle Blake
p. 367 #2 courtesy of Susan Sharpe

Cover design, cover photo, and photos pp. 19, 21 (photo 2), 22 (photos 1 & 2), 27
(photo 1), 28, 62, 64, 88 (photo 1), 90, 112, 113, 120, 122-124, 131, 132, 137, 147,
228, 229, 236, 237, 239, 242, 261, 294-296, 299-302, 306, 309, 323, and 367 #1 by
the author.

For Soko

1993-2006

Other books by Nicole Wilde:

Living with Wolfdogs

Wolfdogs A-Z: Behavior, Training & More

So You Want to be a Dog Trainer

It's Not the Dogs, It's the People! A Dog Trainer's Guide to Training Humans (available in book or audio CD)

One on One: A Dog Trainer's Guide to Private Lessons

Getting a Grip on Aggression Cases

Energy Healing for Dogs

Don't Leave Me! Step-by-Step Help for Your Dog's Separation Anxiety

Acknowledgements

I would like to thank:

Mychelle Blake for review, tech support, and more. I owe you margaritas!

Paul Owens for manuscript review, and for continuing to show the world what can be accomplished through peaceful, non-violent training methods.

James O'Heare for patiently answering my questions.

Cheryl Kolus for sharing copies of the DAP studies.

My editor, Leslie "Glinda the Good" Bockian. Your skill and dedication made this manuscript sparkle. Your patience, enthusiasm for the project, sense of humor, and friendship mean more than I can say.

Laura Bourhenne for reviewing the manuscript and for patiently playing Protocol Model. Your training skills made the shoots a breeze. Thanks too to Cliff and the fabulous four-footed Bourhennes for modeling.

Ian Dunbar, as always. Thanks for your ongoing support and for bringing positive training methods to the masses. Without you this book would not have been possible.

Christine Lee for technical support and being so generous with your time.

Lynne Gifford for the photo session with cover boy Maestro (a.k.a. "Foo").

My wonderful, talented husband, C.C., for the illustrations and for all the things I could never hope to put into words. You're the best.

All the dogs and wolves who have taught me so much over the years: the shelter dogs, rescues, clients' dogs, and my own four-footed family.

Most of all, my smart, sweet, fearful girl Soko who passed during the writing of this book. You taught me so much, and I know you are finally at peace and chasing balls over the Rainbow Bridge.

Table of Contents

Part III: Skills

Part IV: Modifying Fearful Behavior

Part V: Treatment of Specific Fears

Part VI: Complementary Therapies

Introduction

Buffy, a five-year-old Cocker Spaniel, is the apple of her owner's eye. The two live in a home with a large back yard in a lovely suburban community, where Buffy enjoys playing with the neighborhood dogs and children. Life is one big pooch paradise—except for Thursday afternoons, when the garbage is collected. As soon as Buffy hears the far-off rumble of the truck, she dives for cover and begins to tremble uncontrollably. Nothing—not even her favorite chew toy—can coax her from beneath the bed. Her owner feels sorry for Buffy, and wishes she could explain that the garbage truck is nothing to fear.

Murphy is a typical two-year-old Golden Retriever. He exudes good cheer, and seems to be perpetually thinking *the sky is blue, the birds are singing—life is good!* Murphy loves to go just about anywhere: the park, training class, the pet supply store. Anywhere, that is, except the veterinarian's office. Once inside the clinic doors Murphy does a reverse Superman, transforming from a confident bundle of energy into an anxious bundle of nerves. Although his owner strokes him gently and tells him that everything will be okay, Murphy is not convinced.

The young, professional couple who own Max, an eighteen-month-old terrier mix, laughingly refer to him as their "only child." Max has never been around children, except for those he encounters on daily walks through his urban neighborhood. Kids make Max nervous. As a puppy, he would cringe and hide behind his owners' legs whenever a child tried to pet him. Once he entered adolescence and gained a bit of confidence, Max began to growl at children to stay away—and it worked. Max's owners are worried, as his transition into adulthood seems to be accompanied by a transition into aggressive behavior toward children.

These stories are not unusual. Dogs of every breed, size, gender, and background can have fear issues. Some dogs fear specific sounds, such as thunder; some are anxious about being touched or groomed; and some are afraid to ride in cars. Some dogs fear being left alone, while others would prefer that strangers leave them alone, thank you very much! And although some dogs appear to be reactive or aggressive toward unfamiliar people or dogs, in the majority of cases the behavior is actually fear-based.

As the owner of a fearful dog, you know how terribly frustrating it can be to watch your dog suffer, without knowing how to help. But take heart. You are about to gain valuable skills that will help you address your dog's fears. You will learn about the causes of fearful behavior, how to identify what triggers your dog's fears, how to recognize even the subtlest signs of stress in your dog, how *your* attitude and behavior can influence your dog's reactions, and how to apply behavior modification programs that really work. You will discover complementary therapies that can be used in conjunction with behavior modification to improve your results even further, and will learn when to call on the assistance of a professional. In short, you will understand how to handle the challenges of living with a fearful dog.

Although I am a Certified Professional Dog Trainer and behavior specialist, my background involves extensive work with wolves and wolfdogs (also known as wolf hybrids). I served for many years as executive director of a rescue center for those amazing canines, almost all of whom began their lives as somebody's pet. For obvious reasons, pure wolves and part-wolves do not make stellar pets, and the thirty who lived at the rescue center were destined to be permanent residents. A few of the "doggier" ones were social and outgoing. The majority, however, were extremely shy and afraid of people. It was my job and my privilege to spend time daily with those sensitive, fascinating creatures. My greatest reward was watching them learn to relax and trust people so that their stay at the center could be more comfortable.

I am also a "dog mom." Soko, my thirteen-year-old German Shepherd, has been with me since the age of seven weeks. Over the years, she has displayed a canine cornucopia of fear-related issues. Some are probably at least partially genetic, while others were acquired through experience. Soko's temperament is what many would describe as fearful, skittish, and even neurotic. Through the years we have worked hand-in-paw to overcome many of her issues. As a result, Soko has been able to enjoy a quality life with me, my husband, and Mojo, our other fur-child. Soko has been an excellent teacher. As you might have guessed, helping dogs to overcome their fears is a subject that is close to my heart.

Living with Soko, spending time with the wolves, and helping my clients' fearful dogs has given me a unique perspective and a wealth of experience on which to base the advice you will find in these pages. The concepts, techniques, and protocols can be applied to most fear-related issues. The most common fears—fear of unfamiliar dogs or unfamiliar people—are explored in depth. You will also find chapters on how to address specific fears such as those of thunderstorms, stairs, objects, being brushed, riding in the car, visiting the veterinarian's office, and even fear of one specific family member.

The book is set up so that you can read it from cover to cover or flip directly to the section that applies to your dog. Regardless of your dog's particular issues, I suggest a thorough initial reading so as not to miss any salient points.

Above all, be patient with your dog. Changing the underlying emotions associated with fearful behavior takes time. Although not all dogs will be able to conquer their fears completely, be assured that regardless of the cause, you *will* be able to make a difference and help your dog to feel more confident and relaxed. And in most cases, you will be able to help your dog overcome his fears altogether.

Fear Factors

A Word Before we Get Started...*Aggression*

This book is aimed at helping dogs who exhibit fearful behavior, including that which manifests as mild to moderate aggression. It is helpful to understand how fearful behavior, if left untreated, can evolve into fear-based aggression. And it is important to be aware of the potential consequences should your dog bite another dog or person, whether the aggression was fear-based or not.

Karen Overall, a well-known behaviorist, defines fear as "a feeling of apprehension associated with the presence or proximity of an object, individual, social situation, or class of the above."[1] How do dogs respond to feelings of apprehension? A puppy, when presented with someone or something she perceives as frightening, is more likely to run and hide than to stand her ground and fight. But as pups approach adolescence at approximately six to eight months of age, hormonal changes occur and confidence begins to grow. Just as human teenagers tend to test social boundaries and challenge authority, an adolescent dog who previously cowered at the approach of a stranger might now stand her ground and issue a warning growl.

True aggression carries the intent to cause harm; the action is offensive rather than defensive. For example, a dog who truly means to cause injury will lunge directly at a person without hesitation. A fearful dog, on the other hand, is more likely to stand at a distance, barking as if to convey, *Stay away from me, you big scary thing. Don't make me come over there!* What the fearful dog really wants is to increase the distance between herself and the person who is scaring her. And it works! The person moves away. Each time the dog's actions achieve this gratifying result, the perception that barking is effective is reinforced.

Canine confidence continues to increase through adolescence into early adulthood. By the time a dog reaches full adulthood at two to three years of age, multiple experiences may have reinforced the perception that "aggressive" displays work. The dog's progressively more intense repertoire may now include air-snapping (biting at the air without making contact with the subject), snarling, lunging, or even biting.

If you are not sure whether your dog's behavior is motivated by fear or by true aggression, if she has become progressively more reactive with other dogs or people, or if she has already bitten a person or dog, engage the services of a professional canine behavior specialist immediately. (See *Chapter 12* for recommendations on how to locate a qualified professional.) The sooner you intervene, the better your chances of modifying the behavior before it escalates further. If your dog injures another dog or person, there can be serious repercussions. You could be sued, lose your home, lose your homeowner's insurance—and your dog could be confiscated and euthanized.

This is not meant to suggest that every fearful dog will become aggressive. On the contrary, many fearful dogs never act in an aggressive manner unless they are forced to defend themselves. Regardless, it is commendable that you are addressing your dog's fear issues as early and as thoroughly as possible. And kudos to you for having the compassion to help your dog live a happier, more relaxed life.

1   Overall, Karen. *Clinical Behavioral Medicine for Small Animals.* Missouri: Mosby 1997

Anxieties, Fears and Phobias

Anxieties, fears and phobias are all part of a continuum referred to as "fear." Anxiety characterizes the low end of the spectrum. Next come mild, moderate, and then intense fears, and finally, at the far end, full-blown phobias. While the general term "fear issues" is used throughout this book, it is important to understand the distinction between the three.

Anxiety is a feeling of apprehension, an anticipation of future danger—in other words, a concern that something bad might happen. A dog may experience anxiety for no apparent reason; or, it may occur in specific situations only. Some dogs, for example, are anxious in new environments or when meeting unfamiliar dogs or people. Anxiety in unfamiliar situations can sometimes be traced to a lack of early socialization, although the cause is not always so obvious.

Unfortunately, anxiety is often the product of past unpleasant experiences. A dog who has been attacked by another dog might feel anxious on walks, and vigilantly scan the streets ahead, muscles tensed, anticipating the appearance of another dog. A dog who has been summoned by his owner in an unpleasant tone of voice and then been harshly reprimanded is likely to feel anxious whenever he hears his owner use that tone.

Anxiety differs from fear in that it is not dependent on the presence of a specific fear-inducing thing or person. Anxiety deals with what *could* happen, not what *is* happening at the time. Words such as *nervous* or *apprehensive* may be used in place of "anxious." Treatment for anxious dogs includes teaching relaxation skills, providing strong leadership and a stable home environment, and teaching behaviors that build confidence.

Fear is a feeling of apprehension as well, but the emotion is associated with the actual presence of something or someone that frightens the dog. Dogs may fear people, other dogs, objects, sounds, motions, or even specific environments. Fear and avoidance are instinctive responses in certain situations. For example, dogs naturally fear fire, and will flee in the face of a blaze. Dogs and other animals fear that which is unknown or unfamiliar—an instinct designed to keep them safe.

While some fear reactions are instinctive, others are learned. The good news is that if a fear has been learned, there is a good chance it can be unlearned. Let's say your dog has come to fear the nail clippers because he had an unpleasant nail-trimming experience. By exposing him to the clippers in a gradual manner and pairing them with something pleasant (for example, super-yummy treats), you could help your dog to overcome his fear. (Fear of nail-clipping is discussed in detail in *Chapter 38*.)

Phobias are profound fear reactions that are out of proportion to the actual threat. A dog who is thunder-phobic, for example, will panic at the sound and may flee blindly, unable to think clearly, crashing into anything in his path. A dog who is phobic about being left alone may become extremely destructive, or if left in a small, confined area such as a crate, thrash about wildly and even mutilate himself. Whereas fears tend to develop gradually, phobias are sudden and intense from the start and require only one exposure to induce the full-blown reaction.

Phobias do not improve with gradual repeated exposures to the cause of the fear in the way that some common fear issues can. Management— making sure the dog does not get exposed to whatever sends him into a panic—is the first line of defense. In some cases phobias can be addressed with behavior modification and management, often in conjunction with complementary therapies that may include pharmacological intervention. In other cases behavior modification is not possible, and management and short-term medication are the appropriate solutions.

Causes and Prevention

A woman takes two dogs to an off-leash dog park. The first one—a veritable social butterfly—races from dog to dog and person to person, tail wagging, inviting play and affection. The second dog remains close to the woman, reluctant to make contact with anyone, human or canine. The dog's body language broadcasts anxiety.

Why would two dogs in the identical situation react in completely different ways? It is possible that the second dog lacked early socialization, while the first had been introduced to many new people, dogs, and places as a young pup. Or perhaps the second dog was genetically predisposed to being afraid in new situations, while the first was not. It can be difficult to determine the root cause of a dog's fear, especially if the dog was adopted as an adult and her previous history is unknown. But regardless of what your dog fears, the cause will fall into one, and possibly more than one, of the following six categories:

1. Genetics. Just like people, dogs are born with a genetic blueprint. Genetic predisposition to specific traits is what allows breeders to "breed for temperament"—to select the aspects of personality they want to be prevalent in their lines. As canine behavior consultant and author Steven R. Lindsay states, "Emotional stressors affecting the mother during gestation, together with excessively stressful postnatal conditions, may exert a lifelong detrimental influence on the way dogs cope with fear- and anger-provoking situations" and "Together, heredity and adverse prenatal and postnatal stressors may destine many young dogs to express reactive traits and tendencies before they open their eyes..."[1] In other words, breeders can have an effect on the pups' temperaments via careful management of the dam's environment and attention to her stress levels.

Of course, we cannot tell by observing a dog exactly what percentage of her behavior is due to genetics versus learning and experience. Spending time with a pup's sire and dam can offer insight into the pup's temperament. If one or both of the parents seem "skittish" or wary, chances are good that if the pup has the same type of temperament, the fear issues are at least partially genetic.

A pup who is genetically predisposed to being fearful may hold her body stiffly when being picked up or held, and is likely to be cautious around new people, animals, and situations. Some genetically fearful pups seem to be constantly anxious, just waiting for something scary to happen. These "globally fearful" pups startle at almost any sudden sound, touch, or motion, and their primary reaction toward anything unfamiliar is fear. Trainers sometimes refer to this type of overly reactive temperament as "skittish" or "spooky."

One segment of the traditional temperament test for puppies is to drop a ring of keys on the ground. The desired reaction is for the pup to startle but then quickly recover. A genetically fearful pup will flinch or cower, but rather than making a fast recovery, might instead run away, hide, or experience an extended period of anxiety. This tendency toward slow startle recovery will be evident in the dog's everyday interactions. While a pup with a stable temperament might cock her head inquisitively at the sound of thunder, a genetically fearful pup is more likely to dash to the nearest corner, lie down, and shake uncontrollably.

> Clinical and early laboratory tests suggest that some dogs are genetically more likely than others to develop noise phobias, and that they have an auditory sensitivity to particular sounds. However, this genetic tendency might not be apparent at birth. In fact, according to a 1991 study, the fear of particular sounds normally appears after the age of one year.[2]

Breed is another aspect of genetics that can contribute to a dog's temperament. Golden Retrievers, for example, are normally calm and relaxed around new dogs, people, and experiences. Some breeds—Chihuahuas, for example—are more predisposed to having a generally nervous or fearful disposition. While the Retriever is saying, "Come on in, let me take your coat, have a cup of coffee!" the Chihuahua barks (from her vantage point high in her owner's arms), "Who are you? What are you doing here? When are you leaving?" (Of course, not all Chihuahuas are this way, any more than all Golden Retrievers are friendly. A litter of pups of any breed will contain a spectrum of individual temperaments ranging from shy to confident, gregarious to aggressive.) An unfortunate example of the genetic damage that can be done by over-breeding and back-yard breeding is the American-bred German Shepherd. Although there are many good breeders of sound, stable German Shepherds, there are also many poorly bred Shepherds that are extremely skittish; they startle easily, and may even snap at any sudden movement.

Genetically-based fearful tendencies are difficult to overcome completely. However, using behavior modification techniques, progress can be made within the range of what is genetically possible for the individual dog. While a genetically skittish German Shepherd will not ever have the temperament of a genetically confident Golden Retriever, with behavior modification and other therapies, the intensity of the fear can be decreased.

2. Lack of Socialization. When a dog displays fearful behavior around people, it is often assumed that the dog was abused, especially if her history is unknown. But in fact, a lack of early socialization is the more likely culprit. Many behaviorists believe that this early deficit is the primary reason dogs develop fear issues, especially toward strangers, other dogs, or new environments. Remember that dogs have a genetically programmed fear of the unfamiliar, an instinct designed to keep them safe. The engagement of that response is almost wholly avoidable by making most things dogs will encounter—dogs, people, places, sounds, touch, and movement—familiar through early and frequent exposure.

Many veterinarians warn owners against taking pups anywhere outside of the home and back yard until the pup has been fully vaccinated—normally at sixteen weeks—due to the possibility of contracting disease. It is true that parvo and distemper can be fatal. Because these diseases can be contracted by a pup walking where an infected dog has been, owners must exercise caution. (Oddly enough, some veterinarians do not warn owners to keep pups off the waiting room floor, which is where sick dogs are most likely to be found!) Although an early quarantine period may prevent illness, it also prevents puppies from being exposed to the sights and sounds of the outdoors and from meeting other dogs and people, unless they come to the home. Owners of "winter pups" must make an extra effort to take their pups out to socialize even though the weather might not be inviting.

The window for optimum socialization—the period in which a puppy can be exposed to new things without experiencing a lasting fear imprint—has been estimated to be from four to twelve weeks. As Steve Lindsay states, "After week 5, puppies become progressively more cautious and hesitant about making new social contacts—a growing fearful tendency that appears to peak with the close of the socialization period at 12 weeks."[3] It's not that pups cannot be exposed to new things after the age of twelve weeks, but the further from that age, the more difficult it becomes for a pup to accept the unfamiliar.

With the optimum socialization window closing at twelve weeks and recommended post-vaccination socialization beginning at sixteen weeks, things can get confusing. Early socialization is *crucial*. A large percentage of behavior problems are preventable with proper early socialization. I am not suggesting that you disregard your vet's advice and I certainly do not advocate taking an unvaccinated pup to dog parks or other places that are frequented by hordes of dogs. But there are places you can safely take your pup to socialize, such as the homes of friends who have puppy-friendly, healthy dogs, or to outdoor shopping malls where there are many people and few dogs. Standing outside a pet supply store with your pup in your arms is a surefire way to ensure that she will meet many people—after all, who could resist greeting that adorable bundle of fur?

Puppy socialization classes are another avenue to safe, early exposure. Many trainers now accept canine students under the age of four months; vaccination requirements vary. You could also drive your pup around town when you do errands, allowing for "meet and greet" stops along the way.

Socialization must not only begin early, but should continue throughout a dog's life. The first two years are especially crucial, as the dog moves through adolescence and into early adulthood. All too often the fearful avoidance behavior of a young pup evolves into fear-reactive—also called fear-aggressive—behavior as the pup enters adolescence. Predictably, people move away from a threatening display, and the dog learns that it works, which in turn increases the likelihood of the dog performing the behavior again. (By the way, dogs are much faster than humans. "The dog would have bitten me if I hadn't pulled my hand away!" is a common, but false, statement. If a dog means to make contact, she will.) At that point many an owner stops taking the dog out in public for fear of how the dog will react to other people or dogs. Ironically, this results in a dog becoming even less social. If left untreated, fear-reactive behavior can escalate into biting and eventually into inflicting serious harm. It is often at that point that a trainer is called, or the dog might be surrendered to a shelter or euthanized. The sad part is that in many cases the cycle is completely preventable.

So where does this leave you if you have adopted an adult dog or were not able to provide early or ongoing socialization? If your dog's issues are mild, they may be overcome through *habituation*—getting your dog comfortable with new dogs and people through frequent and consistent exposure to them. Daily walks are helpful in this regard, as are the previously mentioned "meet and greets" as you travel around town doing your errands. If your dog's issues are moderate to severe, the good news is that fear issues stemming from inadequate early socialization are usually very responsive to behavior modification.

3. *Abuse.*   While abuse is a less common reason for fear issues than lack of socialization, it unfortunately does happen. Having been abused is certainly a legitimate reason for a dog to fear people. Some unfortunate dogs have been kicked, slapped, or otherwise physically mistreated as a result of anger, frustration, misguided attempts at training or discipline, or simple cruelty. Abused dogs may be hypersensitive to the movement of hands or feet, especially those coming toward them.

I once worked with a Doberman who had been rescued from a home where he had been kicked whenever he urinated on the carpet. I was called in because Thunder was attacking people's feet. Apparently Thunder's plan was to take the offensive before those mean, unpredictable things could hurt him! With behavior modification exercises, patience, and kindness, Thunder's new owners were able to gain his trust. Thunder learned that no one would hurt him in his safe, new home. Once his fear was alleviated, his behavior changed.

4. Traumatic Experience. We have all heard of people who have experienced a traumatic event and never quite recovered. Some traumas are so intense that they strongly influence future behavior. A war veteran might flinch at loud noises or sudden movements. Someone who has suffered a terrible car accident might be too traumatized to drive or even ride in a car again. Dogs, too, can develop intense fear issues as the result of a traumatic experience. A dog who is standing next to a car that backfires might develop a fear of loud or sharp noises. A dog who was attacked by another dog as a pup might grow up feeling that other dogs are not to be trusted. (This is an excellent reason to be hyper-vigilant if you take your dog to dog parks, as many owners do not understand or take responsibility for their own dogs' actions.)

Many trainers and behaviorists believe that dogs experience "fear periods." These periods are specific time frames in a dog's development during which exposure to something frightening will have more of a lasting impact than if the dog been exposed to it at any other time. Behaviorists who accept the idea of fear periods place the first one at roughly eight to ten weeks of age, and the second at seventeen to twenty-one weeks. Some believe there are third and fourth fear periods as well. Others behaviorists believe there really are no such things as fear periods, but rather that the suggested periods coincide with major physiological changes in a dog's body. Physiological change is stressful and when the body is under stress, potentially frightening or unpleasant occurrences can have more of an impact. For example, if someone is rude to you on a day when you were feeling stressed to begin with, your response is likely to be more intense than if the same incident occurred when you were feeling calm and happy. Regardless of whether fear periods exist, it makes sense to ensure that your pup's initial exposures to unfamiliar people, dogs, places, and things are pleasant no matter when they occur, so that your pup is not traumatized.

When the 1994 earthquake hit southern California, Soko was a year old. We were living just south of Northridge—the epicenter of the quake, as it turned out. Our house shook so violently that nothing inside was left standing. We were without electricity for days. Soko was absolutely petrified during the quake and its many aftershocks. In fact, she became sensitized—progressively more frightened—with each aftershock. Unfortunately, she also made an instant association between the freight-train sound/shaking and the flickering shadows created by the candles we had been forced to use. It took a long time and much behavioral assistance to overcome Soko's fear of flickering shadows, but we can now set a romantic dinner table and she will lie calmly nearby. While a traumatic experience can cause intense, long-lasting fears, those fears are often responsive to behavior modification.

5. Learned or Associative Fears. The old question of "nature versus nurture" to explain behavior is moot, because the answer is really "both of the above." The way a dog reacts to her environment as she matures is a combination of genetics and experience. Some fears develop as a result of experiences during which the dog creates associations. For example, Dazzle the Sheltie is afraid of being examined by the vet, and snaps at her. The vet advises Dazzle's owners to purchase a muzzle. At the next vet exam, his owners muzzle Dazzle as requested. After a few repetitions of this routine, Dazzle associates the muzzle with vet exams, and becomes fearful of the muzzle itself.

Whether a learned association is created immediately or after a few pairings depends on the individual dog. Smart dogs tend to create associations quickly. When a dog learns something after only one repetition, it is called "one-trial learning." While that talent comes in handy when learning obedience skills, it can be both a blessing and a curse for a fearful dog.

Some fear responses created by learned associations require a bit of detective work to unravel. Take, for example, a dog who enjoys spending time in the back yard. One day, the dog is frightened by the sound of a nearby truck backfiring, and associates the experience with the back yard. Because the owners were not present when the incident occurred, they are left to wonder why their dog suddenly refuses to set foot in the yard!

I once had a client whose three-year-old dog suddenly refused to eliminate in her usual small corner of the back yard. Upon further investigation it was revealed that new sprinkler heads had recently been installed, one of which was in the center of the dog's elimination area. The sprinkler heads were set to pop up and spray automatically, and the dog was afraid of the sudden motion and the water. Changing the location of the offending sprinkler head solved the problem. Not all learned associations are so easily resolved, but if a fear has been learned and the cause can be uncovered, chances are the association can be broken.

6. Pain/Illness Fears related to pain or illness are seen most often in senior dogs, although they can manifest in dogs of any age. The symptoms of certain medical conditions, such as hypothyroidism, can include fear and apprehensiveness.[4] A dog with a physical condition such as hip dysplasia or arthritis might seem frightened of being touched on the rear (or become aggressive when touched in that area), when in reality the touch is causing pain. Because dogs rely heavily on their senses of sight and hearing, a dog who becomes vision- or hearing-impaired might feel vulnerable and become frightened of sudden movements or sounds.

Any illness—or simply feeling unwell—can affect mood and behavior, in dogs and people. If you suspect that your dog has a medical condition, or she has developed a sudden, inexplicable change in behavior, consult your veterinarian. Fears stemming from pain or illness are best handled by treating the underlying condition, making the dog as comfortable as possible, and managing the environment to keep everyone safe.

~ * ~ * ~ * ~ *~ * ~ * ~ * ~ *~ * ~ * ~ * ~ * ~ *~ * ~ * ~

Even if you do not have information about your dog's background or previous experiences, you *can* change her perceptions, and therefore responses, to the things that frighten her. In the chapters that follow, you will learn specific techniques that will help to turn your fearful fido into a calm canine.

1   Lindsay, Steven R. *Handbook of Applied Dog Behavior and Training, Volume III*. Iowa: Blackwell, 2005
2   Schull-Selcer, E.A. and Stagg, W. (1991) Advances in the understanding and treatment of noise phobias. *Veterinary Clinics of North America* 21(2):353-367.

3   Lindsay, *Handbook of Applied Dog Behavior and Training, Volume 1*. Iowa: Blackwell, 2000

4   Aronson, L.P. (1998). Thyroid testing. *Beardie Bulletin*, August.

Tail End Wrap-Up

Causes of canine fear and prognosis for behavior modification:

🐾 GENETICS (including breed tendencies): progress can be made within the range of what is genetically possible for the individual dog.

🐾 LACK OF SOCIALIZATION: most often modifiable through habituation or behavior modification.

🐾 ABUSE: treatable with love, patience, and behavior modification.

🐾 TRAUMATIC EXPERIENCE: often very responsive to behavior modification.

🐾 LEARNED OR ASSOCIATIVE FEARS: if a fear was learned, there is a good chance it can be unlearned.

🐾 PAIN OR ILLNESS: best addressed with appropriate veterinary care and management.

The Face of Fear

Dogs express fear through body language and vocalization. To effectively modify your dog's fearful behavior, you must become familiar with his body language and fear response patterns. Learning your dog's characteristic responses will allow you to recognize when his fear is being triggered, even at the lowest level. With practice, you will be able to intervene immediately and break the chain of escalating anxiety so the reaction does not become extreme. If your dog tends to display fear by defensively lunging or biting, you will be able to short-circuit the process before harm can be done. Recognizing and monitoring your dog's reactions is also crucial when practicing behavior modification exercises, so that you can adjust the protocols based on your observations.

The first observable sign that your dog is afraid might be as subtle as a flick of the ear, a twitch of the lip, or a slight tensing of the musculature. As fear levels increase, these and other signals become more obvious.

Common Audible Signals	Common Visible Signals	Miscellaneous Subtle Signals
whining	dilated pupils	sweaty paw pads
whimpering	tensed muscles	shedding fur/dandruff
growling	trembling	"clingy"/leaning on owner
barking	pacing	restlessness, hyperactivity
howling	extreme salivation/	vigilantly scans environment
yelping	drooling *or*	shallow breathing or panting
screaming	decreased salivation	"shaking off" (as if wet)
	rapid *or* very slow	stretching
	blinking	moving very slowly
	yawning	

Extreme: anal sac expression, loss of bladder/sphincter control, vomiting

Dogs who are habitually anxious may develop repetitive behaviors such as licking at paws or chewing at other body parts. Repetitive stress-related behaviors are called *stereotypies* (pronounced "stereo-tip-ees"). If ritualized, chronic, and difficult to interrupt, they are termed *obsessive-compulsive disorders* (OCDs). While stereotypies may disappear with increased exercise and mental stimulation, OCDs are best treated with professional assistance, as they may require pharmacological intervention.

Body Language

Like any other language, canine body language must be studied in order to become fluent. Instead of learning individual words, you must first learn the significance of each individual body part's position and movement. One body part—for example, the tail—can convey volumes about a dog's emotional state. Then, just as words are combined into sentences, individual body signals must be interpreted in conjunction with others to paint a full picture of the dog's internal state. Learning to read your dog's body language is a labor of love that will open the door to improved understanding and communication. Once you are fluent, you will be able to interpret his emotional states correctly, even as they fluctuate from moment to moment.

Ears and Tail: The most widely recognized canine fear posture is distinguished by flattened ears and a tucked tail. The degree to which these signals occur is in direct correlation to the degree of fear the dog is experiencing. A dog who takes notice of a potential threat might flick an ear back and lower his tail slightly, but reassume a more relaxed posture once he has determined there is no need for concern. A dog who is extremely frightened is more likely to flatten his ears against his skull and curl his tail completely under so it covers the ano-genital region.

Becoming familiar with the position of your dog's ears when he is feeling relaxed will help you to recognize when the ears are held back in a fearful or submissive response, or held forward in a confident or even aggressive display. If you have a flop-eared dog such as a Cocker Spaniel, changes in ear position will not be as obvious as they are in a prick-eared dog such as a Siberian Husky. Begin to take note of the position of your dog's ears when he meets other dogs and people, and when he encounters something that frightens him.

Note the body language of the fearful/submissive pup on the right. The ears are laid back, the eyes elongated; the tongue protrudes slightly (more on that soon), and a paw is raised in a gesture of appeasement.

It is also important to note the normal, relaxed position of your dog's tail. The tails of some breeds, such as Basset Hounds and Beagles, are set moderately high and curve slightly. Some spitz-type breeds, such as Alaskan Malamutes and Akitas, have extremely high-set tails that curl over the back. Many sighthounds, such as Greyhounds and Whippets, have low-set tails that are normally held in a low position; for some, a tucked tail is normal. Other breeds, such as Labrador Retrievers and Golden Retrievers, normally hold their thickly furred, low-set tails parallel to the ground. Becoming familiar with your dog's normal tail set will help you to recognize when it is held higher or lower than usual, which will tip you off to any change in your dog's emotions.

Cropping the ears and docking the tail inhibit a dog's ability to communicate clearly with other dogs. These cosmetic procedures are unnecessary, painful, and can result in surgical complications. Without a sound medical reason to do so, they should be avoided.

In addition to position, the movement of a dog's tail provides clues about how the dog is feeling. There is a common misconception that a wagging tail is always attached to a happy dog. A Golden Retriever's tail, when he is happy (which seems to be 99.8% of the time), is held parallel to the ground and wags loosely in a wide, swooping arc. But if that same dog were anxious or fearful, the tail would be held lower, wag faster, and make a smaller arc.

A dog will sometimes hold his tail higher than usual and wag it stiffly, like a flag, in a tight arc. The rest of the body will be tense and motionless. Many confident dogs display this type of highly alert body language when meeting other dogs. It can also indicate a certain playful cockiness. At my house, the "cocky tail" is usually attached to Mojo, my beloved twelve-year-old German Shepherd/Rottweiler/Malamute mix. Mojo's cocky tail is obvious whenever he is being playfully antagonistic toward Soko—for example, when he plants himself between her and her favorite resting spot. Body still, tail high and wagging stiffly, you can almost hear his inner Clint Eastwood: *Do you feel lucky, punk? Well, do ya?*

Eyes: The eyes of a relaxed, confident dog will be opened wide, but not overly so. The eyes of a dog who is nervous or anxious will appear smaller and elongated. Eyebrows may be raised in an expression of concern (much as in humans), and wrinkling may appear on the forehead. The pupils of a very frightened dog will be dilated. In cases of extreme fear, the eyes may be opened very wide with a lot of the whites showing. This is sometimes referred to as "whale eye."

Note the dilated pupils with whites showing, the tightly closed mouth, and ear laid back.

Mouth: When relaxed, many dogs hold their mouths partially open in a way that resembles a grin. However, the mouth will close momentarily when the dog is frightened or trying to determine whether there is a real threat. Some dogs also puff out the flews—the fleshy areas above the upper lips—on one or both sides. Once the dog has determined that there is nothing to worry about, the facial muscles will relax and that wonderful grin will return.

A fearful display may include a retraction of the corners of the mouth. The mouth will be partially or completely closed, with no teeth showing. This does not resemble your dog's normal, relaxed grin.

Above: Mouth closed, lips retracted. Ears laid back, eyes elongated.

Right: Eyes look "worried." Mouth closed, puffy flews.

Pilorerection: Piloerection—raised hackles, hair standing on end—is frequently misinterpreted as a sure indication of aggression. While it is true that piloerection often accompanies an aggressive display, it can also manifest as the result of excitement or fear.

When dogs are frightened, they may raise their hackles to make themselves look bigger and more intimidating. As noted ethologist and author Dr. Roger Abrantes says, "The fearful, submissive and surprised dog probably raises its hackles to frighten its opponent. If it succeeds in making its opponent hesitate for a moment it will have a better chance to prepare its defense, or flee."[1]

A lovely example of piloerection and "cocky tail," courtesy of my boy Mojo.

(That's Soko in the foreground, trying to stay out of it!)

Weight distribution: A more subtle aspect of canine body language involves the distribution of body weight. The weight of a dog who is feeling relaxed will be distributed evenly over the front and back legs. A dog who is displaying dominance or aggression will often appear to be leaning forward, the weight apportioned more heavily over the front legs. A fearful dog's weight, however, will be distributed more heavily over the back legs, as though the entire body is leaning backward. Backward leaning may be accompanied by a lowering of the body, as though the dog is cringing or trying to appear smaller. A dog who is extremely frightened might flatten himself completely against the ground. A dog who stretches his muzzle forward to investigate something he is unsure about might not have his weight distributed over his back end, but his back legs are likely to be splayed, giving the impression of a dog who is nervous and ready to flee at any moment.

Weight distributed more heavily over back legs; tail low, wagging in small, tight arc. Ears laid back, eyes elongated, mouth tightly closed.

Weight back, body lowered, ears back, eyes showing whites, tail tucked, front paw slightly raised.

*Compare the weight distribution of these two dogs, along
with tail position and proximity of the body to the ground.*

Fight or Flight Response

The involuntary, instinctual reaction to fight or flee in the face of perceived
danger is known as the "fight or flight" response. When this life-preserving
response is triggered via the sympathetic nervous system, physiological
changes occur in an instant. Sequences of nerve cells fire and adrenaline
and other stress hormones are released into the bloodstream. Heartbeat
and respiration increase and digestion slows so blood can be shunted
away from the stomach to the limbs. These internal changes are designed
to protect the dog from harm by preparing the body to fight or to run.

When a serious threat appears at close range but there is room to flee, a
dog will normally choose flight. If restrained at the time (for example,
by a leash), a dog who desires to flee might instead cower, attempt to
hide, or strain to get as far away from the threat as possible. When no
form of flight is available, a serious, close-range threat is likely to result
in a fight. Any dog, no matter how mild-mannered, may bite if left with
no other choice but to defend himself.

Note: Once your dog's system has been flooded with stress hormones,
be alert! Stress hormones do not leave the system immediately, so if
something else should frighten your dog after the first incident, chances
of a strong reaction are increased.

The way a dog reacts to a fear-inducing situation may be breed-
related. For example, a 1958 study showed that when frightened,
Beagles freeze, while terriers run around frantically.[2]

There are two other responses dogs may display when confronted with danger. The first is simply to freeze in place. Freezing may happen when the fear is at a low level or the threat is at a distance; it gives the dog a moment to assess the situation and consider his options. The second is known as "fidget/fool around." A dog may search around on the ground or perform other canine equivalents of human fidgeting, or bounce or wiggle about, acting in a way we would term silly. While these behaviors might appear pointless, they have a definite purpose—to diffuse a threatening situation. Dogs may go into fidget/fool around mode when trying to get another dog or person to stop acting in a threatening manner.

Fear or Aggression?

The next time your dog encounters an unfamiliar dog or person, note the distribution of his body weight, as well as other body language. Are his ears pinned back, tail lowered, body leaning backward, with weight distributed more heavily over the back legs? Is he barking or growling, but backing away at the same time? If either of those descriptions fits your dog, his motivation is most likely fear. The growling and barking in this case is meant to increase the distance between your dog and whatever is scaring him.

The stance of a dog who truly intends to harm another will appear "forward" as opposed to a back-leaning, fear-reactive stance. In a classic confident display of aggression, a dog's ears are forward, the tail is held high, and body weight is distributed heavily over the front legs. The lips may be retracted vertically in an *agonistic pucker*—this fright-inducing bit of canine body language can be seen on television programs where wolves respond to a threat by baring their teeth. The agonistic pucker differs from the fearful, closed-mouth, corners-retracted display. In the latter, the teeth are not seen; in the former, the lips are retracted vertically to show the front teeth. An agonistic pucker may be accompanied by a deep snarl. While barking may be a function of either aggression or fear, snarling is always a sign of aggression.

Some dogs, when confronted with an unfamiliar dog or person, are conflicted about how to respond. The dog might lunge in and then dart away, vocalizing in a threatening manner but not really wanting to connect. Or the dog might approach a person to solicit petting, but once in close proximity, become afraid and react by either darting away or becoming defensively aggressive and snapping at the person. The possibility of this close-range defensive behavior is a good reason not to force your dog to be petted by people with whom he is not comfortable.

This wolf pup knows the meaning of an agonistic pucker, and responds by laying ears back, raising a paw, and leaning away.

Under no circumstances is it appropriate to punish growling. Doing so suppresses a dog's primary way of communicating that he is uncomfortable, which can lead to biting without warning. If your dog growls, the wisest course of action is to diffuse the situation (for example, by walking away slowly) and then to address the underlying cause of the distress, with the assistance of a professional if necessary.

Cutoff Signals

Picture a group of young boys running and playing. The play gradually becomes rougher and rowdier, and light physical contact turns to pushing and shoving. Finally, one child, feeling overwhelmed by the others, cries, "Time out!" Cutoff signals are the canine equivalent of calling for a time out—they prevent situations from escalating into conflict.

A dog may employ cutoff signals to convey that he is not a threat, to indicate discomfort, or simply because he is stressed. The signals are often used when dogs are in social situations with other dogs or people—although humans are not nearly as good at reading the signals as are other dogs. Wolves use cutoff signals quite efficiently to communicate with other wolves. In fact, wolf ethologists have found the highly efficient social signals to be a major reason that disagreements between wolves seldom escalate into full-blown aggression.

When I first read Norwegian behaviorist Turid Rugaas' book *On Talking Terms with Dogs: Calming Signals* (see *Resources*), I was happily surprised to discover that not only did she list the same signals I had observed in my work with wolves, but that she had identified others as well. (Rugaas uses the term "calming signals" rather than "cutoff signals.") According to Rugaas, twenty-eight signals have been identified. Although they range from subtle to obvious, with practice you can learn to notice even the most minute signals.

Following are descriptions of common cutoff signals. Once you begin to notice them, you may discover that your dog displays at least one or two signals whenever he is nervous or fearful.

Yawning: Yawning is a natural behavior for dogs. Just as with people, yawning is often a simple indication of being tired. But a dog may also yawn when worried or anxious, to signal submission, or to convey that he is not a threat. The yawn may be repetitive or appear in combination with other stress signals.

I once observed a group obedience class where a man was training his large, beautiful German Shepherd. Every time the dog did something her owner didn't like, he jerked the leash roughly, causing the choke chain to tighten. Each time she was corrected in this manner, the dog yawned and looked away; the poor thing was becoming stressed by the corrections and by the owner's obvious frustration. Unfortunately, the man was completely unaware of how his dog was feeling. His comment about the yawning was a disgusted, "Ah, she's bored with training." Noticing what is going on in the environment whenever your dog yawns can shed light on what makes him afraid or uncomfortable. Be observant of your dog's interactions with people and other dogs; you will be amazed at how much communication is contained in a yawn.

Lip-Licking: A dog licking the lips of another is often indicative of submissive behavior, but in this case we are talking about a dog licking his own lips. I have often observed lip-licking in fearful wolves and I see it frequently in my clients' fearful dogs. The licks may be upward toward the nose or downward over the lower lip, and may be singular or repetitive, fast or slow.

Licking lips, head turned,   *Brave enough to face the camera,*
eyes averted.   *but still, a lip-lick.*

The next time you see a child hugging a dog, notice whether the dog licks his lips. Although humans interpret hugs as affection, canines do not. In fact, restraint makes many dogs uncomfortable. Other instances in which you might see dogs licking their lips are upon meeting unfamiliar dogs or people, when feeling anxious in a specific environment (for example, at the vet's office or in the car), or when having a camera pointed at them. I have quite a few photographs of wolves who were licking their lips at the moment I shot the photo—and it wasn't because they thought I was Little Red Riding Hood! Most owners of fearful dogs have at least a few photos of their fur-kid "sticking his tongue out at the camera." This is not to suggest that any time your dog licks his lips it means he is afraid; physical cues must always be read in context and in relation to other cues.

None of these pups is quite brave enough to face the camera,
and one is yawning. Think he's just sleepy?

Turning Away, Averting Eyes: Imagine that one sunny day, you walk out your front door to find a grizzly bear on your porch. Would you feel more comfortable if the bear were turned to the side, or facing you head-on? It doesn't take an ethologist to figure out that the sideways presentation would make you less uncomfortable; it's instinctual. Dogs turn away to send the signal "I am not a threat." They may also turn away when confronted with something that frightens them or makes them uncomfortable. Turning away may involve the head or the entire body. A turned head is often accompanied by an averted gaze, as a direct stare is a threat in the animal kingdom. Fearful or insecure dogs find it difficult to look people or other dogs in the eye, just as insecure people find it difficult to make direct eye contact with others.

I once observed a man in a pet store who was attempting to get his Akita to lie down. The man had given the verbal command three times in a row, with increasingly escalating volume. Finally, exasperated, he leaned over the dog, stared him in the eye and bellowed, "Down!" The dog lay down—but only after turning his body to face completely away from the man. Watch your dog carefully in his daily interactions and notice what causes him to turn his head or body away; it might be greetings from visitors, meeting other dogs, or entering unfamiliar locations. If you find your dog turning away from you (or yawning or licking his lips) frequently during training exercises, consider whether your voice could be softer or your overall approach more gentle.

Scratch and Sniff: Turning away is sometimes accompanied by scratching. It is as though the dog is saying, "I'll be right with you, I just have this pesky itch!" Or the dog might suddenly discover something fascinating on the ground and sniff: "I'd love to address you directly, but—ooh, lookie here!" Sniffing may or may not be accompanied by turning away, but the dog's nose will always be pointed toward the ground rather than held high as when scenting the breeze.

When watching my dogs roughhouse, I can actually predict the moment when Soko is going to develop a sudden itch or discover some fabulous, invisible object on the ground. It inevitably occurs just after Mojo begins to get too rough. Soko's actions are meant to convey "Please chill out!" Mojo will sometimes comply, and sometimes not. If he gets too out of control, Mom steps in and gently reminds both dogs who the real alpha female is!

In addition to being valuable indicators of canine stress levels, calming signals can be used by people to encourage dogs to relax. No, I'm not suggesting that you take up scratching yourself in public—but you can use yawning and lip-licking to your advantage. The next time your dog seems anxious, get his attention, then yawn or lick your lips. You might be surprised at the change in his demeanor; he might even mirror the signals back to you. When working to socialize fearful wolves at the rescue center I often used a combination of turning away, averting eyes, lip-licking, and yawning to show that I was not a threat. The wolves would visibly relax and sometimes even dare to come closer. Practice using calming signals with your dog. Not every dog will respond to a human's use of calming signals, but if your dog does, use them whenever you notice the first signs of anxiety.

Reading your dog's body language, along with noticing calming signals, will become easier with practice. Before you know it you will be fluent in "dog," which will make you that much more effective at helping your fur-kid overcome his fears.

1   Abrantes, R. *Dog Language: An Encyclopedia of Canine Behaviour* Washington: Dogwise Publishing, 1997
2   H. Mahut. "Breed differences in the dog's emotional behavior". Can. Journal of Psychology 12(1)35-44, 1958

 # Tail End Wrap-Up

- Learning to recognize your dog's body language and stress signals is crucial to helping him overcome his fears.

- Begin to notice your dog's natural ear, mouth, and tail positions and in what contexts they change.

- Watch for piloerection and distribution of body weight when your dog encounters other dogs or people.

- Avoid putting your dog in situations where he has no choice but to defend himself.

- Watch for stress signals like yawning, lip-licking, freezing in place, turning away, scratching, and sniffing.

- Use your awareness of your dog's body language to avoid situations that cause him undue stress.

Body Language of the Two-Legged

Shasta, a six-month-old Labrador Retriever, has come to dislike Saturday evenings. That, she has learned, is when people come to visit. This particular evening, a couple is ensconced on the sofa across from the hearth where Shasta is sitting. The petite blonde keeps her hands folded neatly on her lap as she speaks softly to Shasta's owner. The woman does not worry Shasta. The man is tall and muscular, wears a baseball cap, and speaks so loudly and gestures so often that one might think he was at an actual ballgame. The man makes Shasta very uneasy. It seems as though he could explode into action at any moment. Shasta keeps a wary eye on him. The couple has brought their five-year-old son—a bundle of restless energy. Each time Shasta begins to relax and lie down, the boy approaches and looms over her, reaches to pat her on the head, or makes strange noises and waves his hands in her face. Finally, Shasta slinks off into another room. Her owner apologizes to the visitors, saying, "Shasta's funny that way. She just seems to take to some people more than others."

There is nothing "funny" about Shasta's behavior. In fact, the way she views strangers is absolutely normal for fearful dogs. Understanding how human body language affects canines and sharing that knowledge with others will enable you to make your dog more comfortable, keep everyone safe, and help your dog to learn that humans aren't such frightening beasts after all!

Work That Body! Seven Ways to Whittle Away Fear

The following tips on human body language are applicable when interacting with any dog, but are especially important when dealing with a fearful dog. Adopt these mannerisms and teach others who interact with your dog to do so as well:

1. *Let the dog come to you.* If your dog is frightened, *she* must be allowed to decide whether or not to approach. Don't restrain your dog and force her to accept contact from others. Remember the "fight or flight" response; if you take away the opportunity for flight, your dog's choices are limited.

2. *Turn to the side.* Facing a dog directly is more confrontational than keeping your body turned partially or completely to the side; even turning your head to the side will make a frightened dog feel less anxious.

3. *No staring, please!* A direct stare is a threat in the animal kingdom (and on New York City subways!). It is perfectly fine to look at your dog; just soften your expression and don't "hard stare" directly into her eyes. Do not allow children to put their faces near your dog's face or to stare into her eyes.

4. *Don't hover.* Leaning over a dog can cause the dog to become afraid and possibly defensive. The one time I was bitten while working in a Los Angeles city animal shelter happened when I went to return an adorable, fluffy white dog to her pen. While placing her on the ground, I inadvertently reached over her equally adorable little pen mate— who jumped up and bit me in the face.

5. *Pet appropriately.* Approaching dogs by patting them on the head is ill-advised. Envision the interaction from the dog's point of view; a palm approaching from above can be alarming. I do a demonstration with kids to teach them how to pet dogs properly. The child plays the role of the dog; I tell the child that I will pet him in two different ways, and he is to tell me which is nicer. First, I reach my hand slowly toward the child's cheek and stroke it, smiling and softly saying, "Good dog!" Next, I bring my hand brusquely palm-down over the child's head repeatedly, while loudly saying, "Good dog, good dog!" Kids almost invariably like the first method better. If dogs could answer for themselves, nine out of ten dogs would vote

for the first method as well! It's not that dogs should never be petted on top of the head, but that head-patting (or petting over the dog's shoulders, back, or rump) should not be used as an initial approach. It is wiser to make a fist, hold it under the dog's nose to allow her to sniff, then pet the dog on the chest, moving gradually to the sides of the face and other body parts, assuming the dog is comfortable. Likewise, a hand moving in quickly to grab for a dog's collar is more potentially fear-inducing than a hand moving slowly to a dog's chest, scratching it, then moving up to take hold of the collar.

6. *Stoop, don't swoop.* Small dogs in particular are often swooped down upon when people want to pick them up. Fast, direct, overhead movements are much more frightening than slow, indirect ones. To lift a small dog, crouch down, pet the dog for a moment, then gently slip your hands under her belly and chest, and lift.

7. *Watch your smile.* While humans interpret a smile as friendly, a dog might not be as fond of seeing your pearly whites. A show of teeth is, after all, a threat in the animal kingdom. A friend of mine once accompanied me to visit the wolves at the rescue center. She patiently sat on the ground, motionless. Finally, a large, black wolf approached to investigate. Unable to contain herself, she broke out in a huge, toothy grin. The wolf darted away as though she had raised a hand to hit him. The lesson? Save the dazzling toothpaste smile for charming your dates and accepting awards. Smile at canines with a closed mouth.

In an upcoming chapter you will learn how to use human body language to help your dog become more comfortable with visitors, and to address specific fears. For now, be aware of your own body language when interacting with your dog and teach others to modify theirs as needed.

 # Tail End Wrap-Up

BODY LANGUAGE BASICS:

- Let your dog make the choice to approach.

- Turning to the side makes dogs feel more comfortable than facing them directly.

- Don't stare.

- Don't hover.

- Pet appropriately.

- Stoop, don't swoop, to pick dogs up.

- No dazzling toothpaste smiles!

Part II

The Firm Foundation Program

Training

Leadership

Physical Well-Being

Management

The Firm Foundation Program

In the *Skills* section, you will learn how to teach your dog behaviors that can help him cope in fear-inducing situations. But first, you must build a firm foundation upon which learning can take place. Just like children, dogs must be physically and mentally sound in order to learn. The goal of the Firm Foundation Program is to set the stage for learning and confidence-building by providing a supportive home environment.

Four Pillars of the Firm Foundation Program

1. Management
2. Physical Well-Being
3. Leadership
4. Training

You may already be employing some of the program's tenets. If you find them to be very different from you and your dog's current lifestyle, don't worry; you needn't change everything at once. Start by making one or two small changes, and as your dog becomes comfortable with those, make a few more.

You might find that following the Firm Foundation Program requires that you change a few of your own habits and some of the ways you interact with your dog. Don't expect overnight changes in either one of you. Relax and take it slowly. The program is aimed at relieving stress in the home environment, not causing it! You should find that within the first few weeks on the program, your dog will become more relaxed in general—and you just might, too.

Management:
Home, Peaceful Home

Dogs who are skittish in general, or specifically sound- or motion-sensitive, do not do well in social environments with lots of noise and chaotic activity. I have visited homes where a parent yelling at a child or a heated argument between spouses caused the dog to cower or tremble. The people were completely unaware that their raised voices were causing the dogs to react fearfully. At one home, the couple's five- and seven-year-old sons frequently had friends over to play. The boys would wrestle noisily, run through the house, whoop, holler, and crash into furniture. While it was great fun for the kids, the high-volume roughhousing was too much for the poor dog, who would cower in the corner or flee the room altogether.

Of course, you are not expected to—nor should you have to—change your entire lifestyle for your dog. People argue, friends visit—life happens. But be sensitive to your dog's sensitivities. For example, if your dog is afraid of the beeping sounds made by your cell phone, go into another room or step outside to use it. If your dog cringes whenever voices are raised in anger, try to modify your behavior. (Besides, doing so could only benefit your family dynamic.) These concessions need not be permanent, but until you have learned how to address your dog's sensitivities, keeping as peaceful a home environment as possible is key.

Sensitization

In the phenomenon known as *sensitization*, a dog becomes more and more frightened of something with repeated exposures. For example, the first time Baxter the Border Collie hears the mechanical whirring of the garbage truck picking up trash, he becomes alert and appears a bit worried.

With each subsequent trash pickup, his fear becomes more intense until finally he runs, hides under a bed, and drools at the first hint of the sound. Not all dogs become sensitized to sounds or other things that frighten them, but the possibility is another good reason to be aware of what scares your dog and to keep her exposures to those things minimal while the underlying issues are being addressed.

Routine is Queen

Imagine that you have been transplanted to a remote jungle. The natives do not speak your language, nor you theirs. You are surrounded by wild animals, strange sounds, and unfamiliar customs. It seems that everything changes from one day to the next. You have no idea when you will be fed, where you are being led at any given time, or which sounds or sights might indicate danger. Not exactly reassuring, is it? Contrast that with how you would feel if, after a week, you had learned through repetition and association what constituted a normal daily routine. You would know when to expect a meal, which animals were dangerous, and that morning outings meant gathering firewood and evening outings meant hunting. Knowing what to expect would engender confidence and help to reduce your fear and anxiety. It's the same for dogs. The better a dog can predict what is going to happen on a day-to-day basis, the more of a chance she has to develop a sense of security and confidence.

Try to keep your dog's daily routine relatively stable. It helps a dog to know at what times she will be fed, when she will be taken for a walk or to the park to run, and when to expect your departures and returns. One caveat: be sure to vary the routine as well. Yes, I realize that sounds contradictory! But an "established routine" need not mean that your dog is fed at exactly 7:00 a.m. and 4:00 p.m. each day, or that you return home at exactly 5:00 p.m. every day. Dogs have a very dependable inner clock. If your dog is used to activities happening at exact times, any variation in the routine could cause anxiety. To prevent that from happening, feed your dog at 7:00 a.m. one day and 7:30 a.m. the next; return home earlier or later (half an hour to an hour) a few days a week. These variations are likely to occur naturally anyway. The goal is for your dog to know what to expect on a daily basis, yet to be comfortable if the routine varies.

The Lookout Post

Does your dog have a "lookout post" in the house or yard where she reacts to passersby by barking out a doggy rendition of "Hit the road, Jack"? Although you might not realize it, each time that happens, she is being reinforced for her behavior. Look at it from your dog's point of view: she is not comfortable with passersby, so she barks to make them disappear. And lo and behold, it works! She barks, and the intruders move out of sight. Because the behavior is self-rewarding, it is likely to continue. The problem is that with each incident, adrenaline and other stress hormones are flooding your dog's system so that her anxiety level spikes. The cumulative effect can be a dog who is perpetually stressed and on guard.

If your dog barks at passersby when you are at home, call her to you, praise her for coming, then ask for a sit, a down, or whatever other obedience skill or trick she knows. Reward her by offering a chew toy or engaging her in a fun activity.

It is likely that your dog is also reacting to passersby during the day when you are gone. Those uninterrupted bouts of barking might go on for minutes at a time, your dog's stress levels increasing with every passing second. Limit your dog's visual access by leaving curtains drawn or blinds closed over traffic-facing windows. If you do not want to leave the window covered when you are gone, block your dog's access to the room altogether. If your dog's window to the world isn't a window at all, but a street-facing gate or other part of your yard, either keep her indoors (in a small, enclosed area if necessary) when you are gone, or put up a physical barrier outdoors to block her view so she has a chance to relax.

If your dog is afraid of or reactive to sounds (for example, neighborhood construction or other dogs barking) when you are absent, leave her indoors with a television or radio playing to help screen out the sound. Be sure to play the television or radio when you are home as well, so the sound does not become associated only with your absence.

Crates are Great

It is important for your dog to have a place to take refuge whenever she feels anxious or afraid. Perhaps her favorite hideout is under a desk or behind a couch. Many dogs choose small, enclosed spaces because they offer a feeling of security; that's one reason crates are so useful.

Chapter 32 discusses different types of crates and how to introduce your dog to a crate, even if she is fearful of it. It is absolutely worth your time and effort to crate train your dog; it will make life easier for you, and give your dog a safe, secure sanctuary.

Calm is Cool

The way you respond when your dog becomes anxious or fearful will have a direct impact on her emotional state. Of course, in the case of an extreme, full-blown phobic reaction, an immediate response is required; either the dog must be removed from the area, or the cause of the fear must be removed. But in less extreme cases, such as a dog who has a nervous disposition in general and chronically solicits attention and reassurance, the proper response can be less obvious. While you want to reassure your dog, it is important that you not contribute to her anxious state of mind. Don't pick your dog up and coddle her, cooing in a concerned voice, "Poor baby, what's wrong?" Although it may be a function of maternal (or paternal) instinct to do so, dogs who are indulged in this manner never learn to stand on their own four paws. It is wiser to say, "Don't be silly, it's okay" in an unconcerned, non-committal tone. You are not being uncaring; on the contrary, you are helping your dog to gain confidence. Once she sees that you, the fearless leader, are not worried, she can relax. Practice this composed, nonchalant response—it will come in handy when you work with your dog to address specific fears.

Make an effort to notice and reward any relaxed or confident behavior with attention and affection. It might seem silly to reward your dog for simply lying there calmly, but what you are really rewarding is her calm emotional state. Reward by softly praising, petting, or even offering a treat. Let your dog know that calm is cool.

By making your home a true sanctuary, you will provide a safe setting in which your dog can relax and develop confidence.

Tail End Wrap-Up

🐾 Minimize your dog's exposure to things that frighten her.

🐾 Maintain a daily routine so your dog knows what to expect, but vary it slightly now and then.

🐾 If your dog has a lookout post and is reactive toward passersby, limit her visual access.

🐾 Meet your dog's concerns with a cool, confident demeanor.

🐾 Reward your dog for calm, relaxed behavior.

Nutrition

Nutrition affects behavior in both dogs and people. Ever been around kids who have eaten too much junk food? Just as all that sugar can cause kids to become hyperactive, cranky, and out of control, poor nutrition can contribute to canine behavior issues. A dog with a nervous disposition will feel even more anxious if he has excess sugar and unhealthful chemicals flooding his system.

Good nutrition contributes to a solid foundation upon which calmer behavior can rest. Many owners I work with are thrilled to see the behavioral changes that take place after just a few weeks of feeding a more healthful diet. Feeding a food that is valuable nutritionally will result in improved behavior and better all-around health for your dog.

> If your dog has a medical condition, discuss any potential dietary changes with your veterinarian.

Become Label Able

There are so many dog foods on the market, and so many claims made by manufacturers, that it can be confusing to figure out which foods are truly nutritious. One food is said to have scientifically balanced ingredients, while another claims to turn back the hands of time to restore your dog to a younger, healthier state. (Heck, if there were truth in advertising, no woman would have a single wrinkle!) Learning to read labels will allow you to bypass exaggerated advertising claims and get a realistic idea of the product's quality.

By law, dog food manufacturers must list ingredients in descending order by bulk weight. For example, a bag of dry kibble that lists the first three ingredients as "chicken meal, chicken by-product meal, rice" has more chicken meal than any other ingredient. Because dogs are primarily carnivores (technically they're omnivores, able to eat both animal products and plant foods), the first two ingredients should contain meat.

The most common meat sources used in dog foods in the United States are chicken, turkey, lamb, and beef. There are three grades of meat. Using chicken as an example, the highest grade is simply labeled "chicken." This indicates a whole meat source—the clean flesh of slaughtered chickens—and is limited to lean muscle tissue. A step below that is "chicken meal," which is made from rendered muscle and tissue. (Rendering is the process that separates fat-soluble from water-soluble materials, removes most of the water, and may destroy or alter some of the natural enzymes and proteins found in raw ingredients.) If "meal" is listed, the source should be identified, rather than the vaguely descriptive "poultry meal" or "meat meal."

The lowest level of quality in our example would be "chicken by-products." Chicken by-products may contain heads, feet, undeveloped eggs, and intestines. Dog foods that contain by-products, especially when they appear high on the list of ingredients, are not of high quality. (For more on what really goes into pre-packaged dog foods, read *Food Pets Die For*—see *Resources*.)

Avoid dog foods that contain large amounts of corn. Corn is a common allergen that has been known to cause itchy skin as well as hyperactive behavior.

Have you ever noticed how calm and even lethargic people become after a Thanksgiving dinner? That's because turkey contains tryptophan, an amino acid that is a precursor to serotonin, a mood-affecting neurotransmitter found in the brains of both dogs and people. James O'Heare, Ph.D., author and president of Cynology College, calls serotonin "the happy messenger" and believes that increasing its levels in a dog's brain may significantly reduce stress, anxiety, and aggression. Corn, on the other hand, is high in the amino acid tyrosine. O'Heare refers to tyrosine as the "anti-tryptophan." Because corn makes it harder for the amino acids necessary for the production of serotonin to pass through the blood-brain barrier, it is not conducive to a calm state of mind.

According to O'Heare, one way to increase serotonin levels is to feed a meal of pure carbohydrates such as brown rice and vegetables, along with a B complex vitamin (or vitamin B6 individually at 1 mg./kg body weight per day), within an hour or so after a small meal of kibble. If your dog will not eat the pure carbohydrate meal, he suggests mixing it in with the kibble, or finding a diet with as low a protein source as possible (16% protein would be optimal). Once behavior improves (through behavior modification along with good nutrition), you may use a lower-protein kibble on its own.[1]

Other ingredients to avoid include artificial colors or flavors, and any that are not identified by source (for example, "animal fat"). Also, read the ingredient line that begins "preserved with..." The desirable preservatives are vitamins E (sometimes listed as "mixed tocopherols") and C (often called "ascorbic acid"). The unhealthful, potentially cancer-causing preservatives are BHA, BHT, and ethoxyquin.

> Beware! Some sneaky manufacturers break down less-than-ideal ingredients into parts so they can be listed separately and therefore appear lower on the ingredients list. For example, the list might read "chicken meal, ground corn, corn meal, corn gluten meal." In reality, if all of the corn products were grouped together, there would be more corn than chicken by bulk weight, so corn would have to be listed first.

In general, dog foods found at the supermarket are of lower quality than those found at pet supply stores. Better foods are higher in initial cost, but because they contain more nutrients, less is fed per meal. And because the body is able to absorb more of the nutrients, less waste product is produced—an advantage for the poop-scoopers among us. Besides, feeding a high quality food is an investment in your dog's health. Spending a bit more now might well save you the cost of veterinary visits in the future. (And look at it this way—at least you don't have to send your fur-kids to college!)

If you decide to switch foods, do it gradually over the course of a week, adding in more of the new food little by little as you decrease the amount of the old. Switching too rapidly or constantly changing foods carries the risk of causing gastrointestinal problems. Be sure to read the recommended feeding guidelines for the new food, as they may differ from those of your old brand.

It's in the Can

Many owners feed dry kibble only. Some opt for canned food instead, while others feed a mixture of the two. There has long been a perception that canned foods are less nutritious, but more and more manufacturers are now producing canned foods of superior quality. As long as a high quality food is chosen, canned-only can be a perfectly healthful option and is one that many dogs prefer. In fact, canned foods tend to be fresher than dry kibble, have higher quality ingredients, and contain fewer chemicals and preservatives. And canned foods almost always contain a higher percentage of meat than does dry kibble.

Just as with dry foods, quality varies greatly from brand to brand, so a bit of label-sleuthing is necessary. Look for a whole meat source to be listed as the first ingredient. Some mid-to-lower quality foods list water as the first ingredient. A premium canned food will use meat broth, poultry broth, or fish broth in place of water. The same label rules that apply when evaluating the ingredients in kibble apply when evaluating those in canned foods.

The Whole Dog Journal periodically reviews canned and dry foods and lists its top picks. A visit to www.whole-dog-journal.com will yield a listing of past articles that are available for download.

In the Raw

Some owners forego processed food altogether in favor of a raw diet. The staple of this type of diet is raw, meaty bones—chicken or turkey backs and necks, cow femur "marrow bones," and other forms of raw meat. The diet normally includes pulverized raw vegetables and other healthful foods as well. Proponents of raw feeding credit the diet with everything from enhanced canine health and increased longevity to improved behavior and even recovery from disease. Some veterinarians and owners are concerned about the possibility of a bone perforating a dog's intestine or stomach, or a dog breaking teeth or choking on a bone. These problems can be avoided by grinding the meat, bones and all.

The most popular canine raw diet goes by the unfortunate acronym BARF—Biologically Appropriate Raw Food, or Bones And Raw Food. (One of the most popular authors on the subject is Ian Billinghurst. For his and other books on raw feeding, see *Resources*.) If you plan to try a raw diet, research carefully to ensure that you are feeding the correct balance and giving proper supplementation. Always use safe handling procedures, and check with your veterinarian to make sure that your nutritional plan will be safe for your dog.

Commercial Frozen Diets

A number of companies offer meat-based frozen dog foods. The products are convenient and make it easy to ensure that your dog is getting the right nutritional balance. For those reasons, I feed a pre-prepared frozen diet (Darwin's Natural Pet Products—meals consist of hormone-and-antibiotic-free meat, ground bone, veggies, organ meats, and vitamins. It's delivered to my door, and I just defrost a pouch at mealtimes. See *Resources*.) Alternatively, you could opt for freeze-dried meals, or mixtures of vegetables and other nutrients that can be added to a meat-based diet. (Go to www.whole-dog-journal.com to download articles on pre-prepared raw diets.)

Home Cookin'

Some kindly, industrious owners cook for their dogs. Personally, my culinary skills stop at macaroni and cheese. But boiled chicken, vegetables, and other healthful foods are infinitely more nutritious for your dog than what is found in most dry dog foods. If you choose to feed a homemade diet, pay careful attention to nutritional balance and consider whether supplements are necessary. *Dr. Pitcairn's Complete Guide to Natural Health for Dogs & Cats* has excellent information on cooking for dogs. The book contains recipes, information on supplementation, and considerations for dogs with special medical needs. (For Dr. Pitcairn's book and others on canine nutrition, see *Resources*.)

1 O'Heare, J. *Canine Neuropsychology*. Canada: Dog Psych, 2003

 # Tail End Wrap-Up

- Nutrition affects your dog's health *and* his behavior.

- The first two ingredients in your dog's food should be meats, preferably whole sources such as "chicken."

- You should avoid:

    - Foods with lots of by-products or corn
    - Foods with artificial coloring or flavoring
    - Foods that do not list the specific source of an ingredient (for example, "animal fat")
    - The preservatives BHA, BHT, and ethoxyquin

- Switch foods gradually, over the course of a week.

- Research options such as quality canned foods, raw diets, frozen diets, and home-cooked diets.

- If your dog has a medical condition, consult your veterinarian regarding any dietary changes.

Physical Exercise

I live in Los Angeles, where freeway traffic can get pretty intense; it is not unusual to be cut off by other drivers. If someone makes a rude traffic maneuver when I happen to be anxious or not in the best of moods, my temper is likely to flare. But if the same type of incident occurs after I have finished working out at the gym, my reaction is much less volatile. Why? Because exercise causes a chain of chemical reactions in the body and brain that promote a feeling of calm. After exercising, most people feel more serene and have less nervous energy to direct at others.

The exercise/calming mechanism works in essentially the same way in both dogs and people. Have you ever noticed how relaxed your dog is after a long, tiring walk? Sure, she's weary from the walk, but thanks to the chemical reactions triggered by the exercise, there is also a lovely state of calm settled over her like a warm blanket. Achieving that calm, relaxed state is doubly important for anxious, fearful dogs. Keeping your dog well exercised will allow her to stay relaxed and receptive to learning, and will make your behavior modification efforts more successful.

Check with your veterinarian before allowing your dog to participate in any exercise program or sport. Dogs with injured or weak shoulders, knees, ankles, or hips should not engage in any activity that involves jumping, or compete in any strenuous sport.

Walks

The amount of exercise your dog needs depends on her breed, size, age, and physical condition. An adolescent Labrador Retriever, for example, requires much more exercise—an hour a day minimum, assuming good health—than does a nine-year-old Newfoundland. One of the easiest ways to exercise your dog is to take her for walks. Daily walks are beneficial on two levels, as they provide not only physical exercise, but mental stimulation in the form of scintillating scents. To a dog, sniffing where other dogs have left their marks is like reading a community bulletin board: *Hmm, an adolescent male has moved into the neighborhood. Aah, Fifi was here—ooh la la! I'd know that scent anywhere!* Taking your dog for daily walks provides a great excuse for you to get out and exercise as well.

Hikes

To dogs, hiking trails are like paths through a fabulous doggy amusement park. A hike provides the opportunity to romp over hills and play among copses of shady trees, checking out plant life, watering holes, and a cornucopia of natural scents along the way. If your dog is apt to be nervous her first time in a wooded area, bring along plenty of treats and her favorite toy for comfort. Keep the first few outings brief, and tailor hikes to your dog's comfort level and physical capabilities. Follow posted rules and always be aware of your surroundings.

If your dog is fearful or reactive with other dogs or people, even if off-leash hiking is allowed, keep your dog on leash. Until your dog's issues are resolved, hike during hours when you are less likely to encounter others.

Walking and hiking both provide mental and physical stimulation, as well as an opportunity for calm, peaceful bonding time. Plan outings when the weather is cool and always bring along water for both of you.

Aerobic Exercise

Walks and hikes are fine, but what about more intense aerobic exercise? If you have a back yard, or a nearby park that allows dogs to run off-leash, a hearty workout is easy to provide; toss a ball, soft Frisbee®, or whatever your dog likes to fetch. If your dog is reliable off-leash (meaning she comes every time you call) and is dog-friendly, allowing her to play with other dogs at the park is a great form of exercise.

If you are lucky enough to have a swimming pool, you have a built-in exercise facility! Swimming is great cardiovascular exercise, and strengthens muscles without stressing joints (especially good for dogs with arthritis or other joint-related conditions). Assuming your dog is in good physical health, other options include jogging, or running alongside a bicycle attached by a device made for that purpose (see *Resources*).

At dog parks and other dog-friendly areas, monitor your dog's interactions with others. Some dogs, although allowed to romp off-leash, are not dog-friendly. Even if all the dogs seem friendly, play can sometimes escalate into skirmishes and even full-out fights. You are your dog's guardian and must be her advocate. If an interaction makes you uncomfortable, either say something or take your dog and move to another part of the park. If necessary, leave altogether.

Indoor Exercise

Tug: Tug-of-war—that exhilarating game where you hold one end of a rope toy, towel, or other object and allow your dog to tug at the other end—is a great way to provide exercise. Tug has the added benefit of building canine confidence. You might have heard that "playing tug will make dogs aggressive." That's an old myth. The game should, however, have rules and structure. A prerequisite to a proper game of tug is that your dog understands "Leave it." This phrase cues your dog to open her mouth and release the object she is holding. If your dog does not yet understand this cue, teach it using the instructions that follow.

How to Teach "Leave it"

Place a treat in your closed fist and hold it directly in front of your dog's nose. Wait. She will probably nudge and mouth it in an attempt to get the treat. Don't move your hand! When your dog backs off, even for a second, say, "Yes!" then open the fist, praise, and give her the treat. Repeat until you can predict that your dog will back off within a few seconds of your presenting the fist.

Next, hold a treat in your closed fist as before. Allow your dog to sniff for a second, then say, "Leave it!" (This is one instance in which it is acceptable for your voice to be slightly gruff. After all, when you eventually use the cue to tell your dog to leave something alone—like an object on a countertop or on the floor—it is unlikely that you will use a pleasant, singsong voice.) Your dog should back off. Say, "Yes!" and give her the treat and praise.

(For instructions on how to apply this skill to objects on countertops and floors, see the *Train Your Dog: The Positive, Gentle Method* DVD in the *Resources* section.)

Once your dog consistently responds to "Leave it!" as soon as you give the verbal cue, try it with the tug toy instead of the treat. Hold the tug toy (preferably a braided rope) at both ends and allow your dog to put her mouth on the middle section. Don't move your hands. After a second or two, say, "Leave it!" As soon as your dog backs off, reward with praise and a treat. Repeat a few times. Once your dog is doing well, it's time to play! Offer your dog the middle part of the toy. You may move the toy gently from side to side, but allow your dog to do most of the tugging. (Don't pull the toy in an upward direction, as it could hurt your dog's neck.) Periodically during play, freeze in place—stop *all* motion—and then say, "Leave it!" Assuming your dog has had enough practice, she should spit out the toy and back away. Given a few extra seconds, she may automatically sit as well. Praise your dog, then say, "Take it!" and resume the game. (If your dog does not release the toy on request, put off playing tug until she has had more practice at "Leave it.")

If your dog's teeth touch your skin at any point during the game, say, "Too bad!" and put the toy away. Your dog will learn quickly that teeth contacting skin ends the game, and she will become much better at keeping her teeth on the toy. (Your dog might growl during this game; that is perfectly normal. If you are concerned that her behavior might be anything other than normal play, consult a professional trainer.) Allow your dog to win once in a while—it's a good way to help her build confidence. When you are finished playing, put the toy away.

Chewing: Recreational chewing provides exercise for your dog's jaws, is an excellent outlet for excess energy, and has the important benefit of being a canine stress-reliever. Some dogs, whenever they feel anxious, find their favorite chew toy and carry it around the way Linus of the Peanuts™ comic strip carries his comfort blanket.

Make appropriate chew toys available regularly. Avoid rawhide and pig ears, as they can be dangerous if large pieces are ingested without being thoroughly chewed. (Compressed rawhide is a safer version of the original.) A better alternative would be "bully sticks," also known as "pizzle sticks." Bully sticks are natural, do not pull apart in large pieces the way rawhide does, and are widely available at pet supply stores. Always monitor your dog with chew items, as even "safe" ones can become dangerous if the last, small piece is ingested whole. You will learn about my very favorite chew item, the Kong®, in the next chapter.

When You're Too Busy

Many dog owners work, have social obligations, or just plain don't have the time or the inclination to exercise their dogs. Doggy daycare centers offer an excellent solution. Doggy daycare is just what the name implies— it's like child daycare, but for dogs! Those lucky dogs get to romp with each other, play with toys, engage in fun activities, and rest periodically. The advantages of a well-run daycare are many. Because dogs are carefully screened for temperament before they are allowed to join, the chances of aggressive encounters are lessened. Dogs learn to interact with others of various breeds, sizes, and ages, all in a safe environment. Most dogs love it! Owners love it too, as there is nothing like a day of daycare to leave a dog pleasantly worn out, and therefore calm. And that calm often lasts well into the next day; we had many owners at the daycare where I worked who dropped their dogs off every other day, and reaped the benefits all week long.

Less expensive alternatives to doggy daycare include hiring a professional dog walker, friend, neighbor, or student to take your dog for a nice, long walk during the day. Alternately, the person could drop by for an hour to play with your dog in the house or yard. Do you have a friend or neighbor whose dog is in need of company during the day? Assuming both of your homes are dog-safe (that is, there is a secure back yard fence and if there is a swimming pool it is partitioned off) and the dogs get along well, you could switch off locations for supervised play dates.

Exercise Tips

- If your dog is not accustomed to regular exercise, start slowly and build duration and intensity gradually, just as you would if *you* were starting a new exercise program.

- Don't count on your dog to tell you when she is tired. Many dogs will run and chase balls to the point of exhaustion if allowed.

- It is important that, just like a human athlete, your dog's muscles be warmed up before pursuing vigorous activity. Give your dog a brief warm-up walk, and gently massage her muscles before starting the activity; give her a brief cool-down walk afterward. Whenever possible, take long walks or jogs on dirt trails or asphalt roads rather than on concrete, as concrete is much harder on a dog's joints (and on yours).

- When playing retrieve games, be careful not to toss the item too high in the air, as your dog could injure her back upon landing after a vertical jump.

Dog Sports

Dog sports are a fun way to provide your dog with exercise and improve her coordination. Best of all for fearful dogs, dog sports are wonderful for increasing canine confidence.

Agility

Agility is one of the most popular dog sports, and for good reason. It provides dogs with physical exercise and mental stimulation, is a great way to build confidence, and is fun for owners as well. Dogs learn to weave through poles, crawl through tunnels, leap through tires and over jumps, scale an A-frame (a wooden ramp that resembles the letter A), tip a teeter-totter (seesaw), and even walk across a beam set a few feet off the ground. Once a dog has learned to navigate each obstacle, she runs a course with the owner running alongside giving directions. Dogs can eventually compete for the fastest time and finesse in navigating the obstacles, although lessons can be taken solely for fun. Agility not only builds confidence through acquisition of new skills and literally overcoming obstacles, but also improves communication and trust between dog and owner.

Your dog must be in good physical shape to do agility. Dogs under the age of eighteen months are not usually accepted into classes because the impact of the jumps could injure their still-developing skeletal systems; but some groups offer safe, age-appropriate introductory classes for younger dogs. As with any type of class, training methods vary and some instructors are better than others. Be sure to watch a class before joining to check that the instructor uses gentle motivational methods. Note whether the class is organized and well run, and whether the dogs and people seem to be having fun.

If you would rather not get involved in a structured class, or your dog is not comfortable around other dogs or people just yet, consider setting up a mini-agility course in your back yard. Purchase a pre-made kit such as the Dog Games Agility Starter kit (available at pet supply stores or via a Google search), or make your own using the book *Do-It-Yourself Agility Equipment* (see *Resources*). Even teaching your dog to walk over lengths of PVC pipe laid out in various configurations can increase confidence. In fact, Ttouch practitioners (more on Ttouch in *Chapter 45*) use a "Confidence Course" and a "Playground" scenario for that very purpose.

Tracking

For a fun, low-impact activity, consider tracking. In a tracking trial, a trail of scent is laid out and a dog must follow it to find a specific article. The skill is normally taught in a class environment, but if you would prefer that your dog have the fun, stimulation, and confidence-building of tracking without the social interaction, read *Fun Nosework for Dogs* by Roy Hunter (see *Resources*) to learn how to set up tracking games in your home or yard.

Freestyle

There are few things as fun and relaxing as dancing. Freestyle is a fairly new sport that involves dancing—with your dog! First, dogs are taught basic skills such as backing up, walking sideways, weaving through owners' legs, and turning in a circle. Then the fun starts, as dogs and owners work the skills into choreographed routines set to music. Freestyle competitions are great fun, with dog/owner teams dressing up in costumes and performing creative routines set to everything from country music to rock 'n' roll.

Freestyle can be taught to very young dogs, and is also a good choice for dogs who are older or unable to handle the physical requirements of sports like agility. As with agility, communication between dog and owner is key. The strengthening of the dog/owner bond, along with the confidence that comes from mastering each skill, make Freestyle another great sport for less-than-confident dogs. If your dog is comfortable around other dogs and people, consider joining a class and entering competitions. Or, if you prefer, learn and practice in your own home. (See *Resources* for more information.)

Rally, Rally, Oh! Oh! Oh!

While competition obedience is a long-established and well-respected sport, its stringent rules can be too stressful for some anxious dogs. Enter Rally Obedience, also known as Rally O. Rally O incorporates obedience and agility into a completely new, creative, confidence-boosting sport that is fun for dogs and people. The exercises are similar to those found at the "Novice" level of obedience competition, but the sport is easier and gentler in that it is more about fun than precision—a definite plus for anxious dogs.

Handlers walk dogs through a course that includes a number of stops. At each one, a sign indicates which task is required. (Handlers get to walk the course alone first so they know what to expect.) Tasks range from simply walking at a fast pace to the next stop, to making a 180-degree turn, to circling around a series of cones. In APDT-style Rally, the handler is encouraged to use verbal praise, petting, and even food treats. The APDT (Association of Pet Dog Trainers) version of the sport has more relaxed rules than the AKC (American Kennel Club) version. (See *Resources* for contact information on both.) Timed and non-timed courses, along with two levels of difficulty, allow dogs to progress at their own pace. Because the courses constantly change, they remain challenging and fun.

These are just a few examples of enjoyable ways to exercise your dog; there are many others. Check with your local obedience and breed clubs, along with the organizations listed in the *Resources* section, for referrals to groups in your area.

Tail End Wrap-Up

Exercise has many physical benefits for dogs. It is especially important for anxious dogs, as it promotes a calm, peaceful state of mind. Dog sports not only provide physical exercise and mental stimulation, but also build canine confidence.

🐾   Check with your veterinarian to be sure the form of exercise you choose is appropriate and safe for your dog.

🐾   Ways to provide your dog with exercise include:

- Walking – with you or a hired walker
- Hiking
- Swimming
- Jogging alongside you
- Running alongside a bicycle (use attachment)
- Chasing a ball or other throw toy
- Playing with other dogs at a park, friend's house, or doggy daycare
- Playing tug
- Chewing
- Agility
- Tracking
- Freestyle
- Rally O
- Other dog sports

Mental Stimulation

Think back to the last time you worked through a brain-teaser puzzle, or solved a problem that required you to think creatively. Chances are, although you were left with a sense of accomplishment, you also felt a bit worn out afterward. Mental exertion can be as tiring as physical exercise, and sometimes even more so. For anxious dogs, mental exertion can be extremely beneficial, as it encourages a calm state of mind.

A dog whose mind is under-stimulated is more likely to be anxious and to display that anxiety by chewing on inappropriate objects, pacing, whining, barking, and exhibiting restlessness or hyperactivity. On the other hand, a dog who uses his mind, along with getting adequate physical exercise, will be much calmer. Let's look at some ways you can provide your dog with mental stimulation.

Show Me the Treats! Interactive Food Dispensers

Interactive food/treat dispensers are a great way to engage your dog's problem-solving skills. These clever devices come in various shapes and sizes, and are meant to be filled with kibble or small, non-gooey treats. Your dog's job is to figure out how to maneuver the dispenser using his nose and paws to get the goodies to fall out.

Consider feeding your dog's meals in a food dispenser. If you think about it, wolves, relatives of the dog, have to work hard for their food. When wolves hunt big game, they are successful only about ten percent of the time; that's a lot of exertion! And here we are, thousands of years later, a dish of kibble in hand, saying, "Bon appetit!" ...Heck, make 'em work for it! Besides, coaxing a meal from a dispenser bit by bit will keep your dog busy for roughly ten to thirty minutes, which is helpful if you have "morning rush hour" at your house. The dispensers can also be filled with small, dry treats, which is a good way to provide mental stimulation on the days you are not able to train or take your dog for a walk.

The *Molecuball*™ (available at pet supply stores and online) is one of my favorite food dispensers. So named because it is shaped like—you guessed it—a molecule, this nifty device is made of a durable, non-toxic thermoplastic, with a hole at the top. The ball comes in three sizes. The size of the hole and the shape of the ball keep things challenging, but not so difficult that your dog will lose interest. To ensure that your dog does not chew through it, leave the ball with him only at mealtimes or while dispensing treats.

For a more challenging food delivery device, check out the *Buster Cube*® (available at pet supply stores and online). This hard plastic cube conceals four internal chambers. Kibble or other small, dry treats are poured through a hole at the top and then distributed internally by shaking the cube. The insertion hole can be turned to increase or decrease the difficulty level. This device is the perfect choice for extremely intelligent dogs who are good at problem-solving. However, the cube is made of a very hard plastic and might not be the best choice if you have an extremely strong, rambunctious dog and/or antique or fragile furniture. A friend's Pit Bull likes nothing better than to whack the cube into the wall repeatedly, and Mojo has actually disemboweled one or two. Still, for any but the most destructive dogs, the Buster Cube® is a good choice.

Molecuball™   *Buster Cube*®

No discussion of canine food dispensers would be complete without mentioning my very favorite, the *Kong*®. This fabulous creation is made of extremely tough rubber—the black version is even tougher than the red—and is shaped like a snowman. There is a small hole at the top and a larger one on the bottom. Simply plug the top hole with a small, moldable treat or thick substance such as peanut butter, then flip it over and stuff the large cavity. (The product comes in a variety of sizes; be careful not to buy one that's too small, as you won't have much of a cavity in which to stuff goodies.) The idea is to create layers using a mortar-like substance such as peanut butter, cream cheese, or canned dog food between looser layers of dog cookies or kibble. That way the contents do not fall out easily, and the dog is kept busy trying to figure out how to get to them.

You can create a frozen Kong® by filling the cavity and placing the finished product in the freezer. Freezing ensures that the fun will last a long time, and it's great mental stimulation for hot days. You can also feed your dog his meals in the Kong®: Plug the small hole with a soft, moist treat or a bit of peanut butter. Measure out the kibble and either mix it with wet food and spoon in the entire mixture, or alternate layers of wet and dry food, starting with a spoonful of wet and ending in a layer of wet to hold it all inside.

How long will it take your dog to plunder the Kong's hidden treasure? That depends on how tightly it is packed, and on your dog's energy level and tenacity. A loosely packed Kong® might be excavated in under ten minutes. Tightly packed or frozen, it could last over an hour. If your dog has never practiced this type of excavation before, go easy. Pack layers loosely and leave a dog cookie or other treat sticking out so that he has immediate success. As his skills improve, pack layers more tightly to make things more challenging. If your dog is anxious about being left alone, leaving him with a well-stuffed Kong® will occupy him during the crucial initial departure phase, and the chewing will provide stress relief.

If you find yourself using interactive treat dispensers often, cut back on the quantity of food in your dog's regular meals so that weight gain does not become a problem.

The calm focus that comes over a dog as he happily goes about his excavation project is lovely. In fact, one of my clients called this wonderful invention a "puppy pacifier"—and she's right. My personal prediction is that your dogs, like mine, will soon become confirmed Kongaholics! Contact the manufacturer directly for a pamphlet of stuffing recipes (see *Resources*). The Kong®, along with many other fascinating interactive food dispensers, is available through pet supply stores and online.

The fabulous Kong®, being enjoyed by Mojo.

Kibble Toss

Kibble Toss is a creative way to turn feeding time into mental stimulation. The game makes use of your dog's natural scenting ability and provides an urban version of hunting for food. Measure out enough kibble for a meal, then *whoosh!* Toss it all over the yard. While that might seem odd, the game is great fun for dogs! Your dog will happily track through the grass, nose to the ground, tail wagging as he discovers each tasty morsel. If you do not have a yard, the living room or kitchen floor will suffice. *Note:* Do not play this game with multiple dogs if they have a tendency to fight over food, or if one is likely to bully the other out of his share.

Hidden Treasure

Hidden Treasure is a hide and seek game, where you hide something and your dog must find it. The game can be played indoors or out and engages your dog "scentally" as well as mentally. Setting up a Hidden Treasure game before you leave the house will give your dog something productive to do while you are gone, and can be a great stress-reliever for home-alone dogs.

The "treasure" can be a chew bone, Kong®, or other food-dispensing device. To teach your dog how to play, toss the treasure just a foot or two away in clear sight and say, "Find it!" When your dog runs to it make a big fuss, praise him, and allow him to chew at it for a few minutes. Repeat the sequence a few times, tossing the item a bit further away each time. Then either have someone restrain your dog with a leash, tether him (attach a leash to a sturdy piece of furniture and clip it to his regular flat collar) or ask him to stay, and place the treasure on the floor a few feet away. Release your dog and tell him to find it. Place the treasure a bit further away each time so that it eventually ends up across the room.

Now comes the "hidden" part. Restrain your dog as before while you place the treasure in a spot where it is semi-hidden but still easy to spot (for example, peeking out from under a sofa cushion or a newspaper laid on the floor). Release your dog and say, "Find it!" If he runs to the treasure, praise him and allow him to have it. If he does not run to it, give him a few moments to figure it out. If necessary, help him by standing near where the item is hidden. If your dog truly cannot find the item, start over, but make it easier. Once your dog is successful, make the treasure more and more difficult to find, until it is completely hidden.

Once your dog understands the game, hide the treasure in one room while he is just around the corner, then release him to find it. Progress to hiding it in one room while he is in the next, then hiding it in other rooms so that he has to search the house. You can even incorporate your back yard into the game. Once your dog is accustomed to finding the treasure while you are present, hide it, then just before you leave, tell him to find it. You can even hide multiple items if you are going to be gone for a while. Just be careful not to hide things so well that you come home to a house that looks like Hurricane Fido has hit!

Wanna Go for a Ride?

To dogs, a car ride is a moving smorgasbord of scent. Dogs love to stick their noses out the window as they catch the scent of trees, other animals, people, and just about everything else in the environment that we humans barely notice. There is a visual component to car rides as well, as your dog is exposed to things he does not see every day. A car ride provides not only mental stimulation, but fun!

Taking your dog along to do errands or visit friends is a great way to get him out and about, especially if you do not have much time for walks or other outdoor activities. Just be sure not to leave him in the car on a hot day for any length of time, and to keep windows lowered just enough as you ride that he can stick his nose out but not his entire head—dogs can be blinded by flying debris. Adding regular car rides to your dog's life will help to keep him mentally stimulated and therefore calmer in general.

Clicker Training

Clicker training is included here rather than in the training section because it is so mentally stimulating. This non-coercive training method has been used with marine mammals including dolphins and killer whales, and exotic animals such as lions, and tigers, and bears—oh, my! Clicker training is also an excellent way to train dogs and, because it requires them to think and figure things out, is a great way to build confidence.

A clicker is a small, plastic box with a metal tab that makes a clicking sound when pressed. The click acts as a marker to let a dog know the exact moment he is doing something correctly. Let's say you were teaching your dog to lie down. You might lure him into position with a food treat, then click at the moment his body was flat on the floor to tell him that was the exact position you wanted. A click is faster and more precise than words, and always sounds exactly the same. Why would a dog care about a click? Because every click is followed by a treat! Dogs must figure out how to earn a click in order to get a treat—that's where the mental stimulation comes in. It is fascinating to watch a dog "get it" and begin to offer the desired behavior in hopes of earning a click and treat.

If your dog is sound-sensitive, use a soft click, such as that of a ballpoint pen, in place of a standard clicker. There is also a clicker called the "i-click" that has a softer sound than a regular clicker (see *Resources*). Alternately, you may substitute a short, "Yes!" in place of a click.

Clicking can be used in conjunction with luring as described. But the real fun comes when it is used to shape behaviors. This is where your dog's mental wheels really start turning! In *shaping*, you reward small bits of behavior—*successive approximations*—to reach a goal. Shaping is like the kids' game "Hot and Cold," where the subject is told by the rest of the group when she is getting "hotter" or "colder" as she wanders closer to or farther from a pre-selected object. In shaping there is no "colder," but the click serves as a "hotter" signal that helps to shape the subject's movements toward the final goal. For example, to teach your dog to go to his bed, you might first click and treat for a mere glance toward the bed. Once your dog was repeatedly looking toward the bed, you might hold out for any slight movement toward the bed (for example, one paw moving forward) before clicking and treating. You would continue to click small, progressive increments until your dog had one paw on the bed, then two, and so forth, until he was standing completely on the bed. This would all be done without verbal encouragement (except for praise while delivering the treat). Once your dog understood the desired behavior and began to go to the bed on his own, you would say, "Go to bed" just before he did so. You would soon be able to ask your dog to go to bed with successful results.

Even more fascinating than shaping is *capturing*. Capturing means clicking a naturally occurring behavior. Let's say you want your dog to walk nicely beside you rather than pulling on the leash. Every time your dog happens to walk next to you, you click to mark the moment and then reward with a treat. Your dog would soon learn that the most valuable place to be is by your side. Capturing can also help you to train behaviors that would be difficult to elicit. Let's say you want to put stretching on a verbal cue. It might be difficult to encourage your dog to stretch, but you've noticed that your dog stretches every time he stands up after taking a nap. Capture it! Simply click and treat every stretch. A clicker-savvy dog is always trying to figure out what he did to earn the click, so your dog will soon begin to offer the behavior. Once he does, add the verbal cue—say, "Stretch!" or, if you'd prefer, something creative like "Bow to the Queen!"—just as he begins to stretch. Using capturing, you could even teach your dog to yawn, sneeze, or belch on cue, although I would advise against the latter—who wants a dog offering *that*?!!

Note: Throughout this book, the verbal marker, "Yes!" is used instead of an actual click. If you would like, assuming your dog is not afraid of the sound, you may substitute a click for the verbal marker.

The principles of clicker training might seem odd or backward if you have trained dogs in a traditional manner, especially if you are accustomed to physically manipulative methods such as pushing your dog's rear to the ground to teach sit. But clicker training is worth taking the time to explore. The method is not only fascinating, creative, and effective, but offers a whole new way to communicate with your dog. And clicker training is an extremely valuable tool for building canine confidence. (To learn more about the fascinating art of clicker training, see *Resources*.)

 Tail End Wrap-Up

🐾 Use interactive food dispensers to feed meals and deliver treats.

🐾 Play Kibble Toss with meals.

🐾 Set up Hidden Treasure games when you are home and before you leave the house.

🐾 Take your dog along for car rides, even just to do errands.

🐾 Give clicker training a try!

Leadership

Imagine that you are planning a trip to a foreign country, and you must choose between two tour guides. The first candidate, Adam, knows the territory well, speaks the language, and appears knowledgeable. He is relaxed and exudes an air of confidence. Bob, your alternate choice, has never been to the country and, for that matter, has not been a tour guide for very long. Bob appears apprehensive about the excursion, and nervously offers his assurance that he will try to do his best. Fast forward a week into your trip: you are walking through a quaint bazaar when you hear an explosion. What should you do? With Adam at the helm, you would feel assured that he would handle the situation and keep you safe. But had you chosen to place Bob in charge, you might feel the need to take your safety into your own hands. While Bob's demeanor does not encourage feelings of safety or security, Adam's strong aura of leadership does. Now consider how crucial it is to encourage those feelings in a fearful dog.

A dog who regards his human as a strong leader will feel more secure in threatening situations. For example, Shiloh the Shetland Sheepdog is nervous when strangers approach on the street. Without confidence in his owner, Shiloh might feel the need to take matters into his own paws, barking and lunging furiously to drive the stranger away. But if he sees his owner as a capable leader, Shiloh can relax and let her handle the situation. Leadership has its benefits for you, the owner, as well. If you feel that you have more control over your dog, you will be able to remain calmer when confronted with potentially anxiety-producing situations.

Good leaders use psychology rather than physical force to lead and teach. There is no need to prove to your dog that you are in charge by being physically overpowering. In a pack of wolves, it is the middle-ranking pack members, the "alpha wanna-be's," who constantly squabble in attempts to prove their status. A true alpha ("top dog") has nothing to prove. Interestingly, the same phenomenon can be seen in human social groups—just observe office politics sometime!

The Language of Leadership

The unruffled, self-assured manner of a strong leader is reflected in her tone of voice and body language. Speech is succinct. Instructions are clear and direct. A good leader is fair, consistent, and patient. Although it might be difficult to define a good leader by listing personality traits and mannerisms, the aura of a true leader is unmistakable. Even if you do not naturally exude leadership qualities, you can learn to approximate them well enough that your dog will be convinced that you are in charge. Here's how:

- Maintain an air of calm confidence. Whenever you feel yourself becoming tense, take a few deep breaths.

- Give verbal cues once in an even tone of voice. Do not repeat cues with escalating volume! Your dog can hear a potato chip hit the carpet in the next room—she heard your request the first time.

- Keep verbal cues simple; do not surround them with extraneous chatter. It's not, "Hey Buddy, come on, come here now!" It's, "Buddy, come!"

- Be clear in your hand signals and body language. Do not use unnecessary movements. Stand tall and communicate calmly and clearly.

- If your dog does not respond to a verbal cue immediately (assuming it is one she understands and has practiced), count to 30 silently. If she complies during that time, reward her. The time between the cue and the response—known as *latency*—will get shorter with repeated attempts. If your dog does not comply, a consequence should follow. The consequence might be your walking away and ignoring her for two minutes, withdrawing a potential reward (like the treat you were about to give), or gently placing her into the requested position.

- If you must interrupt a behavior, use a soft but sharp "Eh-eh!" rather than a frantic or whining "No, no, noooo, stop doing that right now!" Once your dog has ceased the inappropriate behavior, calmly redirect her to another activity such as chewing an appropriate chew toy. (Ask for a sit before giving her the chew toy so she is being rewarded for the sit rather than for the inappropriate activity.)

Dominance

Sassy is a typical nine-month-old Golden Retriever. She blasts through doorways ahead of her owner, jumps enthusiastically on guests, and as of late, has developed selective hearing. Some people would label Sassy as "dominant." Unfortunately, the concept of dominance has been overblown and misused terribly in dog training over the years. The fact is, none of the aforementioned behaviors makes Sassy "dominant." They do, however, describe a typical pushy adolescent in serious need of some manners. (Sassy's behavior, by the way, does not make her "stubborn" either. Dogs who are called "stubborn" are often quite intelligent, so much so that they get bored easily and simply need a good reason to do as asked.)

It can be detrimental to your relationship with your dog to label her as "dominant," because in doing so you will come to view everything she does in that context. While your dog might be pushy or have an "alpha" type personality, that does not mean she lives in a perpetual state of plotting to overthrow your kingdom—or even that she wants to be top dog in all situations. As with children, dogs feel more secure having rules and boundaries. Just as you would with a child, teach your dog proper manners. Training should not be a battle of wills, but a loving, learning process with you at the helm. That's where the Leadership Program can help.

Leadership Program

The Leadership Program is not a training exercise to be practiced here and there, but a set of rules and habits to adopt into your daily routine. Leadership means that *you* make the rules and control the resources. *You* decide when it is time for your dog to eat, play, or be petted, and whether she gets access to the couch and other privileges. In other words, you have more influence over your dog's behavior than vice versa.

It is key to the success of this program that once guidelines are established they remain firm. All family members must adhere to the program. As with any training program, it is counterproductive to have one "untrainer" in the group who bends the rules and undoes everyone else's hard work. Inconsistency is also confusing and unfair to your dog. Ensure that everyone stays on track by gently reminding each other when someone veers from the plan. Presenting a united front will make expectations clear to your dog and produce fast, reliable results. It can be helpful to post the house rules in a central location, such as on the refrigerator or kitchen bulletin board.

Control the Good Stuff

If you have children, you already know all about managing resources. You control the allowance, the curfew, and if you have teenagers, use of the car (or so you hope!). Humans and canines innately understand that those who control the resources are in charge. With that in mind, your new official title is "The Source of All Good Things." (You've got as many words in your title as The Artist Formerly Known as Prince—now you *know* you're important!) Consider what constitutes a valuable resource to your dog. Let's see…he's not getting an allowance, and we're certainly not going to hand over the car keys…but wait! There's food, play, and other valuable resources you can easily control.

Food

Because food is literally life or death to dogs, it is important that your dog understand that it comes from you. Unfortunately, many dogs believe this most precious resource comes from that small, circular object that is somehow always magically full. Free-feeding (leaving food constantly available) is no way to establish leadership. Unless you work extremely long hours, there is no reason to free-feed. (While water is also an important resource, it should always be readily available.)

In addition to scheduled feedings helping to establish leadership, they can also act as a diagnostic tool. If your dog normally eats immediately and finishes all her food, the day she turns her nose up at a meal you will know something is awry. That very thing happened with Mojo last year. Ever since he was a pup, Mojo has wolfed down his food (and any other dog's food he could get his paws on). The day he walked away from a meal, I took him directly to the vet—and it was a good thing, too, because he was quite ill. The rejection of his regular meal alerted me that he was sick, and in fact, it might have saved his life.

In a wolf pack, the leader usually eats first. In some literature, that information somehow got translated to the admonition to always eat before your dog eats. I knew one woman who was meticulous about always eating a cracker in front of her dog before allowing him to eat his meal. That is not necessary! Feed your dog whenever it is convenient for you, whether that happens to be before or after your own meal. You are in charge, so you decide when things happen. The rules themselves are not as important as the fact that you are making them.

To switch your dog from free-feeding to scheduled feedings, offer a meal in the morning at whatever time is convenient. Leave the food down for ten to fifteen minutes, then pick up the uneaten portion and put it away. A dog who is accustomed to food being available throughout the day is probably not going to have eaten very much. That's fine. At the next feeding (for example, dinner time), offer food again. Wait ten to fifteen minutes, then remove the uneaten portion. It is perfectly normal to feel that you are being a mean dog-mom or -dad during this transitional phase. But no dog is going to starve herself. Your dog will soon come to realize that food is available for a limited time only, and your former grazer will soon eat whenever a meal is offered.

Hand-Feeding

Some dogs, even those with fear issues, can be pushy and obnoxious. They crowd our personal space, bark, jump, or get mouthy when they do not get their way. Pushy dogs are pretty sure they know who's in charge— and it's not us. If that describes your dog, jump-start your leadership program by hand-feeding for two weeks. *Oh sure,* you're thinking, *what next? Fan her and feed her caviar?* Actually, hand-feeding does not communicate subservience. On the contrary, you are making it known that the most valuable resource in dogdom comes directly from you, The Source of All Good Things.

If your dog has been free-fed, wait until she is on scheduled feedings to begin hand-feeding. Once she is eating regularly, at each feeding, ask her to sit, then feed her a few bits of kibble. If you feed a wet-dry mixture, use a spoon. Repeat after each mouthful, asking for other familiar behaviors such as shake or down as well, until the meal is finished. If at any point your dog does not comply, wait 30 seconds. If she still has not complied, say, "You must not be hungry!" and put the food away. Return in two minutes and try again. Most dogs will do as asked on the second try in record time. I cannot emphasize strongly enough the psychological impact that hand feeding for two weeks will have on your relationship with your dog. You should notice a change in your dog's willingness to cooperate during training sessions and in her deference to you in general.

Play

If your dog is like most, play is a valuable commodity. Dogs derive great joy from chasing balls, playing tug, and racing around like little fur-covered maniacs. In fact, the dog is often the one who initiates play by dropping a ball or toy in front of the owner. Obedient humans that we are, we comply immediately. What's wrong with this picture?

Part of your being The Source of All Good Things includes being the Provider of Fun. This is not to suggest that your dog be left without toys when alone, but that the really fun, high-value toys be interactive. In other words, your presence and participation are required to make those special toys work. Let's say your dog's favorite chase toy is a rubber ball. Keep the ball hidden away. Whenever *you'd* like, bring it out and offer to play. Play as long as you'd like, then end the game and put the ball away until the next time. Because the best toys and the power to play special games with them are only accessible through you, your status is elevated.

If your dog brings one of her always-available toys and drops it at your feet, whether or not to play is up to you. As you'll soon see in the *Permission Please?* section, if you would like to play, you should ask your dog to do something for you first. If you don't want to play at that particular moment, say, "Not now." Then fold your arms, look up and to the side, and ignore her. (Be sure not to look at or talk to your dog once you've uttered the phrase.) Your dog will soon learn that, "Not now" means she might as well go lie down, because no further interaction will be taking place.

I taught my dogs the meaning of "Not now" when they were pups. It came in especially handy with Soko, who is completely ball-obsessed. She will sometimes lie nearby while my husband and I eat dinner, ball on the floor, looking from me to the ball as if to say, "C'mon, stop eating and throw it already!" I have never once complied in thirteen years, but being the Border-Collie-in-a-German-Shepherd's-body that she is, Soko still holds out hope that it might one day happen. When ignored, she lies there and stares relentlessly. When I finally tire of trying to eat with those big brown eyes boring holes into me, I look at her and calmly say, "Soko, not now." She will immediately pick up her ball, walk to her dog bed in the corner, and lie down with a big, drama-queen sigh.

Location, Location, Location

Real estate agents aren't the only ones who know the value of a fabulous location. Although access to specific areas might not seem like an obvious resource, it is one that many dogs attempt to control. Some dogs lie across doorways to control traffic in and out of a room. Others block access to valued resources. For example, my boy Mojo often bars the way when Soko wants to go to her bed. She doesn't dare pass the huge, bratty, fur-covered roadblock. (Being a brilliant German Shepherd, she instead perks up her ears and barks as though she's heard something outside, then dashes out the doggy door. Mojo invariably follows, at which point Soko darts back inside and claims the bed. Soko deserves an award for Best Performance in a Fido Fake-Out!)

While it is acceptable to a point for dogs to engage in power plays with each other, it is not permissible for them to do so with humans. What do you normally do if your dog is lying across a doorway or otherwise blocking your way? Do you ask her to move? Walk around her? Step over her? As the leader, you should control physical space. Assuming your dog has no aggression issues toward people, do the Shoe Shuffle. (If you have a dog who is likely to react with a growl or worse, consult a professional.) Keep your feet in contact with the floor as though they were attached by magnetic force. Shuffle gently into your dog as though she wasn't there. Most dogs will get up and move immediately. At the least, you will have moved your dog enough to get where you need to go.

Another way to get your dog to leave her doorway sentry post is to stand a few feet away and call her to you. Praise her for coming, then proceed to your original destination. Alternately, if your dog knows "go to your bed," sending her there is another way to remove her from your path. By having your dog accommodate you, rather than the other way around, you are enforcing your leadership status.

Furniture is another valued location. Whether to allow your dog on the couch or bed is a personal decision. Furniture privileges are perfectly acceptable, so long as your dog does not have aggression issues. (A dog who growls or gives the Elvis Lip Curl when asked to dismount should not be on furniture in the first place.) Be sure everyone in the family is in agreement as to which furniture is fair game. It won't do to have Mom let Spike lie on the couch while Dad is at work if Dad prefers that Spike not be allowed on the furniture. Make it a family rule that to gain access to the furniture, your dog must be invited. Simply ask your dog to sit, then pat the couch next to you to invite her up. This simple five-second sequence communicates volumes about your status.

Personal Space

Another type of physical space to consider is that which surrounds your body. Both dogs and people have an awareness of personal space. If you and Granny were both trying to get through a doorway, would you elbow her aside so you could pass through first? Of course not! It wouldn't be safe, and it certainly wouldn't be respectful. If your dog blasts past you at doorways, stairways, or hallways, or crowds your personal space, it doesn't say much for your leadership status. Your dog wouldn't dare behave that way with another dog she regards as higher-ranking, and she shouldn't behave that way with you.

If your dog is a "space invader," teach better manners by using language she understands—body language. If she crowds you when you are standing, use your lower body to gently push her away. If your dog is of medium to large size, you can easily "hip-check" her by jutting your hip out sharply. For a smaller dog, push gently with your lower leg. (Use a gentle shove, not a kick!) Mojo normally has very good manners. But every now and then, when I open the Sacred Cookie Cabinet, he temporarily loses his mind—and his manners. Since Mojo's head is level with my hip, I remind him not to crowd me by using a hip-check, accompanied by a shocked stare and an exclamation of, "Excuse you?!" Mojo will look momentarily startled, then sit and look at me sheepishly as if to say, "Sorry, Mom, lost it for a minute there!"

If you are seated when your dog pushes into your space or tries to climb onto your lap, you can't very well use your lower body to reclaim your space. You can, however, use your arms. Bend your arm and use your forearm to move your dog gently away. Do not speak to her or look at her as you do so; if she had been seeking attention, doing either of those things would be rewarding to her. If using your forearm is not convenient, place your hands on your dog's chest and gently move her away. Be careful not to use a fast, shoving motion. In addition to potentially harming your dog, shoving could be construed as an invitation to bounce back at you and play.

Doorways

If your dog blasts past you at doorways, teach her to wait for permission instead. Practice at a location other than the front door, such as the door leading to the garage. (If you must use the front door to practice, use a long-line—in this case, a leash that is just long enough to allow your dog to reach the door—tethered to a sturdy piece of furniture.) Position your dog approximately six feet back from the door. If she knows sit, ask her to do so. Open the door just a crack. If your dog remains seated (or remains in place if she is not sitting), continue to open the door. If she begins to get up or move forward as the door opens, quickly close it. If your dog moves forward, use your body to block her path. If necessary, walk into her space to cause her to back up to the original starting point. (You will most likely have to use body blocking a few times during initial attempts; that is perfectly normal.) Begin again. Repeat until you can open the door wide with your dog remaining in place. Then step through the doorway and call her to you. With practice, your dog should improve to the point that she consistently pauses at doorways and waits for permission to pass through.

Practice too with the door open wide and you remaining inside, then giving a release word or phrase (such as "Go free!") to let your dog know it is okay to pass through. It does not matter if your dog goes through ahead of you in this case, since it is your decision to allow it. This scenario is helpful for letting your dog out into the yard or other areas when you do not intend to follow.

Many years ago, I used "okay" as a release word. One day I ran into a friend as I was walking my dogs on-leash at the local park. I asked both dogs to sit and stay. My friend and I chatted for a few minutes. As we were taking our leave she said, "Give me a call," to which I replied, "Okay!" Let me tell you, it was no fun being dragged through the dirt by two large dogs who thought I had told them to go free! Don't let this happen to you! Choose any word or phrase you like to release your dog, but stay away from those you use regularly in everyday life.

Permission Please?

Consider all the wonderful things your dog experiences in an average day. She is given food and treats, is taken for walks, gets to chase a ball, and receives attention and affection. Does she have to earn those things, or does she get them all for free? A basic tenet of good leadership is that your dog must earn the things she values. If your dog has even the most basic of obedience skills—sit—Permission Please is easy to apply.

Take a moment to jot down all the things your dog finds valuable; they should be incorporated into your Permission Please program. For example, ask your dog to sit before you put down her food bowl, before a ball is thrown, and before you pet her. If she does not comply after one request, say, "Oh, well!" The food disappears; the ball disappears; she does not get petted. Your dog will soon learn that refusing to cooperate has a consequence. When you try again a short time later, chances are your dog will comply immediately.

Another privilege your dog should earn is a walk. To earn this fabulous outdoor foray, she will be required to sit while you attach the leash. I know, you're thinking *No way! My dog will never sit still to be leashed!* She will, and here's how teach it: Choose a time when you do not actually need to take her out, so you won't be rushed. Hold the leash bunched up so that only the clip is visible. (This short-circuits any attempts to jump up and bite the leash.) Ask your dog to sit, then begin to move the leash clip toward her collar. If she stands, simply straighten up, fold your arms and wait. She might automatically sit; if not, ask her to do so. Proceed calmly, continuing to move the clip toward her collar, straightening up and waiting as necessary until the leash is attached. Remember, *you* have control and all the time in the world. If your dog still won't remain seated after a few minutes, say, "Oh, well!" and walk away. Put the leash away and try again later. Your dog will soon learn that remaining seated is the only way to get what she wants. Additionally, ask your dog to sit before the door is opened. Her compliance earns the walk.

You might not think of attention and affection as resources, but they are probably two of the things your dog values most. While it is true that some dogs do not crave human interaction as much as others, most adore being in close proximity to their human pack members and consider getting a head scratch or tummy rub to be pooch paradise. The problem comes when a dog gets pushy and demands those valuable commodities. If you are one of those well-trained humans who respond to attention-seeking behavior by automatically petting your dog, it's time for some behavior modification—for you.

Whenever your dog solicits petting, if you would like to comply, ask her to sit first. If you are on the couch and your dog is sitting on the floor, paw settled on your leg, big, brown eyes entreating you, ask her to lie down before you pet her. If you do not wish to pet her at that particular moment, say, "Not now." When you are ready to pet your dog, call her to you and pet to your heart's content.

When playing fetch, each time your dog retrieves the ball, ask her to sit before you throw it again. Just as the walk is her reward for sitting at the front door, the next throw of the ball is her reward in fetch. This practice is also helpful for dogs who play "keep-away" once they have possession of the ball. Haven't heard of keep-away? It's that favorite game of canines everywhere: the dog grabs an object and runs, and the silly human gives chase. Don't do it! If your dog won't bring the ball all the way to you, stand with your body turned slightly away and bent slightly forward, pat your leg, and verbally encourage your dog in a high-pitched, friendly voice to bring the ball to you. Once she is close, ask her to sit. Many dogs will spit the ball out as they sit. If yours does, tell her what a good dog she is, then pet her with one hand while reaching for the ball with the other. If she does not spit out the ball, and she knows "Drop it," ask her to do so; or trade a treat for the ball, toss another ball so she drops the one in her mouth, or gently remove the ball from her mouth as you pet and praise her. Now you're ready to continue the game.

~ * ~ * ~ * ~ *~ * ~ * ~ * ~ *~ * ~ * ~ * ~ *~~ * ~ * ~

Whew! You're probably thinking, *That's an awful lot of rules. I don't want to turn my dog's world upside down, or spend all my time doing these things!* Relax. You needn't implement the Leadership Program all at once. Begin with one or two rules and gradually add the rest. Your dog will catch on faster than you think, and you will soon find the new behaviors becoming habits for both of you. The Leadership Program will heighten your status, support your training efforts, teach your dog that she has a strong, capable leader so there is no need to fear, and will help to create a closer bond between you.

Mojo gives Mom a most valued kiss!

 Tail End Wrap-Up

- Use psychology, not physical force, to establish leadership.

- Use the Language of Leadership to be clear and confident in all interactions with your dog.

- Teach your dog that not responding carries a consequence.

- Make sure all family members are consistent with house rules and interactions with your dog.

- Don't free-feed. If your dog is especially pushy, hand-feed for two weeks.

- Save the best interactive toys for when *you* want to play.

- Control access to locations including furniture, doorways, and personal space.

- Have your dog ask Permission Please to earn food, walks, attention/affection, and anything else she finds valuable. You are the Source of All Good Things!

- Above all, be kind, patient, and consistent.

Training

Training is one of the best ways to provide mental stimulation and bolster canine confidence. While self-confidence is important for all dogs, it is crucial for fearful dogs. Training can also teach specific behaviors that can be used to help your dog overcome his fears.

Reward-Based Training

Using positive, gentle methods should be the norm when training any dog, but it is mandatory when training a sensitive or anxious dog. Fortunately, training methods have evolved considerably in the last few decades. Traditional training included "correcting" a dog by delivering jerks or "pops" on a choke chain, along with other forms of physical coercion. Now, however, more and more trainers use non-coercive, reward-based training methods that set dogs up to succeed. Behaviors are broken down into small increments that dogs can understand, with each success rewarded and then built upon. If a correction is necessary, it is *not* a harsh physical one. Dogs learn rapidly, and can be trained to a high degree of reliability, without the use of force. Reward-based training is fun for both dogs and people, and strengthens the dog-owner bond.

Just because reward-based training is gentle does not mean it is permissive. In fact, one of the main tenets is that "every behavior has a consequence." A consequence can be positive or negative. If you ask your dog to sit before the door opens for a walk but he does not comply, a negative consequence would be to say, "Oh, well," unclip the leash and walk away, the opportunity for a walk ended. Rather than incurring a physical punishment, your dog loses something of value. If your dog complies and sits, he gets to go for a walk—a positive consequence.

To Treat or Not to Treat?

Reward-based training normally involves the use of food treats. Some people eschew training with treats, feeling that dogs should work "to please us." That's a lovely thought, but if a dog were offered the choice between a piece of hot dog and a "Good boy!" which do *you* think he'd prefer? Treats are an amazingly useful tool for training new behaviors. *Note:* If your dog has a medical condition, consult your veterinarian regarding appropriate treats.

Some people dislike the notion of using treats because they believe that a dog who has been trained with treats will only respond if treats are present. While that might be true if the training was done improperly, in proper reward-based training, a dog is weaned off treats (either partially or completely) once he is fluent in a behavior. One way to accomplish this is through the use of *random reinforcement*, in which successful responses are rewarded on a random basis (see *Chapter 13*). Real-life rewards can also be used to phase out food treats. For example, a down might earn petting instead of a treat. A dog who spits out the ball when asked to "drop it" is rewarded with the next toss of the ball.

> Reward-based training can produce dogs that are every bit as well trained as those who have been trained using coercive methods. Even better, reward-based training maintains and strengthens the bond of trust between dog and owner, which is essential for fearful dogs.

While many dogs are highly motivated by food, others are more motivated by play. Some dogs love to retrieve, others love to play tug, and some love nothing more than a wild game of chase around the yard. In many situations, play can be substituted for food treats as a reward. A great way to practice skills, once your dog knows them, is to ask for them while playing. For example, while playing a chase game, stop and ask your dog to sit. If he complies, the reward is the continuation of the game. Play training is especially valuable for fearful dogs because it keeps the mood light.

Remember that a reward is not something *you* find valuable, but something *your dog* finds valuable. Take a moment to list your dog's five favorite food rewards, and five favorite non-food rewards, in order of preference. Non-food rewards might include games, riding in the car, tummy rubs, or anything your dog enjoys. Then use the "pretty good" treats when training indoors or in less challenging situations, and the "super-yummy" treats when working outdoors around distractions or in more difficult situations.

Physical Force—Save it for the Gym

Beyond being unethical, unnecessary, and potentially traumatizing to a fearful dog, there are sound reasons to eschew physical punishment (which includes shaking, striking, jerking, kicking, and forcing to the ground):

1. *The application of physical force might temporarily suppress unwanted behavior, but it also causes stress.* The stress caused by punishing a dog might well surface later as a potentially more serious behavior problem. Let's say I have a nervous habit of humming under my breath; each time you hear me hum, you become irritated. Finally, you can stand it no more. I hum one time too many, and you slap me on the back of the head. I stop humming immediately. Did the slap solve the problem? Sure looks like it—but the stress caused by that slap might result in my developing other stress-induced habits, such as biting my nails, or perhaps lashing out whenever people come too close. The underlying problem would have remained, while the symptom was simply replaced with another.

   The psychological damage that can result from physically punishing an already fearful dog should not be underestimated. Dogs who have suffered physical abuse (and harsh physical corrections *are* abusive) take a long time and a lot of gentle guidance to recover. For some dogs, if the trauma is severe, full recovery might not ever be possible.

2. *Physical violence diminishes trust and erodes the dog-owner bond.* You are your dog's protector, his trusted guardian. It is crucial that your dog see you as such, and as a "safe harbor" when things frighten him. If you train with harsh physical corrections, you chance

destroying that precious trust forever. Your dog will come to associate you with unpleasant physical experiences—imagine the impact that would have on an already fearful dog. Once the dog-owner bond has been destroyed, behavior modification becomes difficult, if not impossible.

3. *Defense can turn to offense.* Although a fearful dog might run from a hand that attempts to strike him, if it happens often enough he might eventually begin to defend himself. Training methods involving physical force can result in injury to the human foolish enough to attempt them. Someone, perhaps even a trainer, may have advised you to roll your dog onto his back and growl at him, shake him, or otherwise physically overpower him. But for every person who has managed to get away with those techniques, there are two who did not. Don't make physical force the currency of exchange; the cost of payback is high.

> Some people believe that by rolling a dog onto his back or shaking him by the scruff, they are approximating the behavior of a canine dominating or disciplining another. Therefore, the dog will understand the intention. But dogs know we are not other dogs—something gets lost in the translation. Besides, do you really want to impersonate a dog? I can think of a few canine rituals I'd prefer not to imitate, starting with the infamous getting-to-know-you rear-end sniff!

Equipment to Consider

Just as there are various training techniques, there is a variety of equipment available for walking and training your dog. If your dog is not large or likely to lunge, he could simply wear a correctly fitted flat buckle collar. (Leave enough room for two fingers to lie flat between the collar and your dog's neck.) If your dog has a narrow head (like a sighthound) and can slip out of a flat buckle collar easily, consider a martingale-style collar. Martingales have an extra strip of fabric that makes the collar tighten should a dog try to slip out of it. For small dogs, and those who pull to the point of causing discomfort around the neck with a regular collar, body harnesses can be useful. By decreasing the amount of pulling, body harnesses also make walks much easier for owners.

Front-Clip Body Harness

The front-clip body harness is a fairly new innovation, and an extremely useful one. Its simple design makes it fast and easy to fit, and unlike a traditional body harness where the leash attaches at the dog's back, the attachment ring is at the chest. This configuration allows you better control of your dog's body. If your dog pulls to the end of the leash, the pressure will cause him to arc back around toward you. While body harnesses will not allow you to direct your dog's head, they give better control of the body than traditional harnesses, and most dogs accept them readily. Front-clip harnesses are a good choice for walking and training dogs, fearful or not. Premier's Gentle Leader® Easy Walk™ harness, the most popular brand, is available in pet supply stores and via online retailers. (For other brands, see *Resources*.)

Easy Walk™ Harness

Head Halter

Some fearful dogs, especially large breeds and those who are likely to lunge at other dogs or people, can benefit from head halters. Wearing a head halter drastically reduces the amount of force with which a dog can pull. It's like power steering! A head halter allows you to direct your dog's head (helpful if you need to get his attention in a high-stress situation) and even to close his mouth if necessary. The two most common head halters are the Gentle Leader® and the Halti®.

Gentle Leader®

Halti®

Both are made of lightweight nylon, and consist of a strap that fits over the dog's muzzle and two straps that snap together behind the head. Neither is a "muzzle" in the traditional sense; a dog can still yawn, eat, and bark while wearing a head halter. The leash attaches to a small ring under the dog's chin. There are subtle differences between the two brands: the Gentle Leader® has a single nylon strip that fits around the muzzle, with a plastic clip to keep it snugly in place. The Halti® has two diagonal strips that connect the muzzle strap to the neck straps. Rather than a plastic clip, there is a small metal ring that causes the muzzle strip to tighten when the dog pulls. The newer Halti® models have a safety strap that clips to the dog's flat buckle collar. That way, if the dog pulls out of the head halter, the leash is still attached to the buckle collar.

A short acclimation period is often necessary, since dogs do not naturally like the feel of anything over their muzzle. But the brief adjustment period is worthwhile in the long run. Many owners of fearful dogs find that in addition to making their dogs easier to walk, the head halter has a noticeable calming effect. Manufacturers of the Gentle Leader® call attention to the fact that pups seem to relax when their mothers pick them up by the nape of the neck, and theorize that the head halter has the same effect. Another possible explanation is that the pacifying effect results from the head strap pressing on a natural acupressure calming point. Whatever the reason, many dogs have an obvious relaxation response when wearing a head halter.

> While it is normal for a dog to fuss a bit with a head halter during the acclimation period, a small percentage of dogs completely "shut down," lie motionless, and look miserable. For those dogs, a head halter is not appropriate.

Take care not to jerk your dog on a head halter; his neck could be injured. Head halters are widely available at pet supply stores. A professional trainer can assist with correct fit and proper usage. (For more on head halters, see *Chapter 19*.)

Muzzle

Muzzles are used for dogs who are likely to bite. They can be worn in specific situations such as vet or groomer visits, or when practicing behavior modification exercises. Muzzles may also be used on walks if your dog is likely to lunge or snap at passersby. (For fitting and usage instructions, see *Chapter 19*.)

Tether

A tether is a means of restraining your dog. For our purposes, your dog will only be tethered in your presence. *Tethering your dog outdoors or when leaving him alone can be dangerous and is not recommended.*

A four- to six-foot leash may be used as a tether. If your dog is likely to chew at the leash, coat it with a taste deterrent spray (sold at pet supply stores). If your dog is a serious chewer or is very strong, use a coated steel cable tether instead, with a loop at one end and a clip at the other. It can be difficult to find coated steel cable tethers in shorter lengths in pet supply stores. (To order online, see *Resources*.)

Always use a regular collar for tethering—*never* a choke chain. If your dog has never been tethered before, take the time to acclimate him to it. Provide him with a comfortable bed or mat and a favorite chew item, and remain nearby. If your dog enjoys petting or massage, do so while he is tethered. Practice a few times daily. With repetition, your dog will come to associate good things with being on the tether. If your dog becomes anxious, don't make a fuss. Reassure him briefly in a nonchalant voice that all is well; when he is calm, praise and pet him. Tether your dog three to five times daily while you watch television, work on the computer, or read a book nearby.

Place the tether around the leg of a heavy piece of furniture, then slip the clip through the loop; now that the tether is anchored, attach the clip to your dog's collar (or body harness, if you have a small dog).

Tethers can be used when teaching your dog certain exercises such as "settle" and not to dart out the front door, and can be used to restrain your dog on the spur of the moment when a crate or other confinement area is not available. Again, your dog is only to be tethered in your presence.

Equipment to Avoid

Although some trainers use choke chains (metal chain collars, also known as "slip collars") or pinch/prong collars (metal collars with blunted metal prongs pointing inward), neither is an appropriate choice when training a fearful dog. Both collars work on the principle of "correcting" unwanted behavior by tightening momentarily around the dog's neck. Corrections of this sort could easily frighten a fearful dog. Fallout can be created as well, in the form of unwanted associations. Because dogs associate things that happen within seconds of each other, if a dog is corrected just as he is looking at (or lunging at) something that frightens him—for example, another dog—he could easily associate the other dog with the correction. Now the poor dog is thinking, *I just knew other dogs were trouble!* If this unfortunate timing continues, the dog could develop progressively stronger reactions to other dogs with each encounter.

Another piece of equipment owners of fearful dogs should avoid at all costs is the shock collar (also referred to as the electronic collar or e-collar). The last thing a fearful dog needs is a jolt of electricity at his neck. An anxious, fearful dog could become truly traumatized by the use of a shock collar. If a trainer recommends its use, find another trainer. If you are considering using a shock collar to stop other behaviors such as unwanted barking, consult a positive trainer; there are better options.

One last piece of equipment to be avoided is the retractable (also known as the extendable or "flexi") leash. It is not wise to allow your dog to walk ten or fifteen feet ahead of you, as there would not be much you could do if a dog or person came around a corner and frightened him. Use a standard four-foot leash instead, or if you prefer, a five- or six-foot leash.

Choosing a Professional Trainer

When fear issues are involved, it is vital that you choose a trainer carefully. Because there are no licensing requirements for dog trainers, a great range of expertise and experience exists. Ask for recommendations from friends or your veterinarian, or contact the Association of Pet Dog Trainers (see *Resources*). On the APDT web site, the initials CPDT after a name signifies a Certified Pet Dog Trainer—one who has passed a written exam that tests her knowledge of psychological principles as they pertain to training and behavior, and positive training methods. Once you have a potential trainer in mind, interview the person carefully. Don't be shy about asking questions! A quality professional will not mind and will appreciate that you are being so careful. If you receive abrupt, evasive, or rude responses, keep looking.

What a trainer really does is train *you* to train your dog. Basic obedience skills and manners can be taught in either a home or group setting. A trainer can educate you about your dog's body language, point out canine stress signals, and give feedback about your body language and communication skills so that your dog becomes more comfortable with the training process. A trainer who is competent in working with behavior issues can help you to work through your dog's fears, and coach you on how to teach basic obedience skills as well.

Experience. Asking about length of experience will weed out novices. Keep in mind, however, that a professional who has been training for thirty years might be using outdated methods. Ask how the trainer got her education and experience, and whether she pursues ongoing education. Attending seminars, keeping up with the latest books and videos, and networking with other trainers through professional organizations all indicate a trainer who cares about her craft and is informed about modern training techniques and principles.

Methods. You might have noticed that most training advertisements use catch phrases such as "Positive Training." After all, "Punish Your Pooch" or "We Whack 'Em with a Two-by-Four" probably wouldn't sell. A good way to cut through the advertising lingo is to ask what the trainer would do if a dog did not comply with a request when learning a new behavior. My own answer would be that the dog had obviously been asked for too much too soon, so I would go back to where the dog was last successful and create smaller steps toward the goal. If you get an answer such as, "I would correct the dog; he can't be allowed to get away with that!" keep looking. Ask too what sort of physical corrections are used. Some trainers do not use physical corrections of any kind. Some use mild corrections such as squirt bottles, while others use strong choke chain corrections or other harsh methods. In general, trainers who use food rewards and/or clicker training are apt to be of a positive bent, but ask questions of *any* potential trainer.

Approach to Fear Issues. While a harsh correction or expecting too much too soon might only faze an exuberant, confident dog temporarily, it could do serious damage to the psyche of a fearful dog. Ask specifically about the trainer's approach to working with fearful dogs. This question is key to finding a trainer who is knowledgeable about behavior issues and takes a gentle approach. An enlightened trainer might use words like "desensitize," and phrases like "help your dog to gradually overcome his fears." Trainers who employ more of a strong-arm, correction-based approach that suppresses the symptoms but neglects to address the underlying issues often use phrases like "your dog is just trying to be dominant," "you must show the dog who's boss," and "they must face their fears." Above all, go with your gut. If you and the trainer click and you like her approach, go for it. But if you get an uneasy feeling—even if you can't quite put your finger on the reason—keep searching.

Experienced, knowledgeable trainers who specialize in behavior issues are often able to help dogs with moderate to severe fear issues. If you cannot find a qualified professional in your area, consider contacting a behaviorist. An actual behaviorist—as opposed to a trainer who simply calls himself or herself a behaviorist—has a Ph.D. in Applied Animal Behavior (an Applied Certified Animal Behaviorist) or is a Board Certified Veterinary Behaviorist. It might be difficult to find a certified behaviorist in your area or even in your state, but many will work long-distance either directly with you or through your veterinarian. But even then, interview the potential candidate carefully as to methodology and approach; just because someone is a behaviorist does not mean he or she uses positive, gentle methods. (For referring organizations, see *Resources*.)

Group Classes

If your dog is comfortable around other dogs and people, a group class can be a good training option. Ask about the trainer's experience and methods and whether you can watch a class before signing up. If the trainer refuses, keep looking. Notice whether the dogs and people seem relaxed and happy, and whether the dogs are being handled gently. If possible, speak with students before or after a class to get their feedback as to how the dogs are treated and whether they seem to be learning. In particular, try to question the owners of dogs who appear fearful.

Some instructors allow fearful dogs to work behind a barrier or at a distance until they are more comfortable. This can be extremely helpful. Ask whether the trainer provides this type of setup, and what other provisions are made for fearful dogs. Check out the training environment to determine whether there is enough space to work your dog at a distance if necessary. If you sign up, arrive at class early to allow your dog to investigate the area. Becoming familiar with the area's scents will help him to relax. Arriving early will also ensure that he won't be walking into a room full of dogs, which can be intimidating. Bringing a blanket or dog bed from home which your dog has associated with relaxation (and which you have sprayed with DAP—see *Chapter 47*) can help, as can bringing a favorite chew toy. (Remember, chewing relieves stress!)

I had a client whose Malinois mix, Milly, was one of the most fearful dogs I have ever encountered. The dog seemed almost feral, acting more like a wolf than a dog. I was shocked when her owner told me that Milly had been attending a local group class, as it was difficult to imagine her being near other dogs or people. Unfortunately, the trainer used harsh corrections and did nothing to compensate for Milly's reactions to the environment and the training methods. Every Monday, Milly's owner had to drag her out from under the bed to go to class. The owner was a kind woman, but had not realized that the class was making things worse. She assumed that once enough time had passed, Milly would acclimate; but that was not the case, and they had already attended four series of classes with the same trainer over the span of many months.

On my advice, Milly was pulled out of the class and placed in another where the instructor used gentle, positive methods and understood Milly's fearful behavior. Milly was given a comfortable space to work in and was not pushed past her comfort zone. Within a few short weeks, she was willing to take treats from the instructor and could stand within a few feet of other dogs and people without trembling. Although she will probably never have an outgoing, confident personality, Milly continues to make excellent progress.

The advantage of a group class (other than being less costly than private training) is that your dog will receive exposure to other dogs and people. But if your dog is not quite ready for that level of stimulation, do a few private sessions first. Your trainer should be able to tell you if and when your dog is ready to participate in a group situation.

Do It Yourself

If you do not have the means to hire a trainer or you live in an area where there are no positive trainers available, consider teaching basic obedience skills yourself. There are many good books, videos, and DVDs on the market to assist you (see *Resources*). And don't stop at basic obedience— the more your dog learns, the more confident he will become.

Training Tips

- *Have fun.* When training at home, keep the mood light. Your verbal tone and body language should reflect that training is a pleasant activity, not a chore or a do-or-die mission. Take a few deep breaths before training sessions to relax and focus. If you come home especially stressed after a hard day at work, skip training that day. Dogs pick up on emotional states and your sensitive dog might become stressed as well.

- *Be patient.* If you find that your dog is having trouble learning a new skill, don't get frustrated. Simply back up to the step at which he was last successful and build small steps from there toward your goal.

- *Keep it short.* Aim for three to five training sessions of three to five minutes per day. Short sessions will teach your dog effectively and keep training fun rather than turning it into a drill.

- *Capture the moment.* Some dogs are afraid of the movement of a hand approaching, even to lure with a food treat. A good solution for those dogs is to *capture* behaviors instead. Capturing is easy— simply wait for the behavior to occur naturally. For example, whenever you see your dog sit, say, "Yes!" to mark the exact moment he is doing the right thing, then reward with a treat. Eventually your dog will begin to offer the sit, since he knows it earns a treat. You can then begin to add the verbal cue, "Sit!" right before he sits; you will soon be able to request the behavior.

- *Be aware.* If your dog is uncomfortable with a person, dog, or something in the environment, he may not be able to focus on training. Be attentive to your dog's comfort level and the environment. Begin your training in an area that is comfortable for your dog and work up to more challenging ones.

Corrections

Positive, gentle training does not mean that dogs are allowed to do as they please. So how *do* you correct a fearful dog for inappropriate behavior? Physical corrections are out of the question. Verbal reprimands, however, can be an appropriate choice. When delivering a verbal reprimand, pay attention to your dog's reaction. For example, as Brittany chews the table leg, you utter a sharp, "Eh-eh!" If she stops immediately, great. But if she not only stops but cowers, drops to the ground, or runs from the room, your verbal tone or volume was way too intense. Use the least amount of verbal force that is effective at interrupting the unwanted activity. Even a very soft, "Eh!" can be sufficient.

As explained in *Leadership*, removal of something the dog wants is another type of "correction" for unwanted behavior or lack of compliance. Of course, setting the dog up to succeed from the beginning with good management and training is best, so that fewer reprimands are necessary.

> Pay attention to how you use your voice when requesting that your dog do something. Many people believe they must use loud, stern, authoritarian commands to get their dogs to "obey." Actually, once a dog knows a specific behavior, you can successfully use a whisper or even a hand signal alone as a cue. For everyday communication, a normal tone of voice and inflection are all that are necessary.
>
> If your dog is sensitive to the sound of your voice, be careful of how you praise him as well. Even if he does something fabulous, a loud, enthusiastic, "That was *great*; you're the world's best dog!" might be too much. A softly spoken, "Good boy!" would be a better choice.

Tricky, Tricky

When teaching group classes years ago, I noticed an interesting phenomenon. When students taught their dogs tricks such as shake, roll over, or spin, much laughter and frivolity ensued. But when teaching obedience skills such as stay or down, students became much more intense. They seemed to feel that since these were the "important" things to learn, they'd better get serious and make their dogs comply. But think about the dogs' perspective; it's all tricks to them! Dogs don't know that down or stay are any more "important" than roll over or shake.

Tricks can come in handy in everyday situations. If your dog is starting to become nervous (for example, in the waiting room at the vet's office), run him through a series of tricks. Keep your manner upbeat. Performing the tricks will give your dog something on which to focus, rather than becoming more anxious by the minute.

Tricks are great confidence-builders. Your dog can learn easy tricks like shake and roll over, and more advanced ones such as "say your prayers" (dog sits on floor with front paws on chair, head down over paws) and "turn out the lights." Yes, you can teach your dog to turn out the lights! I taught that particular trick to Mojo using clicker training, and it was great fun. Teach as many tricks as possible! I love the *Take a Bow Wow* series—it teaches a variety of tricks in a fun and easy way using clicker training. (For videos, DVDs, and other instructional sources on trick training, see *Resources*.)

~ * ~ * ~ * ~ *~ * ~ * ~ * ~ *~ * ~ * ~ * ~ *~ * ~ * ~

I cannot emphasize the value of training strongly enough. With patience, kindness, and consistency, you will soon find that you and your dog both look forward to training sessions. Your efforts will be rewarded with a dog who is more responsive to your requests, and calmer and more confident in everyday life.

Tail End Wrap-Up

- Use positive, gentle training methods only.

- Avoid the use of physical force.

- For daily walks and training, use a flat buckle or martingale collar, head halter, or front-clip body harness. Avoid choke chains, pinch collars, and shock collars.

- Use a regular four- to six-foot leash. Avoid retractable leashes.

- Screen professional trainers carefully. Ask questions about experience, training philosophy, equipment and methods used, and special considerations for working with fearful dogs.

- Screen group classes before joining. Observe whether dogs and people seem stressed or relaxed, and interview students before or after class.

- There are many excellent resources available to help you train your dog at home (see *Resources*).

- Teaching tricks is fun and builds confidence.

- Training should not be a chore, but a fun, confidence-boosting, bonding experience for you and your dog.

Part III

~ *Skills* ~

Useful Skills

Misty, a two-year-old Border Collie, is not comfortable with other dogs. Whenever she encounters one on a walk, she barks and lunges. Her owner tries to pull Misty away as he shouts, "Let's go! Let's go!" The barking and lunging intensify. Finally, her owner drags Misty away. He finds the whole experience frustrating and a bit embarrassing, and wonders why Misty "just won't listen."

The reasons for Misty's inability to respond to her owner are simple. First, Misty was never taught what "Let's go" means. For all she knows, when her owner starts yelling, "Let's go!" it means, "Get 'em! I'm here to back you up!" Had Misty been taught the meaning of the words, and had adequate practice at doing what her owner would like when he says, "Let's go," chances would be much better that Misty would comply. The second reason Misty doesn't listen is that she is not *able* to listen when she is highly emotionally aroused. Her owner must learn to interrupt the behavior before it escalates so that Misty can respond.

Parlez-Vous Martian?

All too often we shout instructions at dogs and expect them to understand our meaning. If I walked up to you and demanded, "Beezlebot!" would you understand what I wanted? What if I repeated the word in a more threatening tone? Would it help if I got angry and shouted the word in your face? Chances are, I could shout until I had steam coming out of my ears and all it would do is frustrate us both. It would also probably cause you stress and possibly frighten you as well. You would want to understand what I was saying, but I could be speaking Martian for all you knew.

Now, what if I instead taught you what "Beezlebot!" means? Imagine this: I hold a piece of candy over your head. You reach for the candy with your left hand; I do not let you take it. You reach for it with your right hand; I still do not let you take it. When you finally reach for the candy with both hands I say, "Yes!" and let you have the candy. We repeat the exercise a few times and then, just before you reach for the candy with both hands, I say, "Beezlebot!" After a few repetitions I would be able to say, "Beezlebot!" with you, bright student that you are, responding by lifting your arms over your head. It's that simple. If you want your dog to understand what you would like him to do at a particular time or in a particular situation, teach the skill and *then* attach a verbal cue to it.

Distractions

Just as it would be difficult for you to learn a new language while a marching band played in circles around you, it is difficult for your dog to learn a new task in the presence of distractions. If you have a house full of kids playing noisily, televisions blaring, or other chaos, lock yourself in a quiet room with your dog, even if the only one you can find is the bathroom. Keep practice sessions short—three to five minutes at a time is plenty. Dogs, like people, learn better in small increments. Once your dog is performing the new skill well, work in slightly more distracting areas, such as a room where your kids are watching television. As long as your dog is doing well, add another distraction by having someone stroll slowly past as you practice. Have the person become gradually more and more exciting by working up to walking quickly, talking to your dog, singing, waving arms, and, eventually, running around. (Kids love this game and they make great helpers!) If you have another dog, once your dog is doing well with all of the aforementioned distractions, have someone walk the other dog into the room on leash as you practice.

By practicing around distracting situations in the home, your dog will learn to focus on you regardless of what is happening in the environment. You can then move on to practicing in the back yard or the front of your house, and eventually, to high-distraction environments such as crowded streets or parks.

The Trick to Using Treats

Using food treats is a fast, easy way to communicate what you want and to reward your dog for a job well done. Treats should be small and moist so your dog can eat them quickly. The more difficult the exercise, the higher value the treat should be. While an everyday training treat should suffice in the house, bits of cheese, hot dog, or sliced up dog-food rolls are better choices when working in highly distracting environments.

Once your dog has mastered a particular skill, treats can be given less frequently and then faded out altogether if you wish. This can be accomplished by switching from rewarding every successful repetition to rewarding successes randomly. For example, out of ten successful repetitions of down, your dog is rewarded only for the third, fifth and ninth. The next time around, it might be the fourth and seventh. Your dog will keep playing the game because if he plays long enough, there is a reward. (Ever play the slot machines? Same principle—you keep playing because you *might* win.) Random reinforcement strengthens reliability, because your dog will continue to work for the *possibility* of a reward.

Treats can also be faded out by substituting real-life rewards. For example, if your dog sits when asked at the front door, the reward is the door opening so he can go for a walk. If he lies down when asked, he gets his tummy rubbed.

~ * ~ * ~ * ~ *~ * ~ * ~ * ~ *~ * ~ * ~ * ~ * ~ *~ * ~ * ~

As you practice the skills in this section, be patient with your dog and with yourself. Neither of you is expected to learn everything at once. Some of the skills can be used to keep your dog focused during stressful situations. Some can provide alternative behaviors to the ones your dog currently defaults to under stress. Others will simply help your dog learn how to relax. All of the skills will build confidence and will eventually be used to address your dog's fears.

Settle:
An Exercise in Relaxation

The ability to relax is one of the most beneficial skills a nervous dog can learn. That might sound odd, but like some people, some dogs—especially nervous or anxious ones—find it difficult to remain still and relaxed for any length of time.

Because the body and mind are connected, the body's position and movement can affect the emotional state. If the body is relaxed, the mind and emotions will follow. By teaching your dog to "settle" her body in a relaxed pose and to maintain that pose, you can encourage real relaxation.

Why Settle?

Once your dog has mastered the settle, she can be asked to settle in situations that would normally make her nervous. For example, if your dog is nervous in the veterinarian's or groomer's waiting room, you could ask her to settle. If she is nervous in a group class, asking her to settle between exercises can help to keep her calm. Settle can also be used for dogs who are mildly nervous around visitors.

Settle differs from a formal down-stay. In the latter, a dog is expected to remain lying in a specific position until released. The dog is alert, anticipating the owner's next instructions (for example, to come to the owner). Settle, however, simply requires a dog to lie in a relaxed manner. The dog is allowed to shift her weight, turn her head, or even lie on her side in order to remain comfortable. Once the dog is settled the muscles relax, which is soon accompanied by a feeling of overall relaxation. Dogs may even fall asleep while in a settle.

> Down-stay focuses on maintaining position;
> settle focuses on maintaining relaxation.

Settling Down to Business

To teach settle, choose a time when your dog's energy level is low. Her normal nap time is a good choice, as is after returning from a nice, long walk. If your dog is still overly active despite your best efforts to tire her out, tether her to a solid piece of furniture to teach this exercise. Do *not* tether your dog if she is afraid of being handled around the neck (unless you substitute a body harness for a collar) or of being restrained, or if she becomes stressed when separated from you even by a few feet. If your dog is not tethered, anywhere she chooses to settle is fine.

It is not necessary that your dog learn to settle in one particular spot, since the goal is for her to eventually be able to settle in various environments. But if you have a nice, comfy dog bed, put it to use. If your dog is tethered, place the bed by the tether. The bed will eventually become associated with relaxation, and if you decide to teach "go to your bed" at a future time, you will have laid the groundwork for your dog to remain relaxed once she is on the bed.

Teaching settle is relaxing for people as well, as the easiest way to teach it is to have a seat, get comfy, and wait. Turn on the television if you'd like; this is armchair training! You will be using *shaping*—rewarding small, progressive increments of the desired behavior. (*Note*: If your dog already knows down, you may skip to the next paragraph, ask for a down, and begin with your dog lying down.) Don't stare at your dog, but do watch her out of the corner of your eye. Any time she relaxes her posture a bit (for example, keeps four paws on the floor rather than jumping, or sits rather than standing), mark the moment with a calm "Yes!" then toss her a treat and offer soothing praise. If she remains in position, praise calmly and toss another treat, then go back to watching her out of the corner of your eye.

If your dog stands up or approaches you after being rewarded, ignore her and wait for her to relax again. Each time she does, mark the moment with a calm, "Yes!" and toss a treat, along with giving calm praise.

Let's say your dog went from standing to sitting, you said, "Yes!" and tossed a treat, and she remained seated. You then tossed another treat, along with giving calm praise. If you were to continue to give treats and praise for sitting, your dog would assume that sitting is what you wanted. So instead, after the second treat and praise, wait. Your dog will eventually lie down or make some other noticeable change in posture that signals further relaxation. At that point, say, "Yes!" and treat/praise. Waiting for a bit more relaxed posture each time will result in your dog eventually lying down. Mark and reward the down just as you did the sit, then go back to ignoring her. The end result will be your dog finally *really* relaxing by either rolling her body weight onto one hip, laying her head on the ground, or rolling completely onto her side. Of course, you will mark and reward the posture. Give treats and praise every few seconds, then space them out so they are farther and farther apart. You may also begin to substitute calm praise for every second or third treat. If your dog enjoys massage, you can use a massage as a reward as well.

With practice, it will take less and less time for your dog to lie down and relax. At that point you can add the verbal cue. When your dog is lying down and you see that she is about to roll over onto one hip or completely onto her side say, "Settle" in a calm, soothing voice. Once she settles, reward her. You may also say, "Good settle" in a soothing voice as she lies there, relaxed. If you have been using a tether, once your dog knows the exercise, release her. Practice giving the "Settle" cue when your dog is lying down, then when she is sitting, and finally, when she is standing.

You can help your dog learn to settle even when it's not training time. Watch your dog the next time she lies down. The moment you see that she is about to roll her weight onto one hip, put her head on the floor, or roll onto her side, softly say, "Settle." Once the movement is complete, reward her.

Don't expect your dog to remain lying calmly for an hour the first time! Only you know your dog's energy and anxiety level; if you only achieve a five-second settle the first time, that's fine. Gradually work toward your dog remaining settled for a minute at a time, and then for even longer periods. Practice the exercise in different rooms and areas of your home, and with you standing as well as sitting.

Have you ever caught the aroma of a food you had loved as a child, or a trace of a scent that a long-lost friend had worn? Because scent is so strongly linked with emotions, even the briefest whiff can trigger warm remembrances. Aromatherapy can help your dog to feel more relaxed. Spray a bit of lavender or other calming essence in the room (or on a bandana your dog is wearing) whenever you practice the settle exercise, or when you massage your dog. She will soon come to associate the scent with a state of relaxation. (Lavender is a good choice, as it is calming in and of itself.) You can then spray a bit of the scent on your dog's bandana or collar when you take her places where she might become nervous, when you have visitors over, or in any situation that normally causes mild stress. The scent association will help your dog to relax and settle more readily. (See *Resources* for aromatherapy products.) DAP spray can be substituted for lavender or other scents (see *Chapter 47*).

Alternate method to teach settle, if your dog already knows down: With your dog lying down, hold a treat to her mouth like a magnet until she rolls onto her side. Practice a few times, then add the verbal cue just before making the hand motion.

Take it on the Road

Once your dog has mastered the settle in various rooms of your home, practice in the back yard, front yard, and then in quiet parks and other low-distraction areas. Take your time and don't get frustrated if your dog does not comply immediately. If necessary, go back to practicing in easier environments for a bit longer. Don't expect your dog to remain in settle position for as long as she did at home right away. You'll have to work up to longer settles in public places gradually. Once your dog is settling nicely in quiet public places, it's time to add small distractions. Practice settle in public parks when a few people are around, or in shopping center parking lots at a distance from foot traffic. Always monitor your dog's reactions and don't push too far too fast. As long as your dog is comfortable, work gradually closer to foot traffic, at busier parks, and in other more challenging situations.

To Settle or Not to Settle?

While settle can be helpful in cases of mild fear or anxiety, it should not be used at close range in the face of something that truly frightens your dog. Not only would it be cruel to force your dog to remain close to the source of her fear, but it would be nearly impossible for her to lie down and relax with all that adrenaline flooding her system. Besides, lying down puts your dog in a vulnerable position, which is the last thing she needs when she is already afraid. (Remember that last point if you take your dog to a group class and she refuses to lie down; she may simply be nervous. Working at a distance from the others may help.)

Settle *can* be used in cases where your dog is *mildly* uncomfortable. For example, if she is only slightly anxious around visitors, you could ask her to settle in a comfortable spot away from foot traffic, such as a dog bed in the corner of the room. Settling in the presence of visitors can eventually help your dog to associate them with a state of relaxation. Although that alone might not solve your dog's anxiety about people, helping her to relax around them is a helpful first step. (For more on fear of visitors see *Chapter 28.*)

Tail End Wrap-Up

- Teach settle when your dog is tired or physically worn out.

- Tether your dog, get comfy, and wait for any small sign of relaxation. Mark the moment with a calm "Yes!" toss a treat, and give soothing praise.

- Continue to reward signs of progressive relaxation until your dog is lying down.

- Once you can predict that your dog is about to roll over onto her hip, put her head down, or roll over onto her side, add the verbal cue "Settle" just as she is preparing to do so.

- Reward your dog for remaining in a relaxed settle position; use more frequent rewards at first and then space them out. Massage may be used as a reward as well.

- Practice in various rooms of the house, as well as with you sitting and standing.

- Help your dog to associate a specific scent with settling/ relaxation, then use it to help her relax in stressful situations.

- Have your dog practice settle in progressively more difficult environments, including public places. Build up to her settling around distractions.

- Use settle when you have visitors (if your dog's fear is mild), or in situations or environments in which she is mildly to moderately nervous. Do *not* ask your dog to settle at close range in the face of something that frightens her.

More helpful skills coming up! Relax, "settle," and turn the page...

Attention

When you call your dog's name, how does he respond? Does he stop whatever he is doing at the time and look at you? Or does he go on his merry way...*la-la-la, oooh! These flowers sure smell good!* "Attention" is a skill that describes the former response: When you give your dog a specific verbal cue, he responds by making eye contact regardless of the environment or his focus at the time.

Although "Watch me!" and "Look at me!" are commonly used attention cues, in this case your dog's name will serve as the cue. Teaching your dog to make eye contact whenever you say his name will be helpful in a variety of situations. It can be especially useful on walks if your dog is uncomfortable with other dogs or people, as you will see in upcoming chapters.

The Setup

Choose a quiet, non-distracting environment in which to train. Because fearful dogs avoid eye contact with people they find intimidating, it is important that these exercises be done with someone with whom your dog is comfortable. The person's gaze should always look "soft," as a hard stare is perceived as a threat in the animal kingdom. To soften your gaze, lower your eyelids slightly. If you are not sure what a soft gaze looks like, look in the mirror, smile, and think of how much you love your dog. *That's* a soft gaze.

Lookin' Good!

Stand facing your dog. Your dog may either sit or lie down, facing you. If your dog does not yet know sit or down, he may remain standing. If he wanders off during the exercise, however, tether him by looping a leash around a nearby piece of furniture and attaching it to his collar. (Get him comfortable with being tethered beforehand.) Do not wear a fanny pack, "bait bag" (a nylon pouch designed to hold treats), or other obvious food-dispenser; you want your dog to focus on your eyes, not the prize! Begin by standing—or kneeling, if standing is likely to intimidate your dog—with both hands behind your back and a handful of small, moist treats in one hand. Without making a sound or using any non-verbal encouragement (don't wiggle those eyebrows!), wait for your dog to make eye contact (see *Figure 1*). At the moment he does, say, "Yes!" in a happy tone of voice and follow it immediately with a treat and praise (see *Figure 2*). The "Yes!" should be short and crisp, as it marks the exact moment your dog performed the desired behavior. The treat and praise are his reward. In this exercise, your dog is not required to hold the eye contact for any specific length of time.

Repeat the exercise until the light bulb has gone on over your dog's head and he's "got it." You'll know when that has happened because your dog will practically be staring at you, unwilling to look away.

Figure 1   *Figure 2*

Next, we'll make the exercise a bit more difficult by drawing your dog's attention away from you. Continue to hold the treats in one hand behind your back. Hold a single treat in the other hand and, *without looking at your dog*, move the hand slowly out to the side so it is fully extended, parallel to the floor. Once the arm is fully extended you may look at your dog (see *Figure 3*). Your dog will visually track the motion of your hand and may stare at the treat for a few seconds. Stand still, remain quiet, and wait. (This is the hard part!) At some point your dog will make eye contact, since he has been rewarded repeatedly for doing so (see *Figure 4*).

Figure 3   *Figure 4*

At the moment your dog makes eye contact, even if it's just a brief glance, say, "Yes!" and reward him by giving him the treat that was in your outstretched hand, along with praise.

With subsequent repetitions, it will take your dog less and less time to look at you after tracking the treat. You might even find that he eventually refuses to track the treat visually, continuing to stare at you as if to say, "I'm on to you!" Next, repeat the exercise with the opposite hand. Switching hands helps your dog to generalize that no matter where he is looking, he must always swing his head back around toward you.

Once your dog is making eye contact within a second or two of staring at the treat, it is time to add the verbal cue. Move the treat out to the side as before. Once your arm stops moving and your dog is looking at the treat, wait one second, then call his name in the tone of voice you would normally use. Predictably, your dog will swing his head toward you and make eye contact. Perfect! Say, "Yes!" then treat and praise. Once your dog has become proficient at giving you immediate attention on cue, you can drop the "Yes!" and simply treat and praise.

Now, you may be thinking, *but my dog would have looked at me when I called his name without doing all of this first!* While that might be true, the beauty of these exercises is that they create a *conditioned reflex.* That means once the behavior has been properly and thoroughly conditioned, upon hearing the verbal cue your dog won't stop to think, *hmm, I'm kind of busy sniffing for crumbs right now; can I get back to you?* Instead, he will make eye contact immediately. With practice, your dog will be able to give his immediate attention when asked even in the presence of distractions and in situations that frighten him.

Distraction Action

To teach your dog to respond to your verbal cue regardless of the environment or situation, add distractions gradually. Enlist the help of another person. If you have a child handy, ask if he or she wants to play a game to help train the dog. Kids make great distractions and most really enjoy this exercise. If you don't have a child handy, an adult will do.

As a warm-up, do a couple of repetitions of the arm-out-to-the-side, name-calling exercise that you already practiced. Next, hold some treats behind your back. Don't make eye contact, talk to, or in any way encourage your dog's attention. Have your "distracter" begin by making a slow movement such as stretching her arms above her head or taking a step. When your dog looks toward her, call his name. If he responds by looking at you, say, "Yes!" and treat. If he does not look your way, the distracter should freeze in place and look at you. Remain motionless and wait. It is likely that your dog will follow her gaze and end up looking at you as well. If your dog still does not look at you, call his name again, and when he looks, say, "Yes!" and reward him.

Of course, we ultimately want your dog to respond the *first* time you call his name, which will happen with practice. Here are some potential stumbling blocks and their solutions:

Situation	Solution
Your dog will not take his attention off the distracter.	The distracter's movements should be smaller and slower at first, or the person should stand farther away.
Your dog was not interested in the treats once distractions were introduced.	Use higher value treats. OR Withhold the meal before the next training session.
Other distractions had appeared, making the exercise too difficult.	Find a quieter environment.
Your dog stopped responding.	Stop for now and do shorter practice sessions.

As your dog improves at this exercise, the distracter should increase the intensity by adding faster movements, speaking, and looking at your dog.

General Ize Reporting for Duty

With practice, you will soon find that your dog is responsive even if your distracter is yodeling and turning cartwheels across the carpet. While that is a great accomplishment (for both the dog and the person!), it has been achieved in the context of a "training game" as signaled by the presence of food and by you and the other person acting in a particular way. The next step is to get your dog to respond to your requests for attention in everyday situations.

Your dog must learn to *generalize*—in this case, that an immediate response to your verbal cue is required regardless of circumstance or environment. Begin during a quiet time at home. Stand in your kitchen with treats stashed nearby but out of your dog's sight and scent range (for example, in the fridge). Ignore your dog and wait for him to lose interest in you completely. After a few moments, before he gets too interested in other things, call his name. When he looks at you say, "Yes!" and walk quickly to the treats, praising continually in a cheerful voice ("That was a good dog; what a wonderful job!") until the treat is in his mouth. The happy talk creates a verbal connection between the reward and the behavior so that your dog will understand why he is being rewarded. Practice calling your dog's name at random times when he is not too distracted with other things, in various locations in your home.

Next, begin to call your dog's name when he is slightly distracted (for example, when a person walks through the room or when your dog is pawing at a toy on the floor). If he does not respond, you have expected too much too soon. Go back to a situation in which he was successful, do a few repetitions, then build distractions more gradually. Once your dog is responding reliably, grab some treats and move to an environment where he is likely to be slightly more distracted, such as the back yard. Work inside the home, out in the yard, and when he is ready, on the streets during quiet times. Bring high-value treats along on walks and practice calling your dog's name whenever he is not too distracted. You will not forever be rewarding your dog simply for responding to his name (eventually he will be expected to do more to earn a reward), but for now, continue to use treats.

Don't expect too much too soon. Just because your dog responded brilliantly in your living room does not mean he will immediately look to you on cue while out in public with children running past. Your dog might do well with this exercise for a few days and then have a bad day; that's normal. It takes time to build a response that is reliable in any situation. Practicing in short increments a few times daily will help you to reach that goal.

Now What?

So how can you use a request for eye contact to address your dog's fear issues? As you will see in upcoming chapters, in certain situations where something frightens your dog, you will call his name. Once his attention is focused on you, you will ask for another behavior that will either give him something to focus on, allow you to move him out of the area safely, or do whatever is appropriate at the time. With practice and patience, something wonderful will happen: Rather than becoming reactive or running away when your dog feels threatened, he will anticipate your request for attention, and will begin to look to you automatically.

> Attention means communication, and communication
> means successful behavior modification!

Tail End Wrap-Up

Practice in a quiet, non-distracting environment first.

Practice the both-hands-behind-the-back exercise, marking the moment your dog makes eye contact with a crisp "Yes!" and then treat/praise.

Once your dog is practically staring at you, move on to the one-hand-to-the-side exercise. Practice with the opposite hand as well.

Once your dog is making eye contact within one to two seconds of tracking the out-to-the-side treat, add in calling his name. Say, "Yes!" and treat/praise.

Practice calling your dog with another person acting as a distraction. Keep distractions small at first, then gradually make them bigger as your dog is successful.

Practice calling your dog's name in real-life situations without the obvious presence of treats. Use continuous praise to connect the successful behavior with the reward.

Practice in a quiet, non-distracting indoor environment, then indoors when your dog is slightly distracted. Next, practice in your back yard and then out on the streets. Bring treats along on walks to practice.

Be patient and don't expect too much too soon. At first, don't call your dog's name in any situation where you wouldn't bet me $50 that he will respond! Work up gradually to larger and more intense distractions.

Touch: Right on Target

Dogs can be taught to use a specific body part, such as the nose or a front paw, to touch a specific object or person; this skill is called *targeting*. For our purposes, your dog will learn to touch her nose to the back of your hand in response to the verbal cue "Touch." Though it might seem an odd behavior to teach, this type of targeting has many applications: it can serve as an alternative to behaviors such as lunging or darting away; it can help your dog learn to interact with people and objects with more confidence; and it can help to keep your dog calm and focused during potentially frightening situations.

Targeting is so effective at helping dogs interact with people or objects they fear because it puts the dog in control of the situation. Although the behavior is being requested, the dog is the one who ultimately decides whether to approach and touch the hand or object. This builds confidence and allows progress to be made at a comfortable pace.

Emotions versus Cognition

If you were sitting on your porch doing the Sunday crossword puzzle and a horde of killer bees suddenly swarmed around your head, chances are that "57 across" would remain unsolved as you dashed for safety. Emotions 1: Cognition 0. When you are in a state of extreme fear, it is nearly impossible to think clearly.

When a dog is in a state of absolute panic, the only thing that will help at the time is to remove her from the vicinity of whatever is causing the fear (or vice-versa). In cases of mild to moderate fear, however, targeting can help. Asking your dog to touch your hand in the presence of something that frightens her redirects her attention, thereby short-circuiting the escalating cycle of anxiety. Targeting keeps your dog focused and in cognitive mode by giving her something constructive to do. Additional applications of targeting will be discussed in later chapters. Let's begin by teaching your dog this useful skill.

Teaching Touch

Stand facing your dog. She should be sitting, facing you. If she does not yet know how to sit when asked, she may lie down or stand instead. Hold a few treats in one hand behind your back. With a small motion, extend the empty hand, flat with palm-down, toward your dog. Stop approximately two inches below and slightly to the side of her nose; keep the hand still (see *Figure 1*). Due to the innate canine need to investigate, most dogs will immediately sniff an offered hand. If your dog does not, rub a bit of strong-smelling treat on the back of your fingers and try again.

At the exact moment your dog's nose touches your hand, say, "Yes!" and reward her with a treat and praise (see *Figures 2* and *3*). Just make sure your dog is moving her nose to touch your hand and not the other way around!

Figure 1   *Figure 2*   *Figure 3*

If your dog does not touch your hand, but instead sits there staring as though you've sprouted antlers, the reason is probably one of the following:

Reason	Solution
You did the exercise directly after the attention exercise, so your dog thinks eye contact is what you want.	Stop for now, wait a bit, then try again without doing other exercises first.
Your dog is apprehensive about hands moving toward her.	Sit on the floor with your dog. When you extend your hand, keep it close to the ground.
Your dog has just eaten or is overtired.	Try again before your dog's next meal or when she is more alert.
The treats are not as exciting to your dog as you had thought.	Try bits of hot dog or cheese instead, and increase your odds of success even further by rubbing a bit on your fingers before you begin.

Note: Although hand targeting is traditionally done with a dog touching her nose to the *palm* of the hand, many fearful dogs find the palm-down position less frightening. However, if your dog will not touch your hand with the palm facing down, try it palm-up instead.

Keep things moving: hand is presented, dog touches nose to hand, "Yes!" and treat/praise. Once your dog has eaten the treat, begin the next repetition immediately. If your dog stops and stares at your hand but does not touch it, bring the hand behind your back and present it again, slightly closer to her nose. Or play it sneaky—reach into your pocket as though searching for something, then bring the hand out again. Once your dog is successfully touching your hand, place it in various positions above, below and to the sides of her so she has to reach just a bit further to touch it. (If your dog is frightened of overhead movement, skip the over-the-head touches.) Reward after every successful touch.

Once your dog has touched the offered hand at least five times in a row, add the verbal cue "Touch" just as you present the hand. When nose touches hand, say, "Yes!" and treat/praise.

Moving Right Along

Next, practice having your dog touch your hand as you walk along. Start with your dog standing next to you, on the side you would normally walk her. (We'll use the left side.) Keep all the treats in your right hand; your left hand should be empty. Begin with your elbows bent and hands at chest level. Say, "Let's go," take two steps, then extend your left hand down with the palm flat and the back of the hand facing your dog (if your dog was more comfortable with the palm facing her, turn it toward her instead), and say, "Touch." When she touches, praise and reward by plucking a treat from your right hand and presenting it down by your left side. Try to keep moving along as you feed the treat.

Continue to ask for a touch every few steps, until your dog is happily following you around the room touching your hand when asked. Maintaining continuous movement may be challenging at first, but your technique will become smoother with practice. Remember how complicated driving a car seemed when you first learned? This combination of movements will become automatic as well.

Once you and your dog have mastered the walking touch exercise, it is time to add a leash. Although it might seem odd to have your dog on-leash indoors, it is good practice for real-life outdoor situations. The instructions that follow assume that you are right-handed and normally walk with your dog on your left side. (If you are left-handed or normally walk your dog on the right, reverse the instructions.) Slip the loop of a four-foot leash over the four fingers of your right hand so that it crosses your palm. Holding the leash in this position will allow you to close your fist over it if necessary when working outdoors. The treats should be held in the same palm. (Using a four-foot leash rather than a longer one makes the exercise easier because there is no extra length of leash to bunch up and hold.)

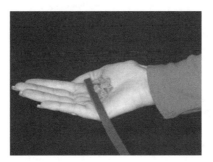

With your dog on your left, the leash should cross the front of your body. You will offer your left hand and ask for a touch, then reward with your left hand as well by picking a treat out of your right hand and delivering it down by your left side. (See the photos on the following page.) The hand nearest your dog is used for both targeting and rewarding.

This exercise gets easier with practice, but if you still find the method of leash-holding and treat delivery unwieldy or uncomfortable, experiment to see what works best for you. You could even use a waist leash, which leaves your hands free altogether (see *Resources*), as long as you are in no danger of being pulled off balance by your dog.

"Touch"   *Pluck treat*   *Deliver treat by side*
           from other hand

Keeping your palm flat as you deliver treats will ensure that your dog does not nip your fingers, even if she becomes stressed or excited. With this method you are almost pushing the treats into your dog's mouth with the flat of your hand.

Practice hand targeting with your dog off-leash first in various rooms of the house, and then on-leash indoors. Next, practice in the back yard off-leash (assuming the yard is enclosed) and then on-leash, and then on walks in your neighborhood (on-leash only, of course!) when you are not likely to encounter many people or dogs. As always, build distractions gradually so that your dog can eventually succeed even in busy, highly distracting environments. Once your dog is proficient, you can drop the "Yes!" and simply treat and praise.

A Touching Combination

In the previous chapter you taught your dog that her name is a cue to give you eye contact. Once your dog has mastered both attention and touch, practice a combination of the two. Call your dog's name. When she looks at you, present your hand and ask her to touch. Practice this in a stationary position and then while walking along together. Begin in the house and then practice on walks during quiet times, gradually building up to working when streets are more crowded.

In real-life situations, you might not always need to use the attention cue before asking for the touch, but it is best to practice both skills together as well as separately. In distracting circumstances, being able to get your dog's attention and then ask for touches will allow you to keep her focused on you, move her calmly and safely away from a situation, or move off a path to allow others to pass.

Other Targets

Your dog can also be taught to touch her nose to targets other than your hand. As you will see, this skill can be useful in addressing fear of a specific object or person. Object targeting is also an important first step in teaching a variety of tricks.

For our purposes, it is best to use either a plastic lid (such as a coffee can lid) or a Post-it®-type sticky notepaper as a target. The notepaper is easy to stick on objects, and the plastic lid may be applied using two-sided tape (don't apply the tape just yet). To teach your dog to touch the target, have her touch your hand a few times first. Then hold the target in the palm of your hand and ask for a touch. Say, "Yes!" as your dog touches the target. Follow with a treat and praise. (Once your dog is proficient at touching a particular target you may drop the "Yes!" but continue to reward with a treat and praise.)

Next you will teach your dog to touch the target when it is not in your hand. Practice each step until your dog is successful before moving on to the one that follows:

1. Practice with the target held in various positions, including above your dog's head (unless overhead movement causes fear) and to either side of her body. Repeat five times.

2. Now hold the target a bit lower with each repetition. The end result should be the target touching the ground with you still holding it. Do five repetitions with the target in this final position.

3. Place the target on the ground, remove your hand (place it behind your back), and ask for a touch. Your dog should touch the target. Repeat five times.

4. Now begin the exercise with you and your dog standing at a short distance from the target. Either toss the target a short distance away (easier if you are using a lid) while you restrain your dog, or have someone else place the target on the floor while you restrain your dog. Then say, "Touch!" and release your dog to go touch the target. Repeat five times.

5. Over the course of a few sessions, move your starting position gradually farther and farther from the target.

What's in a Name?

Soon your dog will be able to use her newly-learned targeting skills in a variety of situations. For now, build your dog's repertoire by teaching her to touch a variety of objects. Hold an object such as a ring of keys in your hand, just as you did with the original target. Ask for a touch. Once your dog has consistently touched the item on cue at least five times, change the cue word from "touch" to the name of the item (for example, "keys"). Because your dog has just touched the item five times in a row, chances are good that she will touch it on the sixth even though you have changed the verbal cue. (If she doesn't, do a few more repetitions before changing the word.) Teaching your dog to target various items will increase her skills and build confidence—not to mention how helpful it will be to have a dog who can find misplaced keys!

 Tail End Wrap-Up

- Targeting can be used to keep your dog focused, build confidence, address fears, teach tricks, and provide an alternative to unwanted behaviors.

- Teach your dog to target the back of your hand with her nose.

- Practice with your hand in various positions, and then while walking with your dog alongside you.

- Practice targeting with your dog on-leash, first indoors and then outside.

- Practice combining the attention and touch cues, first in low- and then in gradually higher-distraction environments.

- Teach your dog to target a plastic lid or sticky notepaper.

- Teach your dog to go to the target from a distance and touch it.

- Teach your dog to target a variety of items.

The Walk-Away:
Avoiding Close Encounters of the Fearful Kind

As you work to help your dog overcome his fears, it is crucial to avoid setbacks. For example, if your dog is afraid of other dogs, it would not be conducive to your progress for him to be surprised by a stray dog bursting out from behind a bush. If your dog fears people, someone rushing up to pet him would not be helpful. Ideally, your dog should not experience any "close encounters of the fearful kind" as you help him to modify his reactions. But real life is not a sterile training environment. Unpredictable things can and will happen, especially outdoors. While you cannot control the outside world, you can plan for contingencies by teaching your dog skills that will help him to cope in the face of the unexpected.

The walk-away is a useful maneuver for removing your dog from a potentially frightening or confrontational situation quickly and without causing stress. The verbal cue "Let's go, let's go!" will signal your dog to focus on you and follow wherever you lead. Depending on the situation, you might then do an about-face and walk your dog away, cross the street, or move to a far area of the sidewalk to allow another dog or person to pass at a tolerable distance. Conflict is avoided, and your program can continue without setbacks.

First, Baby Steps

Practice in a spacious indoor area with as few distractions as possible. Attach a four- to six-foot leash to your dog's collar and stand with him on the side he is accustomed to being on during walks. Hold the leash in the opposite hand so it crosses the front of your body. The leash should remain slack. (A slack leash will resemble the letter "J".)

Keep one treat in the hand that is closest to your dog and the rest of the treats in your other hand. Take a few steps with your dog walking beside you at a normal pace, then extend the hand closest to your dog so it is just in front of his nose. Urge, "Let's go, let's go!" in a high-pitched, excited voice and take a few small, quick steps forward. (If you prefer, you may use, "Hey, hey, hey!" or whatever phrase would naturally come to your lips—just be sure it's brief and easily repeated.) After a few quick steps, reward your dog with the treat and praise. You might find that the leash tightens on your first few attempts so that you are tugging your dog along. That's okay; just avoid any harsh jerking. Your dog will soon get the idea and follow along with the leash remaining slack.

> Have you ever seen a breeder get a litter of pups to follow her? The breeder says, "Pup, pup, pup!" and the pups move right along. High-pitched, repetitive sounds encourage movement, while low-pitched, one-syllable words (for example, "Whoa!") encourage animals to stop moving.

Once your dog has learned that "Let's go, let's go!" means "pay attention, sudden movement is imminent!" and can perform the exercise with the leash remaining slack, it is time to move in other directions. Begin with your dog at your side. Take a few steps, then extend the hand with the treat to your dog's nose and give the verbal cue. This time, instead of moving forward, take a few quick steps diagonally forward to the right. Reward your dog with treats and animated praise as he turns with you, then, without pausing, resume walking at a normal pace. Repeat every 10-15 steps as you walk along. Once your dog is moving along with you nicely, do the same diagonal walk-away but now withhold the reward and praise until you have not only turned, but taken a few steps. Remember to make your praise animated so your dog is encouraged to follow along. As you practice diagonal walk-aways to both the right and the left, your dog's focus and response time will improve.

Once your dog has mastered forward diagonal movement, practice walk-aways at a right angle. If your dog is on your left, move sideways to your right (and vice-versa); you should be moving away from your dog, not toward him. Then practice moving at a right angle in the opposite direction. As always, remember to keep the treat to your dog's nose as you give the verbal cue.

Teaching a diagonal walk-away

About Face!

Once your dog is responding in all of the aforementioned directions without the leash tightening, it is time to practice an about-turn. Begin by taking a few steps, then give the verbal cue. Holding a treat to your dog's nose, make a 180-degree turn—turn to the right if your dog is on your left, and vice-versa. Break the turn into a few small steps rather than pivoting, so it is easier for your dog to follow. You should now be facing the opposite direction from which you started. Finish the turn by taking a few small, quick steps in the new direction, then give your dog the treat and resume walking at a normal pace. It is common for dogs to lag during about-turns at first, so be vigilant about your dog's position and the position of your treat hand. As your dog gets better at staying next to you, make your turns sharper by taking fewer steps, and finally, by pivoting. When you pivot, bend your knees slightly and turn on the balls of your feet.

A full about-face

Once your dog is moving along with you in all directions with the leash slack, it is time to stop using the treat as a lure. As you practice walk-aways in various directions, give the verbal cue and use the same hand movement as before, but without a treat in the hand. Complete the walk-away and take an additional few steps, then give your dog a treat (pluck a treat from the far hand and deliver it down by the side closest to your dog). The movement you originally used to lure your dog to follow along has now become a hand signal, which can be made gradually smaller and smaller as you go—and if you would like, faded out altogether. (To fade out the hand signal, give the verbal cue, pause a second, then give the hand signal. Gradually increase the time between the verbal cue and the hand signal. Your dog will soon learn to anticipate the hand signal and therefore respond to the verbal cue alone.)

Practice Makes Perfect

Next, employ the help of a friend. Practice in an enclosed back yard or on a quiet street, with the friend playing the part of the approaching person/ dog. Start with the person at a distance. Walk toward each other, then give the verbal cue and walk your dog away. Practice walk-aways in various directions. Once your dog is doing well, practice waiting until you are closer to the person to give the verbal cue.

In the event that a stray dog approaches during a walk and you cannot get your dog to walk away with you, or if the stray follows you, toss a handful of treats on the ground near the stray and then walk your dog away calmly and quickly. You could also carry a can of Direct Stop® (available at pet supply stores) as a backup. The product resembles a can of pepper spray but instead sprays citronella. It might not work if dogs are already engaged in a fight, but a quick spray is usually enough to dissuade approaching dogs. Just be sure you're not standing downwind!

Once your dog is proficient at walk-aways in a practice situation, take it on the road. Practice in calm outdoor environments with people and dogs at a distance. Give the verbal cue just as your dog spies another dog or person. You might need to go back to luring with the food treat for the first few repetitions, since the distraction level has increased. Keep using the food reward and praise as your dog moves along with you. Over time, your dog will become conditioned to follow on your cue and the food reward will no longer be necessary. However, keep praising your dog for a job well done.

Always monitor your dog for signs of discomfort. If he is unable to focus on you or begins to bark, whine, or show other signs of distress, you are working too close to others too soon. As he improves, practice giving the cue closer and closer to approaching people/dogs.

When you use the walk-away in real-life situations, be sure to use the same verbal tone you used during practice sessions rather than a tense, worried voice.

Practice the attention, touch, and walk-away skills individually and then in combination. For example: during a walk, call your dog's name, do a walk-away, then ask for touches as you continue walking along. Or call your dog's name, walk him to the side of the road, then ask for touches as someone passes by. Practice during low-traffic times at first and then when streets are likely to be more crowded.

Tail End Wrap-Up

The walk-away helps to avoid confrontation and setbacks, and is useful for moving your dog along in a safe, timely manner.

🐾 Teach the walk-away using a verbal cue such as "Let's go, let's go!" Once your dog has the idea, the leash should remain slack.

🐾 Practice walk-aways straight ahead, to the sides, and diagonally in either direction.

🐾 Practice right-angle walk-aways and about-turns.

🐾 Once your dog is following along easily, stop using the treat as a lure.

🐾 Practice in a safe area with a friend playing the part of an approaching person/dog.

🐾 Practice walk-aways when you see other dogs and people on the streets.

🐾 Practice the walk-away in combination with attention and touch.

Part IV

Modifying Fearful Behavior

18

Behavior Modification
Program Overview

Congratulations on building a firm foundation on which learning and behavior changes can take place, and teaching your dog skills that will soon be put to use. Now it's time to get into the actual behavior modification process. In this section you will find:

- Considerations before embarking on a behavior modification program.

- Keys to success.

- An exercise to help you systematically pinpoint your dog's fears.

- Definitions of terms with easy-to-understand explanations.

- A sample behavior modification program, including a step-by-step protocol.

- How to gauge progress and know when to proceed to the next step.

- An additional type of behavior modification program that will take your success to an even higher level.

The Programs

This section focuses on two common fears: fear of unfamiliar dogs and fear of strangers. Even if your dog is comfortable with other dogs and people, once you understand how the process works, you will be able to apply it to your dog's particular fear issues. (The *Specific Fears* section has ready-made protocols to address individual issues.)

The first type of program you will learn about involves the dynamic duo of *desensitization and counterconditioning*. Don't let those complicated-sounding terms throw you—it's actually pretty simple. If your dog's fear reaction is so strong that she is unable to focus on you, this is where you should start. The program is easy for people and dogs; in fact, your dog will not be expected to do anything but accept treats when you offer them. She will be exposed gradually and safely to the things that frighten her, so that she can become calmer in their presence. You will even help your dog to develop a good association with those things so that her emotional reaction to them changes.

The second program can be employed once your dog is calm enough to focus on you. It involves *operant conditioning*—your dog will be expected to *do* something in order to earn rewards. This is where the skills you have so diligently practiced will come into play.

If your dog's fear reaction is mild to begin with and she is already able to focus on you in the presence of the thing that frightens her, you may be able to skip the first program and begin with the second. Once you have read through both programs it will become clear where to start with your dog.

Don't Cuss, *C.U.S.*
(Commitment, Unity, Safety)

While it is highly commendable that you are willing to make the effort to help your dog, it is also important that you understand what will be involved. Before embarking on any behavior modification program, you and your family should discuss the following:

Commitment

Any program geared toward addressing a dog's fears must progress gradually and incrementally. You should be prepared to do short training sessions throughout the day at home if your dog's fears are based there, or to practice during daily walks if the things your dog fears are normally encountered outdoors. While some fears can be overcome fairly quickly, depending on the cause, severity, and longevity of the issue, rehabilitation may take days, weeks, months, or in extreme cases, even longer.

While you might start to notice progress with an issue such as moderate to severe fear of people in as little as two to three weeks, significant changes might not become apparent for months. That waiting period can be challenging on an emotional level. Consider how difficult it can be to stick to a diet or exercise program if rapid results are not seen! Knowing in advance that progress may take time will help you to avoid frustration. The good news is that once changes begin to take hold, progress is likely to be steady—as long as you are committed to sticking with the program.

Unity

If you are the person who will be primarily responsible for working with your dog, discuss the training plan with those who share your home; it is important that everyone be in agreement. A petitioning child who receives a "yes" from one parent while the other says "no" will not perceive the parents as one strong leadership unit. It is the same with your dog; you must present a united front. That means all family members must understand and implement the house rules and be consistent in their behavior and interactions with your dog. For example, whoever is feeding your dog should ask him to sit first; if it has been decided that he is not allowed on the couch, no one should allow him access; everyone should know how to respond if he becomes frightened on a walk. Making behavior modification a team effort will allow you to support each other throughout the process and will keep motivation high.

Safety

Management

The crux of any desensitization program is gradual, incremental exposure to that which is feared, at an intensity that does not elicit a fearful response. Stringent management will be necessary to keep your dog from being exposed to those things he fears, except when you are working with him. While you cannot control everything that happens outdoors, you can control what goes on in your home to a great extent, and be as cautious as possible outdoors.

If one of the things that frightened your dog was people wearing hats, good management would entail asking visitors to remove their hats before entering your home. If your dog were extremely scared of visitors, you would place him in the yard or another room before visitors arrived. If your dog were afraid of unfamiliar dogs, good management would dictate that until real progress was made, walks would be taken when streets were apt to be less crowded.

Management prevents setbacks and creates an environment that is conducive to successful behavior modification.

If your dog reacts to delivery people by barking, growling, or with any other not-happy-to-see-you type of display, take a moment to put him behind a gate, in another room, or in the back yard before answering the door. Fear-based aggressive behavior grows stronger with repeated episodes; solid management is crucial to stopping the cycle. Remember, if your dog bites another person or dog, legal action could result in the loss of your home, your homeowners's insurance—and your dog's life.

The purpose of management is not only to keep your dog's anxiety level low, but to keep everyone safe. If your dog tends to lunge at or run from people or dogs on the street, your ten-year-old child should not be allowed to walk him. Doing so would not only be potentially dangerous for passersby, but could be harmful to your child. If your dog became reactive, he could knock down and/or drag your child, or even redirect his frustration onto your child, resulting in a bite. That might seem overly precautionary to you, but these types of incidents happen with alarming regularity. A little bit of management goes a long way.

Equipment

On walks, if your dog does not react to people or other dogs by lunging toward them, a front-clip body harness is best. But if he is reactive or drags you along, a head halter is recommended.

Head Halters

Unlike a muzzle, a head halter does not keep a dog's mouth closed or prevent him from biting. It does provide "power steering" by lessening the force with which a dog can pull or lunge. A head halter will allow you to maneuver your dog's head gently toward you to get his attention if necessary. If your dog is fear-reactive, recapturing his attention can interrupt the first step in an escalating chain of arousal that begins with staring at another dog or person. A head halter will also allow you to close your dog's mouth temporarily if needed, by pulling up gently on the leash.

Note: Dogs do not like the feel of anything restricting their muzzle. Many dogs protest at first by pawing at the head halter; that is normal. But if, as previously mentioned, your dog completely "shuts down," a head halter is not right for him. If you are unsure as to whether this tool is appropriate for your dog, consult a professional.

Introducing the Head Halter

A dog should be acclimated to wearing a head halter in a gradual manner, and he *must* be comfortable wearing it before attempting behavior modification exercises around things that frighten him. The instructions that follow are for acclimating a dog to a Gentle Leader™. (To use a Halti™, refer to the instructions that come with the product.) To introduce your dog to the head halter, hold a treat in one hand and hang the muzzle loop of the halter from the other (See *Figure 1*). Place the loop between your dog's nose and the hand with the treat, so that he must stick his nose and mouth through the loop in order to get the treat (see *Figure 2*). Let him have the treat. Repeat a few times. Then, *as* your dog is nibbling at the treat (don't release it!), use your free hand to push the muzzle loop gently back on all sides around your dog's mouth so that it is resting approximately one-half inch below his eyes (See *Figures 3* and *4*). Allow your dog to take the treat. Remove the muzzle loop. Repeat a few times. *Note:* Refer to the Gentle Leader™ product packaging for tips on proper sizing. For instructions on ensuring a correct fit, see www.premier.com.

Next, with the muzzle loop in place in back of your dog's mouth, drop a few treats on the floor; as your dog eats them, release the loop and connect the straps behind his ears (see *Figure 5*). Mission accomplished! (See *Figure 6*.) Feed another treat, then disconnect the straps and remove the halter.

Next, with the head halter in place and the straps connected, attach a four-foot leash with a lightweight, key-chain-style clip to the metal ring that hangs down under your dog's chin. As you walk along, be sure to keep the leash slack. If your dog paws at his face, don't try to comfort him; doing so would only reinforce his behavior. Instead, divert his attention by encouraging him to walk along with you, sit, or perform another behavior he knows. If necessary, as he paws, pull up *very gently* on the leash a foot or so from the head halter so his face raises and he is unable to paw at it. At the *instant* he stops pawing, release the tension so the leash returns to a slack position. Over time, the pawing should lessen; ultimately, your dog won't even notice that the head halter is there.

> *Never* jerk on the leash when using a head halter; doing so could cause serious neck injury.

Fig. 1   Fig. 2   Fig. 3   Fig. 4   Fig. 5   Fig. 6

Muzzles

If your dog has bitten or you feel that he might bite (he lunges at other dogs or people, or his reactive behavior has become progressively more intense), a muzzle can help to keep everyone safe.

A muzzle is also useful if your dog is so fearful of being handled by your veterinarian or groomer that he might snap at them. Depending on the severity of your dog's behavior, a trainer might recommend that he be muzzled during the initial stages of behavior modification. There are some protocols, such as the one that addresses fear of being touched, where a muzzle is appropriate if your dog is likely to bite.

There are two common types of muzzles. A *nylon muzzle*, also referred to as a fabric muzzle or groomer's muzzle, consists of a wide strip of fabric (usually nylon) that encases the dog's mouth and holds it closed. Most nylon muzzles have a small opening at the front; they all have two straps that attach behind the head to keep the muzzle secure. A dog cannot drink, chew anything large, bark, or bite when wearing a nylon muzzle. (If the muzzle has an opening at the front, canned squeeze cheese can be used as a reward.) Because a dog cannot open his mouth to pant, *this type of muzzle should not be used in hot weather*. Nylon muzzles are meant to be worn for short periods of time only; for example, while a dog is being examined by a veterinarian or having his nails trimmed.

A *basket muzzle* resembles an open-weave basket made of wire or plastic. It fits over a dog's nose and mouth and is secured by straps around the head. A basket muzzle allows a dog to open his mouth to pant, so it is safe to use even in hot weather. Many dogs seem more comfortable with a basket muzzle than the nylon type because the mouth is not being held shut. Some basket muzzles even have side slats that allow thinly sliced treats (such as coin-sized hot dog slices) to fit through, so a dog can be rewarded during an exercise.

Both nylon and basket muzzles come in a variety of sizes and are available at some pet supply stores and online (see *Resources*). Be sure to purchase the appropriate size for your dog and fit it correctly; the muzzle should not be so tight that it cuts into his fur, nor so loose that it can move around on his face. Straps should be fitted so that you can barely get one finger between the strap and your dog's head.

> A muzzle is not a solution in and of itself. Muzzles are not meant to be worn for long periods of time, nor should they be left on dogs who are unsupervised.

nylon muzzle   *basket muzzle*

Unless it is an absolute emergency, until your dog is accustomed to wearing a muzzle, do not muzzle him in the presence of the thing that frightens him. You do not want him to form an association between the two and, besides, being muzzled might increase his fear by making him feel unable to defend himself.

Introducing the Muzzle

The instructions that follow are for introducing your dog to a basket muzzle. (For nylon muzzle introduction, see *Chapter 30*.) Use super-yummy treats for this exercise, and remember to relax and breathe so that your dog remains calm as well.

Hold the basket muzzle on the ground with the opening face up. Place a treat in the basket. Hold the muzzle still and allow your dog to stick his nose in to take the treat. Repeat a few times. If your dog will not put his nose into the basket, hold it still on the ground. With your other hand, feed treats a few inches away from the muzzle. With each repetition, move the treat hand closer and closer to the muzzle, until the hand is right next to the muzzle. Then, as long as your dog is comfortable, move the hand so that the treat is at the opening of the muzzle, and then, eventually, inside it.

Once your dog is comfortable taking treats from the muzzle on the ground, hold the muzzle a few inches off the ground and repeat. As long as your dog remains calm and takes the treats, move the muzzle slightly closer to his face with each repetition. Proceed at a pace at which your dog is comfortable; if he balks when the muzzle gets too close, go back to a distance at which he was comfortable, do a few repetitions, then call it a day. At the next session, start a few steps back from the distance at which your dog balked, then proceed gradually, working in even tinier increments than on the previous attempt. Keep in mind that even if you are having great success, there is no reason to rush through all of these steps in one session. Every dog is different. If the whole process takes days, or even a few weeks, that's perfectly fine.

Once your dog is happily sticking his nose into the muzzle as you hold it at face level, it is time to apply the straps. When your dog pokes his nose into the muzzle to get the treat, bring the straps together behind his head so they are touching; do not attempt to attach them. Hold for one second, then release. So long as your dog is at ease, next, hold the straps together for two seconds, then release. At this point you might find it helpful to have someone else with whom your dog is comfortable feed treats as you hold the straps together (assuming the muzzle has side slats). Keep building the time gradually by one-second increments until you can hold the straps together for ten seconds. Next, attach the straps, feed a few treats through the muzzle in rapid succession (if the muzzle does not have side slats, praise and pet instead), then release the straps and remove the muzzle. All treats and praise should stop immediately once the muzzle is removed so that your dog associates good things with wearing it. Gradually build up to leaving the muzzle on for longer periods, up to ten minutes. Again, this process may take days, weeks, or longer depending on your dog and on how often you practice.

> If you feel there is any chance of your dog injuring another dog or person on walks or when working on behavior modification exercises in public places, he should wear a head halter *and* a muzzle. (If this describes your dog, contact a professional to help you work through the protocols that follow.) Introduce each piece of equipment separately. Once your dog is accustomed to each, put the head halter on first with the muzzle over it.

If your dog must be muzzled for walks, you might be concerned that the perception of him as a canine Hannibal Lecter will make you both social pariahs. This is a case where what others think must take a back seat to what is best for your dog. By muzzling your dog, you are being a responsible citizen and keeping the public safe as you work to rehabilitate him. And *you* will be much more relaxed because you will know there is no danger of your dog hurting anyone, which will in turn make your dog more relaxed. If you are worried about looking conspicuous, load your dog into your vehicle and practice in other neighborhoods first. (You should do this anyway if your dog is more reactive on his home turf.) As his behavior improves, you can work gradually closer and closer to your own neighborhood where, with consistent practice, your dog will not need to be muzzled any longer.

With commitment, unity, and safety in place, you will be well prepared to embark on a behavior modification program.

 # Tail End Wrap-Up

🐾 Make sure you have the time to commit to a behavior modification program.

🐾 Discuss the program with family members to ensure that everyone is on the same page.

🐾 Use management to keep everybody safe.

🐾 Use head halters and/or muzzles if necessary.

Keys to Success

You and your dog are about to jump paws-first into a program that will help to overcome her fears. Here are a few keys that will unlock the success of any behavior modification program:

It's All About You

Before we address your dog's behavior, let's discuss *your* behavior when encountering something that frightens your dog. What you do at your end of the leash will have a direct impact on your dog's reaction.

Most owners of frightened or reactive dogs learn to scan the environment vigilantly during walks. Unfortunately, once a potential problem is spotted, many become tense and tighten up on the leash. Some do it purposely to keep the dog close by, while others are not even aware of their actions. Either way, the result is the same; tension is transmitted down the leash and the dog becomes tense as well.

A simple visualization technique can help you to remain calm and keep your body relaxed in the face of whatever scares your dog. In a quiet moment, relax and imagine that you are walking down the street with your dog on leash. You encounter another dog, person, or whatever would normally elicit a fearful response from your dog. Imagine yourself remaining at ease, muscles loose, breathing normally as you and your dog walk steadily past. You are both relaxed and confident. Visualization might seem a bit odd to you, but this self-conditioning technique is used successfully by actors, business people, and professional athletes to improve performance.

You can also set up practice scenarios in the house or yard. Enlist the help of someone with whom your dog is comfortable to play the part of a passerby (even if your dog fears other dogs rather than people, this is good practice for you). Begin with your dog on-leash and the person at a distance. Imagine that you are in a real-life public situation. The goal is to pass each other just as you would on the street, with you and your dog remaining calm. Take a few deep breaths, then walk past the person with an air of calm assurance. Remember to keep the leash slack. With practice, you should see a difference in both your *and* your dog's reactions when you encounter others in public.

Don't be a Grabby Gus!

Some owners, when encountering a person or situation that might cause their dog to become fear-reactive, grab their dog's collar and hold it tightly. While that might make the owner feel more secure, it has the opposite effect on the dog. After all, the dog's option for flight has just been removed! That doesn't leave many choices, and many an owner has been snapped at or even bitten as a result.

Even when collar-grabbing does not result in lashing out at the owner, it can make a dog reactive; it did with Blondie, my neighbor's dog. In the rural canyon where I live, many residents have horses and cattle. As you would expect, the livestock are contained in corrals and stalls. Some neighbors, however, do not see the need for fences or any form of containment for their dogs. In Soko's younger, fitter years, I frequently took her for off-leash walks down our winding dirt road. Her favorite activity (after ball chasing, of course!) was visiting Blondie, our neighbor's sweet Golden Retriever. Soko and Blondie were always delighted to see each other and enjoyed spending time together.

Blondie was, in fact, perfectly friendly with every dog and person she met—a credit to her breed. She would lie in front of her house, enjoying the sunshine and passersby as though she didn't have a care in the world. But that all changed in the space of seconds, thanks to a neighbor's free-roaming Australian Cattle Dogs. The pack of three dashed down the hill from their unfenced property, crossed the road, surrounded Blondie, and attacked her. The incident was horrifying for everyone concerned.

Fortunately, Blondie's injuries were not life-threatening; but after the incident her owners became vigilant about not leaving her outdoors unsupervised.

On a Saturday not long after the attack, Soko and I rounded the bend to where Blondie lived. I was surprised to see her outside, seemingly alone. As we approached, it became clear that a man—as I later discovered, a visitor who had been warned about the incident—was keeping an eye on her. Upon seeing a petite woman approaching with a large, off-leash German Shepherd, he rushed up to Blondie and grabbed her by the collar. I quickly explained that the dogs were friends and that he could release her. The man did not believe me. As Blondie dragged him closer to us, he tightened his grip. At that moment, Blondie became agitated; she started to bark and growl at us. (*This* coming from the dog who would invite you in and make you a sandwich if she could!) Soko and I calmly retreated and gave Blondie a moment to calm down. I asked the man again to release Blondie. After a bit of convincing he finally did, and Blondie rushed over to greet us, friendly as ever.

The moral of the story is that being a Grabby Gus can cause even the nicest of dogs to feel threatened. Grabbing your dog's collar or tightening the leash can not only make her feel trapped, it can actually cause her fear to escalate, and can push reactivity over the edge into aggression. If you find yourself in a threatening situation, breathe deeply and lead your dog away as calmly as possible. If your dog knows the walk-away, use the verbal cue to get her to follow you.

Using Voice to Your Advantage

If you tend to talk to your dog when she becomes afraid, you will be pleased to know that you need not stop. However, you may have to change the *way* you speak. Have you ever seen a child fall down and skin his knee? The mother who rushes over crying, "Oh, honey, are you all right?" is likely to be rewarded with a bout of bawling. The mother who matter-of-factly checks out the knee, ruffles the child's hair, and says casually, "You're fine, kiddo" is more likely to see her child, assured that all is well, return to play.

Like children, dogs take their lead from authority figures. If you do not show concern over something, there is obviously nothing to be concerned ·about. Don't soothe your dog by patting her nervously and saying, "It's okay, don't worry" in a worried tone of voice; doing so is likely to have the opposite of the desired effect. And if you use the phrase often enough in frightening situations, it could even become associated with scary things, resulting in your dog tensing up as soon as she hears the phrase! Instead, use "cheerful chatter." In an unconcerned, cheerful tone of voice, say something like, "Look, it's another dog! We love other dogs!" It really doesn't matter *what* you say—"Malamutes have landed on Mars!" would work just as well (although I can't promise that your neighbors won't look at you strangely). Just make sure that whatever you say sounds cheerful. In a stressful situation, you can also soothe your dog by using long, stretched-out vowel tones such as, "Gooood dog." If you would like to pet your dog, the touches should be long, firm strokes rather than nervous pats.

If you do not normally talk to your dog in public and don't wish to start now, that's fine. Just remain aware of your body language so as not to transmit tension, and breathe. Humming a tune under your breath can help you stay calm. "Who's Afraid of the Big Bad Wolf?" was always my favorite. A friend likes to use the birthday song. Regardless of your musical choice, it's hard to remain tense when humming a silly tune!

Sorry, Hands Off!

While you are out in public diligently working with your dog, you may encounter well-meaning people who want to greet your adorable fur-kid. But if your dog is afraid of people, that greeting could cause a setback to all your hard work.

If someone asks to pet your dog, don't even bother trying the "My dog is afraid of people" approach. Too many people will invariably continue to walk toward your dog, murmuring things like "It's okay; all dogs like me." Instead, respond in a calm but firm tone that you would rather the person not approach. Use a phrase such as "Sorry; my dog is in training right now." (For children, "The doggy is in school right now" works well.) If the person continues to advance toward you, step in front of your dog. Put your hand straight out, palm forward, and say, "Stop. I *don't* want you to touch my dog." You may feel as though you are being rude, but this is about your dog's welfare. An alternative phrase would be, "Stop. She bites." And then there's my personal favorite, "Stop. She has a contagious skin disease." Believe me, *no one* wants to approach when they hear that one!

Just say no! You must be an advocate for your dog.

Give it a Rest

Consider how long it has been since your dog has had a fearful reaction. If she is afraid of other dogs and had a frightening encounter with one just yesterday, wait at least two weeks before starting a behavior modification program that involves other dogs, and keep her from being exposed to them in the meantime. That might mean that instead of your regular neighborhood walks, you temporarily exercise your dog in the back yard, or drive her to an area such as an outdoor mall where dogs are not normally found.

Regardless of what triggers your dog's fears, use management to ensure that she is not exposed to it for a least a few weeks prior to starting the program. This precautionary measure is meant to give your dog's system a chance to de-stress, and will create a level field upon which your behavior modification program can play out successfully. Next, let the programs begin!

Tail End Wrap-Up

- ❧ It is crucial that you remain relaxed when encountering things that frighten your dog. Remember to breathe and keep the leash slack. Practice visualization exercises and rehearse in private settings so you will be ready for the real thing.

- ❧ In a tense situation, don't grab your dog's collar. Instead, use a walk-away along with calm, firm pressure on the leash if necessary to move her out of the area.

- ❧ Use an unconcerned voice and long, smooth petting strokes to reassure your dog.

- ❧ In public, be an advocate for your dog. If she is afraid of people, do not allow them to approach or pet her, regardless of what they say.

- ❧ Make sure your dog has not been exposed to the things that frighten her for a minimum of two weeks before beginning a behavior modification program.

Triggers:
Pinpointing Your Dog's Fears

The more closely you can identify the specific things that frighten your dog—his *triggers*—the more effective you can be at helping him to overcome his fears. Most of us categorize a dog's fears in general terms. You might have noticed, for example, that "Molly is afraid of other dogs" or "Toby is scared of men." But if you did not define those fears more precisely, you might miss the fact that Molly is specifically afraid of large dogs with prick ears, or that Toby is only scared of men who are wearing hats or dark sunglasses. Speaking of hats and sunglasses, both are common triggers of canine fear. A hat changes a person's silhouette— it makes it look *wrong* somehow to a dog—while sunglasses make a person look as though he's got two-inch pupils!

Some dogs' triggers are auditory rather than visual. Some are sound-sensitive in general, while others fear specific noises such as beeping, vacuum cleaners, or thunder. There are other types of fear triggers as well. Some dogs are motion-sensitive, and will dart away any time someone stands suddenly or gestures broadly. Some dogs are so motion-sensitive that they will take flight at the tiniest twitch of a person's muscle! Other dogs are touch-sensitive. While some touch-sensitive dogs fear any type of handling, others fear being touched on a specific body part such as the rear or the paws. A dog might be sound-, motion-, or touch-sensitive, or a combination.

Identify Your Dog's Triggers

Each of the categories that follows lists possible triggers; some include examples to get you thinking. You might find that your dog is afraid of only one or two things in one category, while numerous triggers from another category elicit a fearful response. Jot down each one that applies, and note combinations of triggers as well. For example, if "children" and "fast motion" were pulled from separate categories, your dog's combined trigger might be "children running or bicycling past." Try to be as specific as possible.

Don't worry if the exercise looks a bit daunting—it's actually easy once you get started. Once you've finished, the chart provided will make it simple to organize and prioritize the information.

People

- men
- women
- children (infants, toddlers, kids between certain ages, teenagers)
- elderly
- body type (tall, large, small)
- skin color
- ethnicity
- facial hair
- one specific person
- delivery people (mail carrier, water delivery)
- service people (gardener, pool service)
- veterinarian/vet staff
- groomer
- unfamiliar people

People/Visual Triggers

- hat, cap, hood
- sunglasses
- specific type of clothing (uniform, work boots, scarf)
- carrying large or unusual objects (rake, bucket or mop, umbrella, backpack, purse)
- cane, crutches, walker, wheelchair

People/Body Position and Movement

- directly facing dog
- looking at or staring at dog
- crouching (facing dog, turned to side)
- hovering or leaning over dog
- reaching toward dog (or moving hand over dog's head)
- walking toward dog (direct frontal approach)
- approaching dog from behind
- movement of feet
- any movement at all (person stands up, gestures)
- running (running toward dog, running past)
- moving quickly across dog's field of vision (bicyclist, scooter zooming past)
- jumping
- passing by house

Other Dogs

- male
- female
- intact
- neutered
- size
- color (dark-coated dogs can be more difficult for other dogs to read)
- breed (fear of a specific breed may be due to traumatic experience)
- prick ears (like those of a German Shepherd)
- flop ears (like those of a Beagle)
- cropped ears
- docked tail
- coat (heavy-coated, fine-furred)
- tail carriage (tail held high or curled over back)
- when your dog is on-leash
- other dogs who are off-leash
- unfamiliar dogs

Other Dogs/Interactions

- standing nose to nose with your dog
- looking at or staring at your dog
- walking up to your dog
- approaching from behind
- sniffing your dog's rear
- placing paw or muzzle over your dog's shoulder or back
- jumping
- running
- lunging toward your dog
- canine-specific movements (pawing, play-bowing, wagging tail, leaping about)
- passing by your house
- barking
- whining
- growling
- air-snapping

Motion

- slow movements (person slowly reaching toward dog)
- odd movements (elderly person shuffling past)
- fast or sudden movements (chair being quickly pulled out from a table, swinging door, person standing suddenly)
- overhead movement (flag flapping, ceiling fan)
- movement (as opposed to sound)—cars, trucks, motorcycles, bicycles, scooters, skateboards
- moving light (flashlight, laser pointer, reflection of candles on ceiling)

Distance

- discomfort distance (dog is afraid when other dogs are less than ten feet away; or dog is fine with people across the street but not when passing by on the same side of the street) Estimate your dog's discomfort distance—begin to notice it on walks.

Sound

- specific pitch or tone (high- or low-pitched sounds)
- beeping sounds (pager, microwave, cell phone ring tone)
- flapping sounds (dog door flap, banner blowing in wind)
- deep, motor-driven sounds (central heat turning on, vacuum cleaner, blow-dryer)
- volume (loud music)
- tone of voice (person speaking sternly, "Fluffy, *lie down*!")
- yelling, shouting, or screaming (directed at the dog or not—for example, spouses fighting, kids screaming while playing) Note volume, verbal tone, proximity to dog.
- sudden, unexpected sound (something being dropped)
- crying
- thunder
- fireworks
- aircraft
- cars or trucks
- motorcycles
- cars honking
- sirens
- trash pickup (truck, rolling bins)
- lawn mower
- leaf blower
- musical instrument
- doorbell
- knocking on door
- furniture moving (chair scraping on floor)
- other in-home sounds (drawers or doors opening or closing, refrigerator, floorboards creaking)

Touch

- from above (being patted on head or back, having collar slipped over head)
- surprise touch (does not see approach/approached when asleep)
- light touch/firm touch/rough touch/scratching

- being touched on specific body part (back, rump, head, mouth, paws)
- collar being grabbed
- restraint (being hugged, restrained for vet exam)
- being lifted
- being held in arms or on lap
- having nails clipped
- being brushed
- being bathed
- having teeth brushed

Miscellaneous Triggers

- Sudden Environmental Contrast (SEC) – a person or dog suddenly appears (for example, from around corner) in an otherwise deserted environment
- crowded environments (dog parks, shopping malls)
- unfamiliar environments
- collar, leash, other training equipment
- riding in car
- stairs
- elevators
- escalators
- substrate (sand, gravel, hardwood, smooth or slippery surfaces)
- unfamiliar objects
- specific object (crate, mirror, statue, baby stroller)
- scent (smoke, feces, perfume)
- type of location (small or enclosed spaces, heights)
- specific location (room in the house, a street corner, a friend's home, the vet's office, a house passed on a walk)
- other animals (cats, horses, birds)
- lightning
- rain
- wind
- darkness
- water (sprinklers, garden hoses, wet surfaces)
- swimming pool
- camera or video camera pointed at dog

Long as it is, this list is not comprehensive. Think about the times your dog has reacted fearfully and add any triggers that were not mentioned.

Create a Chart

Now that you have a concrete idea of what your dog fears, it is time to create a chart. This will help you not only to pinpoint your dog's fears, but to become more aware of which triggers to pay attention to in your dog's daily interactions. Use the chart on page 166 to fill in your own responses. As you will see, two sample entries have been provided.

In the *Category* column, list the general category (for example, People). Next, under *Subcategories*, include as many listings from the general category as apply. For example, if your dog were afraid of people, the Subcategories column might include men with facial hair, and children. If the Category listing was Sound, the Subcategory might list thunderstorms, fireworks, and vacuum cleaners.

In the *Specifics* column, clarify the trigger even further. Specifics are particular circumstances that influence your dog's fearful responses. These include environment, time of day, distance, movement, and any other specifics you can recall. Be as descriptive as possible. Let's say you listed Sound under Category and thunder under Subcategories. Under *Specifics*, you might write "when outdoors," "when left alone," or "only after dark." If your dog is afraid of large breed, prick-eared dogs, your Specifics list might include "at the park," "less than ten feet away," "when moving toward us," or "when other dog is not on leash."

Under *Frequency*, note the frequency of your dog's fear reaction when faced with the trigger. Assign A for always, S for sometimes, or O for occasionally. If your dog runs behind your legs every time he sees another dog, for example, choose A for always. Be sure to base your choice on how often your dog reacts when presented with the trigger, rather than on the frequency of encountering it. For example, if you encounter other dogs frequently but your dog only reacts fearfully every now and then, choose O for occasionally. If your dog always reacts fearfully to men with beards but you only see one every now and then, the proper choice would still be A for always, not O for occasionally.

Under *Contributing Factors*, jot down anything else you can think of that might affect your dog's reaction. For example, a dog who is afraid of other dogs while he is leashed might be made more fearful by the owner tightening the leash, or less fearful with a certain person at the end of the leash. A dog who fears thunder might act less fearfully when a crate is made available, or more so when his owner tries to comfort him. Think back to the last few times your dog reacted fearfully. Had he been given less exercise than usual that day? Skipped a meal? Had a stressful experience earlier in the day? Received vaccinations recently? Or perhaps a significant person or other dog was absent at the time. Some dogs react more strongly with the owner present; for others it's the opposite. List *anything* that you feel might have a positive or negative effect, no matter how trivial; even the tiniest factor can contribute to discovering a pattern. Ask others who live with or visit with your dog for input as well. Other people may have noticed triggers and circumstances that you did not; in addition, it can be hard to be objective when you are emotionally involved.

It has long been accepted that vaccinations can cause adverse physical reactions in dogs. Current research is investigating the link between vaccination and adverse emotional reactions, including sudden fear issues. (For more on this topic, see the reference to Jean Dodds' work in *Resources*.)

Reaction pertains to your dog's physical reaction to the trigger. Does the hair stand up on his back? Does he whine? Bark? Drool? Record as objectively as possible what you have seen. Stay away from emotional interpretations such as "she gets worried" or "he goes crazy." Stick to observable physical characteristics, as though you are a video camera recording exactly what you see.

Under *Intensity*, grade the intensity of the reaction, with one signifying the least intense and five, the most. One would describe a very mild reaction, such as a dog's ear flicking backward for a moment. Three would indicate an obvious reaction such as ears back and tail lowered, or if your dog is fear-reactive, mild lunging and barking. Five indicates an extreme, full-blown reaction such as intense panic where the dog cannot seem to control himself. The dog might crash blindly into objects in an attempt to flee, expel his anal glands, or lose control of his bladder and/ or sphincter muscles. (If your dog is having level five reactions, call a professional immediately. It is imperative that your dog receive behavioral assistance and possibly pharmacological intervention as well.)

Next, under *Your Reaction*, record how *you* respond when your dog becomes afraid of that particular trigger. Do you soothe him, cooing, "It's okay," or stroke him softly? Ignore him? Move him away from the trigger? If others have been around when your dog reacts fearfully, ask them to describe what they have seen you do; again, it can be difficult to be objective when you are directly involved. Finally, under *Result*, record your dog's response to your actions. For example, if your reaction was to move your dog away from the trigger, your note in the *Result* column might read "stops shaking, panting decreases."

Form a Summary

Once you have completed the chart, search for similarities among the entries. You might notice that your dog has the most entries in the sound category, or that specific types of dogs frighten him. Take special note of the entries that list higher frequencies and intensities. Now, with the overall picture in mind, construct a few simple sentences that summarize your dog's biggest fears. For example, "Brady has a mid-level fear of men who wear hats or have facial hair. He reacts more strongly in the home than outdoors. Holding Brady by the collar to allow men to greet him has resulted in his becoming more uncomfortable and trying to get away." Or "Dusty has an extreme fear of having her hind-quarters touched. She has air-snapped at a vet tech and will not allow family members to brush her. Any type of forced restraint results in growling."

On the following page are two sample entries from the chart of Hunter the Beagle. Take a moment to review them.

Category	Sub-Cat.	Specifics	Frequency	Contributing Factors	Reaction	Intensity	Your Reaction	Result
People	Men Gardeners	Yard with leaf blower	A	Mom is home	Whines, runs, hides	3	I encourage him to come out	None
People	Women	Housekeeper when vacuuming	A	None	Backs up, ears flatten, barks	2	I yell to be quiet	He gets more upset

Before considering all the variables, Hunter's owner might have thought, *Hunter is afraid of the gardener* or *Hunter just doesn't like the housekeeper*. Now, considering specific factors more carefully, Hunter's owner might ask herself:

1. Is Hunter afraid of other people he sees only once a week or so, or is it these two people in particular?
2. Is Hunter afraid of the service people immediately upon their arrival, or only when they are operating loud equipment? Does he interact with them at other times?
3. Is Hunter afraid of the vacuum cleaner when it is used by family members?
4. Is Hunter afraid of other noises that are similar to the leaf-blower or vacuum?
5. Do the gardener and housekeeper have anything else in common (for example, do both wear caps)?
6. Is it possible that the service people are teasing or mistreating Hunter when no one is at home? (This is a terrible thing to have to consider, but it has been known to happen.)

Asking yourself these types of questions, along with reviewing and updating your chart periodically, will allow you to better treat your dog's fears.

 # Tail End Wrap-Up

🐾 A trigger is anything that causes a fearful response. It may be something your dog sees, hears, smells, touches (or is touched by), or even a specific location or situation.

🐾 Pinpointing your dog's triggers as precisely as possible will allow you to target his fears more efficiently.

🐾 Don't jump to conclusions! Consider all the variables in a situation so the trigger can be correctly identified.

22

Association, Generalization, and How Long will it Take?

Association—The Power of Prediction

Dogs are master prognosticators. Because they associate things that happen in close proximity, they quickly learn that one thing predicts the other. For example, most dogs know that their owner picking up a leash means a walk is imminent—hence the seeming loss of all self-control! A food dish predicts a meal. A gardener predicts the use of a leaf-blower. Some dogs make associations through repeated exposures, while others make the connection the first time. Fearful dogs tend to make associations very quickly.

It is important to determine whether the trigger for your dog's fear is the obvious one. Allow me to share a personal story that illustrates this point. My house is at the end of a long canyon, where winds often whip up to near-hurricane force. Unfortunately, the high winds cause brownouts—temporary losses of electricity. Ironically, the winds were raging as I wrote this chapter, and sure enough, the power went down. What happened next is exactly what is supposed to happen—the computer's backup power supply turned on. Now, the power supply beeps merrily as it goes about its work, which frightens Soko to the point that she will flee the house. Had I not been aware of Soko's fear of beeping sounds, I might have assumed that her nervous demeanor when the wind kicks up is due to a fear of wind. But Soko has never shown any anxiety when we are in the park or on the street, no matter how windy it might be. Her fear of wind is specific to the home location, because she has learned that there is always a lurking possibility that the wind will be followed by the dreaded beeping sound. There are actually two triggers in Soko's situation: the beeping sound itself (of which she is afraid regardless of location), and wind around the home. The moral of the story is to be sure you are identifying your dog's fear trigger correctly, and taking into account any secondary triggers as well.

Generalization

Earlier, you taught your dog some new skills. You then helped him to generalize so that he could perform those skills in different environments and in a variety of circumstances. Your dog should now be able to respond to your request for attention by giving eye contact whether the request is made in your living room, at a busy park, with you sitting in a chair, or in the presence of distractions. But while generalization is of great benefit in training, it can create problems when it comes to fear issues. Take, for example, a dog who has a mildly frightening encounter with another dog at the park. The event elicits a fearful response. Soon after, the same dog has a frightening experience with another dog at a different location; he quickly associates the two incidents. Now the dog feels that unfamiliar dogs, regardless of location, are to be feared. And because he had been on leash for both incidents, the dog now fears being on leash around other dogs as well. While you cannot prevent generalization from happening, you can manage things as carefully as possible to prevent problems, and consider whether generalization is contributing to your dog's fears.

How Long Will It Take?

Several factors will influence how long it will take to work through your dog's fears.

1. *Genetics.* While there is nothing that can be done to change your dog's genetic blueprint, you can still make progress within the range of what is possible for your particular dog.

2. *Early socialization.* A dog who was socialized early in life to various people, places, and things will generally have an easier time recovering from fear issues than one who received little or no early socialization. Again, this may be something you cannot change at this point, but progress can still be made.

3. *Duration and number of exposures.* Consider how long your dog has been living with his fear and how many exposures he has had to the trigger. If your pup was frightened by another dog just once, chances are he will recover fairly quickly. If your dog is an adult who has experienced numerous frightening incidents involving other dogs, rehabilitation will take longer.

4. *Sensitization.* Consider whether sensitization has occurred. As opposed to a dog becoming desensitized through careful gradual exposure, some dogs become *sensitized,* meaning they become more and more frightened each time they randomly encounter the trigger. This possibility is one more reason to manage the home environment so that your dog receives as little exposure to the trigger as possible.

5. *Intensity.* A dog who is only mildly fearful when encountering a trigger has a much better chance of moving through a desensitization program quickly than one who flies into a blind panic.

6. *Type of sensitivity.* How many senses are involved is important in determining a prognosis. For example, a dog who fears thunderstorms is probably afraid of the sound of thunder; but the dog might also fear the flash of lightning that precedes it. And because thunderstorms cause a change in static electricity in the air, the dog's coat might be picking up a static charge, causing the dog to feel small shocks. So the thunderstorm-phobic dog might actually be reacting to sound, sight, and touch. Similarly, a dog who is afraid of fireworks might fear not only the sound, but the sight and the acrid smell. The more senses that are involved, the more difficult the desensitization process, because it must address each component of the fear individually.

7. *Physical and mental state.* Your dog's physical condition and mental state will influence how quickly you are able to make progress. Medical conditions and certain medications can make dogs lethargic or less alert mentally, and can even intensify fearful or aggressive behavior. If your dog is elderly, he might not be as mentally responsive. If he is in pain, or is blind or deaf, progress might not be as fast. But as long as your dog can function to some extent physically and mentally, *progress is still possible.*

Now that you have clearly defined your dog's triggers and have a realistic idea of the factors that affect progress, it is time to move on to some helpful behavior modification techniques.

 Tail End Wrap-Up

🐾 Consider whether your dog has associated other triggers with the initial one. If so, those triggers must be addressed as well.

🐾 Manage the environment carefully so that your dog experiences as few fear-inducing incidents as possible, thereby decreasing the possibility of problems caused by generalization. Be aware of how generalization might be contributing to your dog's fear issues.

🐾 How long rehabilitation will take depends on many factors. Consider the ones listed and how they apply to your dog, in order to determine a realistic time frame.

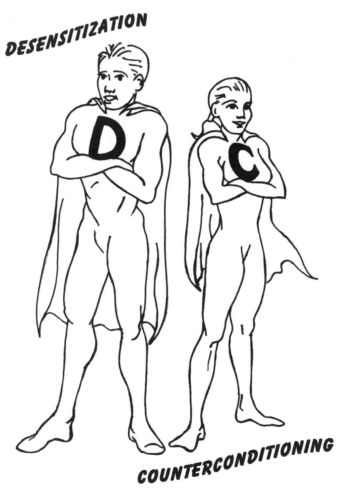

Meet the Techniques

Regardless of what causes a fearful reaction in your dog, there are proven techniques that can be used to address it. Following are brief introductions to the main techniques you will be using.

Desensitization

Desensitization exposes a dog to a fear trigger in a gradual, incremental manner. The process begins at a level low enough to avoid a fearful response, and builds incrementally to the level that originally frightened the dog. Working below the dog's fear reaction threshold allows her to become gradually more comfortable around the trigger until, eventually, she is no longer afraid of it.

Desensitization works on people as well. I, for example, have a fear of horses. (Oh, the irony—being perfectly comfortable with wolves but afraid of horses!) To desensitize me to what I perceive as large, strong, unpredictable animals, you could take me to a horse ranch. First, you could have me watch the horses milling about in the corral from a comfortable distance. As I became a bit more relaxed, you could encourage me to move slightly closer. In the weeks that followed, as long as I remained comfortable during our daily sessions, you could continue to bring me closer and closer to the horses. In time, I would be able to stand right outside the corral. I might eventually feel comfortable enough to stroke a horse's muzzle, and even work up to riding a horse. You would have helped me to work through my fear in a way that allowed me to feel comfortable and safe.

> Desensitization allows dogs to overcome their fears safely and humanely. The desensitization motto is "A little at a time is effective and kind!"

To ensure that exposure is gradual, a desensitization program manipulates factors, or *variables*. Depending on the trigger, variables might include such things as proximity (for example, distance from other dogs); volume (such as that of a stereo); angle of approach (a person walking directly at a dog, for example, as opposed to one walking across the dog's field of vision); and movement (such as a child walking versus running).

Counterconditioning

Counterconditioning seeks to change an unpleasant emotional response to a trigger into a pleasant one. Once the dog's underlying emotional response changes, her reaction toward the trigger will change as well. Counterconditioning is accomplished by pairing a trigger with something the dog perceives as wonderful. For example, if your dog were afraid of other dogs, you would feed her extra-special treats each time she saw another dog. Your dog would eventually associate the presence of other dogs with something wonderful, and her reaction upon encountering another dog would change from *Oh, no!* to *Whoohoo! Something great is about to happen!* Counterconditioning is often paired with desensitization; think of them as behavior modification's Dynamic Duo.

Don't feed the fear! When implementing a desensitization and counterconditioning program, it is crucial that treats or other rewards are paired with the trigger *only when the dog is relaxed.* If your dog were afraid of cars and you simply stood at a curb and fed treats as cars zoomed passed, your dog would very likely have a fearful reaction, despite the treats. A proper approach involves pairing treats with gradual exposure so that your dog remains calm. A program that haphazardly offers treats without regard to the dog's emotional state is likely to be unproductive, and possibly dangerous. If your dog were afraid of people and you coaxed her to approach a stranger to take treats, your dog certainly might approach and take the treats; but she would then find herself in such close proximity to the feared person that she might panic and even bite.

A funny thing happened years ago when I was working to help Soko past her fear of high-pitched beeping sounds. The fear had started with my husband's pager, to which she had never previously reacted. Perhaps the sound had at some point been inadvertently paired with something else that frightened her, like a passing garbage truck. I'll never know, but Soko quickly generalized the fear to the beeping sound made by the microwave. Now, *that* is a problem at my house! Not only that, but because the movement of the microwave door meant a beep was imminent, she became frightened whenever we opened or closed it.

To address the fear, I positioned my husband at the microwave while I stood with Soko in the living room, sliced hot dogs at the ready. The plan was for my husband to open and close the microwave door gently, and I would feed hot dogs. Soko would come to associate the scary microwave with the yummy hot dogs, and the microwave would become a good thing. We would build gradually to the microwave actually beeping. On the first try, my husband opened and closed the door gently and I fed Soko the hot dogs. So far, so good. But on the next repetition, something happened—perhaps a wayward burst of testosterone—and my husband closed the door too roughly. Soko panicked. Can you guess the result? Soko was instantly afraid of hot dogs! Fortunately, that fear didn't last—but be careful when using counterconditioning; if you do not work under your dog's fear threshold, it can backfire!

Classical Conditioning
(also known as Pavlovian conditioning, or associative learning)

Classical conditioning, like counterconditioning, creates an association between things. In classical conditioning, however, a dog does not necessarily have a negative association with one of those things to begin with. The classic example is Pavlov's experiment, where each time a bell was rung, the dog was immediately presented with food. Once the dog made the connection between the sound and the food, she salivated at the sound of the bell alone. (I am fairly sure I have been classically conditioned, as I have the same response when the doorbell rings for pizza delivery.) If your dog is like most, she has been classically conditioned to become excited when she hears the leash jingling, or when she sees you open the cabinet that holds special treats or toys.

Classical conditioning can be extremely useful when working with fearful dogs. One way to use it would be to play a certain piece of music (preferably something soft and melodic, like classical music) each time you massaged your dog; after a time, the music alone would trigger a relaxation response. You could then play the music in situations where your dog was nervous, to help her relax. Likewise, you could condition a specific scent to become associated with relaxation, then dab a bit of that scent on your dog's collar in advance of a potentially stressful situation such as having visitors over or visiting the vet.

Operant Conditioning
(also known as Skinnerian conditioning, or instrumental learning)

Where classical conditioning and counterconditioning are about creating associations, operant conditioning is about consequences—one thing actually *causes* the other. To classically condition your dog to overcome her fear of other dogs, she would not have to do a thing but accept extra-special treats in their presence. Using *operant* conditioning, however, your dog would be expected to *do* something to earn the treats. For example, whenever your dog saw another dog, you would call her name; she would look at you, and be rewarded with the treat.

A behavior that is rewarded is more likely to happen again. When a dog receives a treat for sitting, operant conditioning is at work. The dog is more likely to sit the next time she is asked, because the consequence of complying was pleasant. Dogs are constantly learning through operant conditioning, even though we don't always realize it. If your dog does not like being left alone in the back yard and barks until you let her in, she soon learns that the consequence of barking long enough is being let inside. (Coincidentally, *you* learn that letting her in stops the barking, and you become a well-trained human!)

> Although it might appear that a behavior modification program involves *either* classical or operant conditioning, there is usually an overlap of the two.

Habituation

Although habituation is not included in the programs that follow, as the owner of a fearful dog it is something of which you should be aware. Through *habituation*, a dog becomes more comfortable with a trigger simply through repeated exposures. Let's say a dog is nervous around unfamiliar people because she is confined to the back yard and the family does not get many visitors. If the fear is mild, it might be overcome by nothing more than taking the dog on daily walks. The frequent, consistent exposure would allow the dog to habituate to the presence of unfamiliar people and, eventually, she would no longer fear them.

Note: Habituation will not normally take place if a dog's fear is extreme; in fact, the dog might become sensitized to the trigger, and fear it more with each encounter.

Even when habituation is successful, the owner must guard against the possibility of "spontaneous recovery," in which the dog's fear returns because she has not been exposed to the trigger for a long period of time. This often happens with dogs who have habituated to the presence of other dogs, but then move to an isolated area where they seldom encounter them.

Flooding—Just Say No!

Although flooding is not recommended or used in this book, you may hear it suggested elsewhere—so let's discuss it. Where desensitization soothes, "Let's take it slow and easy," *flooding* snaps, "Just deal with it!" Flooding exposes a dog to a trigger in a way that immerses her, as she is simultaneously prevented from escaping. In one common approach, the dog is made to experience the situation until, after a prolonged fear reaction, she finally becomes exhausted and gives up. If the dog can no longer respond fearfully, the theory goes, she will realize that being in the presence of the trigger is not so scary after all.

Here is an example of how flooding might be applied: I am your subject, and my fear trigger is scorpions. Whenever a scorpion finds its way into my desert home, I practically leap out of my skin! (Hey, I'm an ex-New

Yorker. We're used to cockroaches—but scorpions?!!) To treat my fear, you would lock me in a closet with hundreds of scorpions. Scream and beg though I might, you would not let me out until I was a helpless mess, unable to respond fearfully or in any other way. Sound cruel? You betcha! Besides, I might have a heart attack before I "got over it."

In the television show *Fear Factor*, contestants voluntarily perform stunts such as lying in coffins while giant hissing cockroaches are poured over them. The operant word here is *voluntarily*. Those same contestants who steel their minds and tell the host to let the insects fall where they may would have a totally different reaction had the choice not been their own. It is the same for dogs—*facing fears on a voluntary basis is a completely different experience than being forced to face them.*

As you might have guessed, I do not recommend flooding. Speaking strictly scientifically, under the right circumstances, when administered by an expert, flooding *can* work. However, it would assuredly be a most unpleasant experience for your dog. Flooding carries a huge risk of creating an even more intense fear issue if it fails, along with other fallout: If you were the one applying the technique, you would chance damaging your relationship with your dog by being associated with the experience. (If you were the person who locked me in a closet full of scorpions, I doubt we'd be speaking afterward!) And if you were wrong about your dog's fear being mild or her ability to cope strong, or the technique was applied incorrectly, flooding might even cause your dog permanent psychological damage.

~ * ~ * ~ * ~ *~ * ~ * ~ * ~ *~ * ~ * ~ * ~ * ~ *~ * ~ * ~

Using humane techniques that involve gradual, incremental progress will ensure that your dog feels comfortable and safe as you help her to work through her fears. This approach is not only effective, but will actually strengthen your relationship. Best of all, your dog will soon learn that fear is not a factor for her!

Tail End Wrap-Up

	Desensitization	Exposure to a trigger is done in a manner that is so gradual that a fear response is not elicited.
	Counterconditioning	An unpleasant emotional response is changed to a pleasant one by pairing the trigger with something the dog perceives as wonderful.
	Classical conditioning	An association is created. For example, the jingling of a leash eventually triggers an excited "I'm going for a walk!" response.
	Operant conditioning	One thing causes another; the dog learns that her behavior has consequences. For example, if she barks long enough, someone opens the door to let her in.
	Habituation	A dog becomes less afraid of a trigger through repeated exposures to it. Habituation can work well for mild fears.
	Flooding	The opposite of desensitization. *Do not attempt flooding!*

24

Desensitization and Counterconditioning Program

If your dog's fear issues are extreme or he displays aggressive behavior such as attempting to bite other dogs or people, do not undertake this or any other behavior modification program without the assistance of a professional (see Resources). Be sure too to have your dog thoroughly checked out by a veterinarian. Disorders such as thyroid imbalance have been linked with aggression, and simply being in pain can cause fearful or aggressive behavior.

Now that you and your dog are thoroughly prepared, it is time to begin the first of our behavior modification programs. This program addresses two of the most common triggers—unfamiliar dogs and strangers. Whether your dog hides behind your legs when a person walks by or lunges at passing dogs, this is where you should start. (If your dog's fears have nothing to do with other dogs or people, skip to Part V, *Specific Fears*, to locate the appropriate treatment for your dog's issue.)

The program centers around the slow and easy, amazingly effective Dynamic Duo of desensitization and counterconditioning. We'll take it step by step so that both your dog *and* you are comfortable. Be sure to read through the entire program before you begin.

Setting the Stage

Choose a time of day when you are not likely to encounter many other dogs or people. If your neighborhood is constantly buzzing with kids playing and people walking dogs, or if the streets are not wide enough to maintain much of a distance from other dogs or people, drive your dog to another area. (Another benefit of starting outside your own neighborhood is that if you normally walk your dog along the same route, he might already be nervous about the area due to past frightening experiences.) Choose a location with enough space so that your dog will be comfortable. Two good choices are large parking lots and large, park-like areas.

Bring along plenty of whatever food treat makes your dog think he's in Hound Heaven. Don't be stingy! Use the best, top-of-the-line stuff. Often what dogs consider to be super-high-value treats are not actual dog treats but "human treats:" bits of cheese, pieces of boneless boiled chicken, or hot dog slices. Dry cookies are out—the rule is "the stinkier the better!" To ensure that the treats retain their value, don't use them for normal training exercises or at any time other than when doing behavior modification sessions. You can also improve the chances that your dog will be interested in food during the sessions by having him skip the meal that precedes them.

Treat Tips

- When a dog is extremely frightened he will not eat, no matter how scrumptious the food. If your dog will not take treats, chances are you are working too close to the trigger.

- When a dog is mild to moderately stressed (or excited), he may still take treats, but in a much less gentle manner than when he is relaxed. The pressure with which your dog takes treats can be a useful gauge of his stress level as you work through a behavior modification program. Just watch your fingers! Delivering treats by your side with a flat palm can help (*see p.124*).

- If you are concerned about the effect all those treats might have on your dog's weight, compensate by decreasing the size of his meals or by providing more exercise. If your dog has a health issue that precludes the use of treats altogether, use an improved version of his normal dry dog food: place a portion of the daily ration in a plastic bag, along with some hot dogs or boiled chicken; seal and refrigerate overnight. In the morning, remove the hot dog/chicken. The kibble will have absorbed the odor and become much more enticing! If your dog is on a special diet canned food, remove the contents from the can, cut it into slices, then bake until dry and crunchy.

For the vast majority of dogs, food treats will serve as the high-value reward; but to some dogs, toys are more valuable. If your dog is blasé about boiled chicken but fanatical about playing tug, use the tug toy instead of treats. Keep the toy (preferably a long, braided rope) attached to your belt loop or stuff one end in your pocket. When it's time to reward your dog, whip out the toy and allow him a few quick tugs. If your dog is so-so about sausage but lives for a toss of the ball, reward by tossing him the ball and letting him hold it for a few minutes as you walk along. That said, don't conclude too quickly that your dog is not interested in food on walks; first, try increasing the treat's value and withholding a meal before the walk. If it turns out that your dog is truly more toy-motivated than food-motivated, substitute the toy wherever you see the words "treat" or "reward" in the directions that follow.

Variables

The success of this program is dependent on manipulating a few variables:

Distance. At what distance does your dog react? Does he react if a dog is ten feet away, but show no reaction toward a dog fifty feet away? Does he fear a person walking on the same side of the street but not one across the street? Take notice of your dog's comfort zone in regard to various triggers so you can work under his reactivity threshold.

Angle of Approach. A stranger walking directly toward your dog is potentially more frightening than one who is walking across his field of vision, or one who is moving away from him. Your dog might be comfortable with a person crouching and petting him on the chest, but not with one who is standing and attempting to pet him palm down over the head. Begin to notice which angles of approach frighten your dog.

Speed of Approach. If your dog is afraid of other dogs, another dog running is likely to be more frightening than one who is moving slowly. A hand that darts quickly toward your dog to pet him is more likely to be frightening than a hand that moves slowly.

Trigger Characteristics. Does your dog react fearfully to large dogs with prick ears? Stout men with facial hair? Children who are running and screaming? These variables will be important to keep in mind. Using those examples, you might begin with exposure to flop-eared dogs, smaller men with no facial hair (or, if necessary, women) and children who are sitting quietly. You would then work up slowly to small dogs with prick ears, diminutive men with some facial hair, and children who are walking and talking. Continuing in this way, you would eventually work your way up to the things your dog feared most.

Fab Four Rules for Working with Variables

1. *Break things into small increments.* The distance between your dog and the trigger should become shorter in tiny increments, the angle of approach more direct gradually, and so on.
2. *Whenever you make one variable more difficult, relax the criteria for another.* Say you have worked up to standing with your dog fifteen feet from children who are running past. When you decrease the distance to ten feet, you might revert to having the children walk slowly instead. Whenever you make one aspect of an exercise harder for your dog, make another easier.
3. *Always work under your dog's threshold.* If your dog reacts fearfully during an exercise, reconsider and modify your approach so that he is more comfortable. (The next chapter, *Troubleshooting*, covers what to do if he does have a reaction.)
4. *Move to the next step only when your dog is ready.* How can you be certain that it is time to work a bit closer to the trigger? It's simple: ask your dog. No, I'm not suggesting you coo in Bowser's ear, "Sweetie, how'd you like to go warm up to that cute Cocker Spaniel?" What I mean is, *watch* your dog. Observe his body language and look for signs that he actually seems happy to see the thing that previously frightened him—or that he at least seems relaxed. Perhaps he started out cowering or barking, but has now begun to wag his tail happily (as opposed to an anxious wag) whenever he sees another dog. Or perhaps he simply remains completely calm and unaffected, ears in normal position, with no body tension visible. Great! Be sure the happy or relaxed reaction occurs on a few different occasions before working closer, to ensure that it was not a fluke or a misinterpretation of body language.

But how, you're probably wondering, will your dog go from "Uh-oh!" to "Yipee!" at seeing the trigger? By calling on the other half of the Dynamic Duo—counterconditioning.

Counterconditioning

The trick with counterconditioning is to pay attention to what your dog sees. As soon as he spots another dog or person (whichever triggers his fear)—not when *you* see the trigger but when *your dog* sees it—let the party begin! Feed treats in rapid succession, one after another. Cheerful chatter may accompany the treats but is not absolutely necessary. The treats and cheerful chatter should stop as soon as the trigger disappears.

Your timing in stopping and starting the treats is crucial to creating an association between the presence of the trigger and the pleasant emotion felt by your dog when eating the treats. Keep treats handy, ready to go.

Practice Makes Perfect

When a trigger shows up, it's a party! When the trigger is gone, the party's over. Sounds simple, doesn't it? In theory, it *is* simple. But speaking as someone who has coached many clients on this technique, I can tell you that things sometimes become complicated by nervousness and other emotions—your dog's *and* yours—when working in public. A few rounds of practice in the living room before taking it on the road can help.

To practice at home, enlist the help of a friend with whom your dog is comfortable. The friend's job is to step out from behind a corner, walk across the room, then return and disappear around the same corner again. (If the room has two entrances, the person can enter from one and exit through the other.)

Stand in the room with your dog on-leash, treats at the ready, friend out of sight. Right now the distance at which your friend will appear is not critical, since this is a person your dog knows—the practice is really for you. Keep an eye on your dog. The friend should appear unexpectedly, without calling out or signaling to you first. Begin feeding treats (along with happy chatter if you'd like) as soon as your dog sees the person; stop when the person disappears. Watching your dog, feeding treats in a timely manner, and keeping an eye on the person all at the same time might seem challenging at first, but will quickly become second-nature.

Once you are comfortable doing this exercise in the house, practice outdoors with your friend appearing from around a house or corner. At-home practice sessions, indoors and out, will build your skills and confidence so that when you are ready to work in public, your timing will be precise and you will be able to remain calm in the face of triggers.

Let the Party Begin!

Now you're ready to work in the public place of your choice. Position yourself at a distance from passersby at which your dog is absolutely comfortable and does not have a fearful response. Let's say your dog is afraid of unfamiliar people, and you have decided to practice at your local post office. If your dog is uncomfortable with strangers ten feet away but is comfortable when they are at a distance of thirty feet, stand in the parking lot thirty-five or even forty feet back from the entrance. Feed your dog as soon as a person appears (gets out of a car or exits the post office), then stop when the person moves out of sight (gets into a car or enters the post office). Remember to stay relaxed. Take a few deep breaths if necessary.

You might not be working at a location where you are standing still, but are instead walking around at a park or on a wide street. In that case, start feeding treats as soon as your dogs sees the trigger (dog or person, depending on your dog), then calmly move your dog away, stopping the treats as you do so. If you are on a wide path, moving your dog away might simply mean continuing on your way as the trigger passes in the opposite direction. If the trigger is too close for comfort (such as a stranger walking toward you), do a walk-away to move out of the person's path. Remember to start the treats when your dog sees the trigger, and stop them as you move away.

Note: When you use the walk-away, your dog might not come along as easily as when you practiced at home. Don't jerk on the leash, but if necessary, exert firm pressure as you turn and walk away.

Examples of Proper Treat Timing

- You are walking along with your dog. A woman with a dog is walking toward you, on the same side of the street. You know this approach and proximity will be too much for your dog. As your dog spots the pair, you feed a few treats in rapid succession, then stop treating as you give the walk-away cue and walk with your dog calmly across the street.

- You are sitting on a park bench. A person walking a dog is leaving the park. They are at a distance at which your dog is comfortable. As soon as your dog spots them, you start feeding treats. The pair disappears into a nearby car. The treats stop.

Your first public sessions should be brief. Pay attention to whether your dog becomes agitated after a certain period of time. For example, if you normally take a twenty-minute walk but have noticed that your dog usually becomes agitated after fifteen minutes or so, cut your walks down to ten minutes and build gradually from there.

Sample Protocol

The following is not meant to serve as an exact blueprint, but an example of how to manipulate variables in order to keep your dog comfortable and lessen the chance of a fearful response.

For our purposes, we'll assume that your dog has a fearful response toward unfamiliar people at a distance of twenty feet or less. You are standing with your dog on-leash on a quiet street. You will begin treating/cheerful chatter as soon as your assistant (a friend with whom your dog is *not* comfortable) appears from around a corner, and stop the treating/chatter when she disappears around another corner. Each step of the protocol should be repeated as many times as necessary; you should proceed to the next step only when your dog seems relaxed, happy, or even excited at your assistant's appearance.

"Horizontal" indicates that the assistant walks horizontally across your dog's field of vision. "Diagonal" indicates that she walks toward your dog, but on a diagonal. Of course, it would be physically impossible to maintain the same exact distance (for example, 10 feet) when walking on a diagonal, but the person should adjust the angle to maintain roughly that distance at the point closest to your dog. "Walks at normal pace" indicates the assistant walking at a normal pace without swinging her arms, looking at your dog, talking, or doing anything that would potentially frighten your dog.

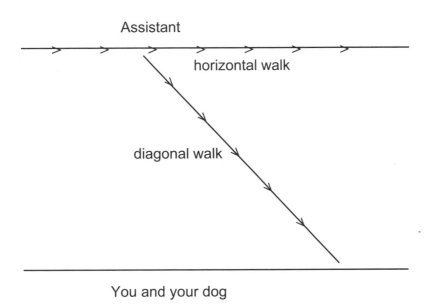

You will notice that whenever the angle of approach changes from horizontal to diagonal, the distance drops back to ease your dog into the more challenging situation. Actions (walking more quickly, swinging arms, glancing briefly at your dog, calling out a greeting) are added in gradually at the beginning but are lumped together more quickly toward the end, because by that time your dog will have had more practice.

Assistant's Distance	Angle of Approach	Assistant's Movement
20 feet	Horizontal	Walks at normal pace
20 feet	Horizontal	Walks a bit more quickly, swings arms
20 feet	Horizontal	Walks quickly, swings arms, glances at dog for 1 second
20 feet	Horizontal	Walks quickly, swings arms, glances at dog for 2 seconds
20 feet	Horizontal	Walks quickly, swings arms, glances at dog for 2 seconds, calls out a greeting
15 feet	Horizontal	Walks at normal pace
15 feet	Horizontal	Walks a bit more quickly, swings arms
15 feet	Horizontal	Walks quickly, swings arms, glances at dog for 1 second
15 feet	Horizontal	Walks quickly, swings arms, glances at dog for 2 seconds
15 feet	Horizontal	Walks quickly, swings arms, glances at dog for 2 seconds, calls out a greeting
20 feet	Diagonal	Walks at normal pace
20 feet	Diagonal	Walks a bit more quickly, swings arms, glances at dog for 1 second

Distance	Approach	Movement
20 feet	Diagonal	Walks quickly, swings arms, glances at dog for 2 seconds calls out a greeting
15 feet	Diagonal	Walks at normal pace
15 feet	Diagonal	Walks a bit more quickly, swings arms, glances at dog for 1 second
15 feet	Diagonal	Walks quickly, swings arms, glances at dog for 2 seconds, calls out a greeting
10 feet	Horizontal	Walks at normal pace
10 feet	Horizontal	Walks a bit more quickly, swings arms, glances at dog for 1 second
10 feet	Horizontal	Moves quickly, swings arms, glances at dog for 2 seconds, calls out a greeting
13 feet	Diagonal	Walks at normal pace
13 feet	Diagonal	Walks a bit more quickly, swings arms, glances at dog for 1 second
13 feet	Diagonal	Walks quickly, swings arms, glances at dog for 2 seconds
13 feet	Diagonal	Walks quickly, swings arms, glances at dog for 2 seconds, calls out a greeting

Don't get overwhelmed by the way a protocol looks on paper—it's actually pretty simple in practice. Just remember to proceed slowly, and if your dog becomes stressed or fearful at any point, go back to the last step at which he was successful and create tiny steps from there. For example, instead of jumping from "walks at normal pace" to "walks a bit more quickly, swings arms, glances at dog" you might insert a step where the person walks faster but does not swing arms or glance at your dog. The other movements would gradually be added, one at a time, as long as your dog remained relaxed.

Again, this sample protocol is only a slice of the pie. To proceed further after the last step, closer proximity would be added gradually. You might also begin to add approaches where the assistant walks directly toward your dog but then veers off horizontally at the halfway point. (This serves as an intermediate step between a diagonal and a direct approach.) Eventually, as your dog was ready, direct approaches would be added.

Just remember, the pace at which you proceed through any behavior modification protocol should be dictated entirely by your dog's responses. You might sail through a protocol during one session, or take weeks to complete a step or two. Once completed, the protocol should be repeated with various people in varying locations to address the issue comprehensively.

Be patient. The most common mistake is moving ahead too soon. Assessing whether your dog looks relaxed and happy at each step will ensure that you proceed at a pace that is safe and comfortable for your dog. Remember the tale of the tortoise and the hare; fast might be flashy, but slow and steady wins the race.

And now, instead of the usual Tail End Wrap-Up, turn the page for a special guest...

Tail End Rap-Pup

Use the best, super-yummy treats
Practice at home before hittin' the streets
Don't be frettin', it's an easy thing
With a little desens. and conditioning!

Time to move on, time to step up
When your dog is lookin' like a happy pup
Take your time, you chill too
Soon things won't scare either of you!

25

Troubleshooting

Whether you are practicing between professional training sessions or carrying out a desensitization and counterconditioning program on your own, problems can arise. Following are two of the most common challenges and how to solve them.

Problem: Your dog will not accept food in the presence of the trigger.

Considerations:

- Your dog might not perceive the treats to be as valuable as you do; or perhaps he simply had a full stomach. In the first case, try more appetizing treats. In the latter, withhold the meal before the next session.

- Consider the angle of approach. If the trigger was coming directly toward you, or toward you on a diagonal, perhaps the approach was too intense. Try setups where the trigger passes by horizontally until your dog is more comfortable.

- Did you become tense and tighten up on the leash? If so, it might have made your dog nervous as well.

- Perhaps your dog simply wasn't feeling well during the exercise.

- Intense fear will not allow a dog to eat. Reassess the distance involved in your dog's comfort zone; he might not be as relaxed as you had thought.

If your dog becomes so fearful upon seeing the trigger that he will not take treats, you can ease him into the process more gradually by adding an intermediary step: Scan the environment ahead as you walk along so that you see the trigger before your dog does. When it appears, begin to feed treats (along with cheerful chatter if you'd like). This differs from the original protocol in that now you are feeding treats as soon as *you* see the trigger, rather than when your dog sees it. Since your dog will already be eating the treats when he spies the trigger, he is likely to continue taking them. And because he is already experiencing pleasant, treat-induced emotions when he sees the trigger, he will associate those emotions with the trigger.

Once your dog has become more relaxed around the trigger (which could be days, weeks, or months depending on your dog), switch to feeding the treats as soon as *your dog* sees the trigger, rather than when you see it.

Problem: Your dog reacts to the trigger.

Despite your best efforts to work within your dog's comfort zone, it is probable that at some point he will react to the trigger. The reaction might be mild, such as freezing in place. It might be moderate, such as growling with hackles up, or attempting to hide behind you. Or the reaction might be severe, involving lunging, barking, or snapping.

- If your dog's reaction is mild, try to get him to take the treats anyway. Yes, that does seem as though you are rewarding the unwanted behavior! However, classical conditioning is a powerful thing, and an association between the treats and the trigger is still being made. Treat for a few seconds, then turn and walk away with your dog.

- The best course of action in the case of an extreme reaction is to remove yourself and your dog from the situation as quickly and calmly as possible. If you have been practicing walk-aways, you should be able to get your dog to come along with you. Since your dog is so aroused, however, you might have to exert a bit of firm pressure (as opposed to a jerk) on the leash.

- Once your dog has had an extreme reaction, the physiological changes that accompany that reaction last for some time. Because your dog's body is still in a state of high alert, it is best to return home afterward in order to avoid a second setback. Later, when you are both calm, reassess your program to figure out why your dog reacted, and modify the protocol accordingly.

Videotape It!

Having someone come along to videotape your sessions can be invaluable. You might find that your body language is not quite as relaxed as you had thought, or that your dog was offering stress signals of which you were unaware. You might realize that your dog's comfort zone is not as large as you had originally estimated, or that a certain type of dog or person causes a stronger reaction than others. Based on your findings, modify your protocol as needed.

 Tail End Wrap-Up

🐾 If your dog will not accept food in the presence of the trigger, consider the cause and modify your approach accordingly.

🐾 Try feeding your dog when *you see* the trigger, before he even notices it.

🐾 If your dog has a mild reaction to the trigger, feed treats anyway, then walk your dog calmly out of the area.

🐾 If your dog has a severe reaction to the trigger, remove yourself and your dog from the area as calmly and quickly as possible.

🐾 Videotaping your sessions can help you to spot details you might have missed.

Operant Conditioning

Your dog may have initially been so emotionally aroused around other dogs or people that she was unable to respond to your requests for attention. In that case, you practiced daily desensitization and counterconditioning sessions, in which she was not expected to do anything more than take treats in the presence of the trigger. Now, assuming your dog is calm enough around the trigger to mentally process information and respond to requests, it is time to move into the operant conditioning phase of the program.

You've Got the Skills

You will be glad to know that you have already taught all of the necessary skills for this phase. If you have been incorporating distractions into your attention exercises, you will now be able to put that practice to good use. On walks, practice with the trigger at a distance. Wait for your dog to notice it. When she does, call her name, using the same tone of voice as you did in practice sessions. When your dog looks at you, extend your hand and ask for a touch; she should touch her nose to your hand. Reward with a treat. Continue to walk along and ask for touches until the trigger has disappeared, or until you have passed the trigger. Over time, practice asking for attention closer and closer to the trigger, until you can pass it calmly at close range. Continue to use the walk-away in the meantime if a trigger is too close for comfort. Following are two examples of how the attention and touch commands might be used:

- Whenever you walk your dog past your neighbor's house where Thor the Doberman lives, Thor barks, resulting in your fear-reactive dog lunging and barking back at him. So you begin practicing across the street from the house, asking for your dog's attention just before Thor becomes visible. As you pass, you ask for and reward touches until you can no longer see Thor. You work gradually closer and closer to the house, until you can pass Thor's domain at close range with your dog paying attention to you instead of him.

- You are walking your dog on a crowded, narrow sidewalk. Remus the Rhodesian Ridgeback and his owner are walking toward you. You do a walk-away to the side, ask your dog to sit, then do touches to keep her focused on you until Remus and his owner have passed.

You might have heard that when a trigger appears, it is best to walk your dog to the side of the road, place her in a sit-stay, and then block her view of the trigger until it has passed. But if your dog is brimming with anxious energy, it might be difficult for her to sit still and do nothing; and because she fears the trigger, she will feel more comfortable if she can see it. After all, if a large, hairy beast suddenly burst through your living room window, would you rather I block your view or allow you to keep an eye on it? By giving your dog something proactive to do such as touches, or a trick she has learned, you will help to keep her calm.

Depending on the situation, you might be able to skip the attention cue and move directly to asking for touches. Always gauge your dog's stress level and proceed accordingly; while you might be able to get touches with the trigger only five feet away, if the trigger were to approach you directly, your dog might not be able to focus on you. Try touches with the attention cue first and then without it to get a feel for your dog's ability to respond under various circumstances. Even if your dog can successfully respond to touch without the attention cue first, keep practicing attention as well, as it will come in handy in many situations.

Anticipation…

You might believe that all you are accomplishing by asking for attention and/or touches is diverting your dog's attention away from the trigger. While you are certainly doing that, you are also teaching your dog what to *do* when she sees a trigger. Because you are practicing attention/touches when encountering the trigger, your dog will learn to anticipate your verbal cue. Let's say your dog's trigger is large men with beards. Each time you pass one on the street, you ask your dog for touches. Your dog soon learns that whenever she sees a large man with a beard, a request to touch your hand will follow. The result will eventually be that when she sees a large man with a beard, she will anticipate your verbal cue and nudge your hand without being asked. (If you have been using the attention/touch combination, she is likely to look at you when she sees the trigger and then touch.) You will have helped your dog to become more confident by giving her perceived control over potential stress-producing situations, and have successfully substituted an acceptable behavior for previous inappropriate ones.

Once your dog begins to automatically touch your hand upon encountering a trigger, you will have a useful gauge of her emotional state. For example, you might not have realized that the dog walking toward you on the sidewalk was causing your dog to feel anxious, until you felt her nudging your hand. Once you were aware of her distress, you could remove her from the other dog's path and evaluate whether your program needs revising.

Do these successes mean that you should now allow your fear-reactive dog to romp freely with others at the local park? Or that your afraid-of-strangers dog may now come along to your kid's crowded baseball game? No! Keep up the good work and don't push your dog too far too fast. Next, we'll discuss how to gauge your progress and just how far you can expect to take your success.

 # Tail End Wrap-Up

🐾 When encountering triggers, stay calm and use the same tone of voice to ask for attention and/or touches as you did in practice sessions.

🐾 Practice using attention and touch separately and together.

🐾 Your dog will eventually anticipate your verbal cue and will give attention/touches whenever she spies a trigger. This is not only a useful alternative behavior, but offers a beneficial gauge of her emotional state.

🐾 Don't jump the gun by putting your dog into a situation for which she is not ready. Keep up daily practice sessions, and celebrate even small successes!

Gauging Success, Making Progress

You know the old expression about not being able to see the forest for the trees. Well, when you are immersed in a program of daily behavior modification practice, it can be difficult to gauge your overall success. To maintain an accurate perspective, it is best to track your progress.

Ways to Keep Track

If you have a willing assistant and a video camera, have the person accompany you on walks once a week to videotape your dog's interactions. The assistant should walk far enough behind or stand at enough of a distance so as not to be distracting. Note the date of each recording. Every three to four weeks, review the tapes. Not only will you remain motivated by seeing the progress you have made, but you might notice something in your dog's body language (or yours) that you had not been aware of, or catch something in your technique that needs modification.

Another way to track progress is to keep a written log. After each practice session jot down the date, how many people or other dogs you encountered, and your dog's reactions. Assign an intensity from one to five, with five being the most intense.

Here are a few sample log entries for Buddy, an Australian Shepherd. Buddy is mildly fearful of people and moderately fearful of other dogs.

Sunday 2/1 Worked in our neighborhood. Saw two people walking dogs and five people without dogs. One woman had two kids with her. All were across the street, approximately 30 feet away. Buddy whined, pulled away and became very agitated when he saw the dogs. Intensity 3-4. Couldn't get him to take treats when he saw the dogs. Not as bad with the people without dogs, intensity 2, took treats. Even looked interested in greeting the kids.

Monday 2/2   In our neighborhood again. Saw two people, neither had dogs. One was across the street, other was on our side of the street. Intensity was only a 1 with the person across the street. The person on our side tried to approach and Buddy's reaction went from 1 to 3 as he whined and hid behind me. The woman wanted to pet him but I told her sorry as I did a walk-away. I've noticed that keeping the leash less tight seems to make Buddy more comfortable in general, but I think we're too close to others in this neighborhood.

Tuesday 2/3   Took Buddy to the local park where dog training classes are held. Parked way back, approx. fifty feet. I started a "treat party" each time someone got out of a car with a dog and stopped as the person disappeared around the corner to the training area. People were moving horizontally past us. Buddy seemed much more relaxed with this setup than he did with others. He seems better away from our neighborhood and with more distance. Intensity 1-2 depending on other dog's activity level. One jumping Lab seemed to be too much. But since Buddy seems more relaxed at the park, we will work there for a few weeks. Once we've made some progress, it's back to our neighborhood but at more of a distance, and we will go out earlier on Sundays to avoid running into so many people at once.

Two weeks later, Buddy's owner recorded this entry:

Tuesday 2/17   Progress! Today we were able to stand twenty feet away at the park, with dogs arriving for class appearing and disappearing around corners. Buddy seems much more comfortable. His mouth is much softer when taking treats, and he did not react more strongly than level 1 today. I was able to get him to look at me and to do touches.

After a few weeks, Buddy's owner will be able to look over her notes and see major progress. With continued practice, Buddy will be able to remain focused enough to give attention to his owner even in closer proximity to the trigger.

Just remember that every dog is different. Your dog's progress will depend on many factors, including how long the fear has existed, as well as its intensity. Gradual improvement is what's important. Whether you choose to videotape your sessions or keep notes, periodic reviews will help you to stay focused and motivated.

Can We Get Closer?

Once you can successfully pass other dogs and people at close range in public, you may wonder what's next. Can you now allow your dog to play with other dogs at the park, or at least stop for getting-to-know-you sniffs on walks? Should you now allow strangers to approach and pet your dog? The short answer is no. Just because your dog is now able to walk calmly alongside you in public without having a fearful or fear-reactive response, that does not mean you should take a giant step for which she is not ready. Besides, is it really necessary for your dog to greet others on walks? You don't stop and chat with every person you pass, and you don't necessarily like every person you meet. So why expect it from your dog? Getting her to be comfortable on walks is a great accomplishment, and for many dogs, that is plenty. (You will, however, learn in the next chapter about how to make your dog more comfortable around visitors in your home.)

I am not suggesting that you cannot get your dog to be even more accepting of people or other dogs, if that is important to you. In many cases, closer contact will be possible. But it is beyond the scope of this book to address "up close and personal" introductions. There are simply too many variables involved and too high a risk of a miscalculation that could result in injury to the dogs or humans involved. If you wish to introduce your dog to other dogs or people at close range, enlist the assistance of a professional (see *Resources*). An experienced trainer can point out minute changes in canine body language, monitor the situation so everyone stays safe, and give you a realistic prognosis as to how much progress you can expect to make. In the meantime, two paws up for you—you've done a great job!

Tail End Wrap-Up

🐾   Track your progress by videotaping sessions and/or keeping a written log.

🐾   Review the tape/log every few weeks to gauge progress, and adjust your program as necessary.

🐾   Don't rush things—slow and steady wins the race.

🐾   If you would like your dog to interact with other dogs or people even more closely, enlist the help of a professional.

Part V

Treatment of Specific Fears

28

Welcome Guests

If your dog is more comfortable with people outdoors than inside the home, before addressing his fear of visitors, use the desensitization and counterconditioning exercises to work with strangers on the street. If there is any chance that your dog will attempt to bite visitors, do not attempt the exercises that follow—enlist the help of a professional instead.

Why do some dogs do well with unfamiliar people in public but fear them in the home? For one thing, people are normally farther away outdoors than they are inside. Proximity to a trigger is, of course, one of the main variables that determines whether a dog will react in a fearful manner. If a fearful dog encounters a guest in a narrow hallway, his flight options are limited.

Door Greetings

Many owners grab their dog's collar at the last moment before answering the door, to prevent the dog from darting outside. Unfortunately, collar grabbing can result in defensive barking, lunging, and even biting.

A common habit of owners of small dogs is to pick the dog up before opening the door. Being ensconced in the owner's arms stops a dog from running out the door, but it can also boost confidence, as height confers a feeling of status. Also, the dog may feel a bit of "status by association." An example of this phenomenon is the insecure child who would never have the nerve to speak out against another, but feels confident enough to do so when he has a big, strong friend backing him up. The fearful dog who is perched high in his owner's arms is confident enough to bark for both of them. But if the owner were to put the dog down, chances are he would bark, but back away out of insecurity at the same time. One reason so many tiny dogs are reactive is that they are constantly in their owners' arms, so they never learn to stand on their own four paws.

Of those dogs who are not normally held for door greetings (I've yet to see a 100-pound Rottweiler in his owner's arms when the door opens), some react to visitors by running and hiding. Others bark, growl, and even lunge at guests. Often when a dog demonstrates the latter reaction, owners assume the dog is protecting the home (being territorial) or protecting them. It is easy to see how that assumption could be made. There is a difference, however, in the body language and behavior of a dog who is fearful and one who is confident and acting in a protective manner. A confident, protective dog will normally move toward a visitor as if to say, *This is* my *home and family—you're not welcome and I'm not kidding!* The dog's weight is likely to be distributed more heavily over the front legs, with ears forward and tail held high. If the dog is barking it will be repetitive, fairly non-stop, and intense in a way that clearly conveys that the dog means business. Alternately, the dog might not make a sound, instead staring with a "hard eye" and head lowered. (Ironically, the second type of display is the more worrisome—the dog is conserving his energy to take action, rather than spending it on barking out a warning.)

A dog who is fearful, on the other hand, might bark and/or growl, but will normally move *away* from visitors. The bark will be more sporadic and less intense—more tentative—than that of a territorial dog. If the dog remains motionless, the body weight will be distributed more heavily over the back legs. The dog's head may be lowered, with ears back and tail held lower than usual. The fearful dog might even alternate lunging/barking and then retreating—a classic approach/avoidance display. In this context, the display conveys conflicting emotions; the dog wants to drive people away, but isn't quite confident enough to do so. It's as though the dog is saying, "Go away, you big, scary beast—don't make me come over there!" as he darts to and fro. In reality, the last thing the dog actually wants to do is approach the person. The intention of fearful dogs who bark and growl is to increase the distance between themselves and the thing they fear.

Management

Good management dictates that while you are working to address your dog's fear of visitors, he not be placed in situations that would make him uncomfortable or trigger a fearful reaction. Management will help to keep your dog's stress levels (and yours) low, and will help to avoid setbacks. Most importantly, good management will keep everyone safe by not placing your dog in a situation where he might feel the need to defend himself.

Let's say your dog, Sage, is comfortable with most women but fears men. Your neighbors, the Johnsons, are coming to visit. Although Joe Johnson is a nice, mild-mannered guy, Sage views him as a potentially dangerous being. Should you force Sage to face his fear? Perhaps hold him in place while Joe pets him? No! That would probably scare Sage and might even result in his becoming *more* fearful of men. Instead, you could make Sage comfortable by placing him in another room or in the back yard *before* the Johnsons arrived. You could also make sure he had something wonderful on which to chew. Providing your dog with a fabulous chew item will not only give him something else to focus on and help to relieve stress via chewing, but it will also help him to associate the presence of visitors with something pleasurable.

If you must place your dog in the back yard, draw the curtains or close the blinds to block his view. If he has been placed in another room, keep a radio playing to screen out the sounds of conversation. These measures are not meant to trick your dog into thinking there are no visitors, but to keep movement and sound to a minimal level so your dog can relax. Even if your dog is comfortable with some visitors, if you are expecting many guests at once use management so your dog does not become overwhelmed.

Set the Stage for Safety

Of course, management alone is not going to solve your dog's issues. While it should be used when necessary, you must also begin to expose your dog to visitors in a safe, gradual manner. Begin by working with the types of visitors with whom your dog is least uncomfortable; that might be women, children, men, or people of slight stature, depending on your dog. Consider *all* of your dog's triggers and keep in mind that combining them can increase the intensity of a reaction. For example, if your dog fears men with facial hair and also fears strangers in the home, a man with facial hair entering your home is likely to trigger a strong reaction.

The exercises on the following pages are for those dogs who show fearful—as opposed to fear-aggressive—reactions to visitors. Again, if you are even remotely concerned that your dog might bite, do not attempt the following—use management for now and consult a professional for assistance.

- Leave your dog off-leash, as a leash limits your dog's fight or flight options. Also, if you are tense, that tension could transmit down the leash to your dog.

- Be sure your dog always has an escape route that allows a wide berth around visitors, and a safe room or crate in which to take refuge.

- If your dog is fearful or wary of children but chooses to remain in the room with them, explain to the kids why the dog is not a good playmate. Supervise children and make sure they have activities to keep them busy so they won't forget and start approaching the dog.

- For dogs who bark at visitors at the door (but do not attempt to bite) teach them that the doorbell ringing is a cue to "go to bed." The "bed" can be a dog bed or mat that you have placed in a far corner of the room, away from where guests congregate. "Go to bed" actually means not only to go to the bed, but to lie down and stay there until instructed otherwise. Once your guests are settled, give your dog a release word so he can choose whether to remain where he is or to approach guests. (To teach "go to bed," see the *Train Your Dog: The Positive, Gentle Method* DVD in *Resources*.)

> Never leave your dog alone unsupervised with visitors; any dog who feels threatened may bite.

Training Your Visitors

Phase I: Bore and Ignore

Norwegian behaviorist Turid Rugaas uses a wonderful analogy to illustrate the way frightened dogs view humans. To paraphrase, Rugaas asks: if a big, green, scary monster entered the room, would you prefer that the monster ignore you, or move toward you with arms extended, making scary monster noises? Most of us would just as soon go unnoticed, thank you very much! Fearful dogs everywhere agree. However, most visitors will want to greet your adorable bundle of fur. That is why you must give clear instructions before they arrive, the most important of which is to *ignore the dog completely*. So as not to make your guests apprehensive, explain why you are doing this, and that your dog is not aggressive. (If a particular visitor is the type to become uncomfortable or not to follow instructions, use management instead.)

It is not enough to ask visitors to "ignore the dog." Your instructions must be specific:

- Don't look at the dog
- Don't talk to the dog
- Don't reach for the dog
- If the dog approaches to sniff, allow it, but don't look at him, talk to him, or reach for him.

Most visitors do fairly well with the first three, but seem to forget everything when the dog approaches to sniff. It's as though they figure, *the dog approached me, so he must want to be petted!* The person reaches for the dog, at which point the dog does the couch-to-corner dash in 0.5 seconds, more convinced than ever that getting close to those unpredictable humans is a bad idea. Monitor all interactions and whenever necessary, gently remind guests of the rules—after all, some humans are more easily trained than others!

With repeated exposures, your dog should become comfortable enough not only to remain in the room with visitors, but to settle when asked. (If you have not taught settle, see *Chapter 14*.) The settle body posture will encourage further relaxation. Just be sure to get your dog settled in an area where he will feel comfortable, away from the center of the action. Settling in the presence of visitors will be as far as some dogs are capable of progressing, and that's fine. If your dog is still a bit fearful but shows an interest in interacting with visitors, continue on to Phase II.

Phase II: Toss a Treat

This phase involves visitors tossing treats to your dog. It is preferable that the person be seated and settled for at least ten minutes before beginning the exercise. Instructions will once again be necessary, as the wrong type of tossing motion could trigger a fear reaction. Arm your guest (this should be done with one person at a time) with small pieces of your dog's favorite treat. The toss should consist of a small, slow, underhand motion, performed without leaning forward or staring at your dog. The treat may be tossed anywhere on the floor, so long as it is at a comfortable enough distance from your guest that your dog will be willing to approach to take it.

Note: Monitor your dog's body language and watch for stress signals—even subtle ones, such as yawning and lip-licking. If your dog seems too uncomfortable, remove him from the area. If he responds to the treat tossing with a mildly fearful reaction, try feeding the treats yourself in the presence of your visitor for a few sessions first. Your dog will still make the association between the visitor's presence and the treats. Once your dog is more at ease, you can go back to visitors tossing treats.

If your dog is willing to take the tossed treats, your visitor may continue to toss them so that your dog must approach a bit more closely each time. *Remember, this is only for dogs who are not fear-reactive.* If your dog is eventually willing to go right up to the visitor to take treats from her hand, great! Just remind the person that even if your dog takes the treats from her hand she is not to look at him directly, reach toward him, or try to pet him. Again, we want your dog to learn that people are safe, even at close range.

Phase III: Reach Out and Touch Someone

If you have not yet taught your dog how to target your hand on the verbal cue "Touch," turn to *Chapter 16*. Once your dog has mastered the skill, you can use it with visitors with whom your dog is comfortable taking treats. First, warm your dog up by having him do a few touches with you. Then show your visitor how to ask for touches. In this case, because your dog is not yet completely comfortable with the person, she should hold a treat in the hand that is to be touched.

Stand next to your seated visitor in order to give your dog more confidence. The person should slowly extend an open hand toward the ground, palm down, with a treat held in place by the thumb. The hand should be held low and slightly to the person's side. Without looking directly at your dog, the visitor should softly say, "Touch!" If your dog touches the hand, the person should say, "Gooood dog" in a soft voice and then slowly turn the hand over to offer the treat. (Alternately, you could start by giving the verbal cue and have the visitor carry out the rest of the exercise.)

Once your dog is more comfortable, switch to having him target the back of the person's open hand without a treat in it. The person should praise and use a slow, gentle movement to reward with a treat from the other hand. The more your dog plays the touch game with visitors, the sooner his reaction to them will become one of happy anticipation rather than anxiety.

If your dog is unwilling to play this game, don't insist on it. *It is never a good idea to force your dog to interact with anyone before he is ready.* Go back to a phase at which your dog feels comfortable for a while (days, weeks, or months, depending on your dog). When you sense that he is becoming more comfortable around visitors, try again.

Permission to Pet

Assess each situation individually, use your best judgement, and don't push too far too fast. If there is a visitor with whom your dog seems completely at ease playing the touch game, tell the person that if your dog approaches she may pet him slowly, on the chest only. That will discourage the type of palm-down, over-the-head petting that frightens so many dogs. (For children, do the two-ways-of-petting demonstration described in *Chapter 5* beforehand to discourage over-the-head petting.)

If your dog is comfortable with the person petting him on the chest, she may pet the side of the face as well. Keep these sessions very short—five seconds of gentle petting is plenty. Tell your guests to avoid petting your dog on the top of the head, shoulders, or back, as the overhead approach is more likely to frighten him.

Tricks to Try

- Have your visitor don one of your overcoats or other articles of clothing before entering your home. The sight and scent of a familiar item may make your dog feel more comfortable.

- If there is a specific scent you wear regularly, have your visitor dab a bit on before entering the home.

- Borrow a friend's friendly dog so your dog can see that dog interacting happily with visitors—the other dog might just convince yours that people are not so scary after all!

- This next trick is called "The Glove of Love." Put on a clean gardening or work glove and feed your dog some yummy treats. Wear the glove to feed your dog's meals, a few bits of kibble at a time. After a week, have a visitor put on the same glove and feed your dog treats. Because the glove has become associated with a safe person and treats, it might just be enough to help your dog transfer that warm, fuzzy feeling to the visitor.

Beware the Butt-Biter!

Have you ever seen a child run up to another from behind, shove or slap him, and then run away? More than likely, the child doing the shoving or slapping would not have the nerve to confront the other child head-on. It's the same with many fearful dogs; they keep their distance when a visitor is seated, but as soon as the person heads for the exit, the dog runs up and nips from behind. People are, after all, so much less frightening from the rear.

If you have a butt-biter (or a dog who is showing signs of being a potential butt-biter), either:

a. put your dog away before guests arrive;
b. put your dog away before guests are ready to leave;
c. put your dog on a leash when guests are ready to leave;
d. teach your dog a solid down-stay and ask him to do so before guests stand up to leave (see *Resources* for obedience training materials); or
e. with your dog on leash, have guests toss treats (using a slow, underhand motion) so they land behind your dog. Practice this first with guests standing still, then eventually, as they walk toward the door. This will help your dog to associate the guest with good things, but will also teach him to stay back when someone walks away.

Keep in mind that butt-biters may strike at times other than when a guest is leaving, such as when someone walks off to use the restroom. Keeping your dog on leash or tethered at a comfortable distance from guests will prevent any mishaps.

~ * ~ * ~ * ~ *~ * ~ * ~ * ~ *~ * ~ * ~ * ~ *~ * ~ * ~

As with all the programs that have been discussed, patience is key. Your dog has been fearful of people for some time and those feelings are not likely to change overnight. But with careful, rcpcatcd exposure to non-threatening people, your dog will soon learn that having visitors over is actually quite a pleasant experience.

 # Tail End Wrap-Up

- Avoid grabbing your dog's collar or picking him up before opening the door. Taking a moment to put your dog elsewhere before you answer the door will prevent unpleasant incidents.

- If your dog is not comfortable with visitors, place him in a safe, out-of-the-way area with a chew toy before they arrive. Screen out visual and auditory disturbances as much as possible.

- Whichever type of interaction you intend your guests to attempt, give explicit instructions and demonstrate for them first what you would like them to do. Be sure to tell them specifically not to reach for your dog if he approaches.

- Never leave your dog unsupervised with visitors.

- Monitor your dog for signs of stress. If he is becoming too anxious or uncomfortable, calmly remove him from the area and put him in another room with a chew toy.

- Beware the butt-biter!

- As always, take your time and move at a pace at which your dog is comfortable.

29

Fear of a Family Member

The Gilberts—James, Kate, and nine-year-old Johnny—are a typical suburban family. They are all very excited about adopting Towanda, a nine-month-old terrier mix, from a local rescue group. Kate looks forward to daily walks with the new family member. The outings will help them to bond and will give Kate a reason to get out and exercise. Johnny can't wait to play and wrestle with his new buddy. James envisions cozy evenings watching television in his recliner, his faithful companion drowsing by his side.

In the weeks that follow, Towanda bonds easily with Kate, and they enjoy their daily excursions. When Kate is home alone during the day, Towanda happily follows her from room to room as Kate goes about her business. Whenever Johnny invites Towanda to wrestle she happily complies, although she won't remain in the room when his rowdy friends come over to play. And what of James' cozy recliner evenings? Unfortunately, Towanda is frightened of James. Although James wouldn't hurt a fly—never mind an adorable bundle of fur like Towanda—she is not convinced. Whenever James moves quickly, gestures, or raises his voice, Towanda skitters away.

Why is Towanda Afraid?

Had Towanda been abused by a man before the Gilberts adopted her? Or had she not been exposed to many men as a young pup? And why does she avoid some of Johnny's friends? The Gilberts don't have the answers, as Towanda's previous history is unknown.

It is not unusual for a dog to bond quickly with most family members, but to fear one particular person—usually the man. The dog might be standoffish or unwilling even to remain in the room when that person appears. If the person attempts to approach or pet the dog, she might cringe or run. Naturally, this behavior can cause feelings of frustration and rejection, and make the rebuffed person feel excluded from the family's newfound circle of joy. If things don't change, the person might eventually develop negative feelings toward the dog. Fortunately, whether the slighted party is a man, woman, or child, there are ways to teach your dog that there is nothing to fear.

Fear of Children

To dogs, kids can seem pretty unpredictable. (Heck, they seem that way to me sometimes!) While adults can be trusted to conduct themselves in a fairly consistent, predictable manner, children are prone to sudden bouts of running, screaming, arm waving, and other outbursts that can frighten dogs. Boys often want to wrestle and roughhouse with dogs, while girls want to hug them. Unfortunately, either of those things can cause a dog to feel afraid.

It is necessary to teach children and dogs how to behave around each other. The following tips will help kids and canines to feel more comfortable with each other and will help to keep everybody safe:

1. Children (roughly age 10 and under) and dogs should never be left together unsupervised. If a large group of active children is scheduled to visit, place your dog in another room before they arrive.

2. Try to schedule supervised dog/child getting-to-know-you sessions when both are pleasantly tired out. A perfect time is after your dog has come back from a nice, long walk and your child is calm as well.

3. Help your dog to associate good things with your child's presence. If your child is old enough to feed your dog, fill the bowl and allow your child to place it on the floor. If your child is not old enough to handle the chore, feed your dog only when your child is in the room. (If your dog is so fearful that she will not eat with your child in the

room, at least present the meal when your child is there.) Your child should accompany you and your dog on walks (assuming your dog enjoys walks), be in the yard when you play fetch (participating by throwing the item if possible), and generally be involved in, or at least present for, whatever activities your dog enjoys most. Your dog will come to associate the presence of your child with enjoyable things and, as a result, will want to be around your child more.

4. Designate a "safe spot" for your dog. The spot can be a dog bed, a crate, or simply a location such as a nook beneath a desk. If the location is portable (such as a dog bed or crate), place it in a corner or against a wall, well away from foot traffic. Reward your dog with petting, praise, affection, and even a treat if you'd like, every time she chooses to go to the spot on her own. Place her chew bones and treats on the spot, give relaxing massages there, and practice the settle exercise there as well. All of these things will help your dog to associate pleasant, safe feelings with the spot. Lead your dog to her safe spot whenever you notice her becoming anxious, until it becomes natural for her to go there on her own.

5. Rules to teach your child:

- Leave the dog alone while she is sleeping. A dog who is startled may snap or bite.
- Leave the dog alone while she is on her safe spot.
- Leave the dog alone when she is eating or has a chew item. The exception would be for your child, under your supervision, to drop tasty bits of cheese or hot dogs in your dog's dish as she eats her regular food. This teaches your dog that your child coming near her food is a good thing. (Do this only if you are sure your dog does not have any food-guarding issues!)
- Never try to take anything away from the dog.
- Never slap, kick, punch, ride, or otherwise assault the dog. And do not make the dog play dress-up!
- When petting, move your hand slowly. Don't pet palm-down over the dog's head, or approach and then jerk your hand away. (Kids often use this approach-withdrawl motion because they want to pet the dog but fear being nipped; unfortunately, the motion teases the

dog into doing just that.) Instead, pet the dog slowly and firmly on the chest and then under the chin or the side of the face (assuming your dog is not touch-sensitive in those areas). For very young children, have them practice on a stuffed animal or your arm first.

- Don't put your face right up to the dog's face and don't stare at her.
- *Do not hug the dog.* While little girls seem to find hugging a necessity of life, many dogs do not enjoy being hugged. To humans, a hug conveys affection; to dogs, a hug translates to restraint, which is frightening. A dog who is being hugged might show signs of stress such as turning her head away, licking her lips, or yawning. While many dogs learn to tolerate being hugged, a fearful dog who is restrained in this manner might bite.
- Always give the dog the choice to play or not. If you want to play but the dog walks away, let her go.
- Never corner the dog (including when she's on the couch or bed) or put her in a position where she has no escape route. Even the nicest of dogs can bite if afraid and cornered.
- If the dog is afraid of your visiting friends, tell them to ignore her for now. (Of course, parents must supervise as well.) Explain that ignoring means not to look at, talk to, or try to touch the dog in any way. If the dog seems distressed, a parent should place her in another room until the visitors have gone.
- If the dog ever shows teeth, growls, or otherwise scares you, call for a parent right away.
- If the dog does something "bad" such as having a potty accident or grabbing one of your toys, don't chase her or try to punish her yourself. Call for a parent right away.

6. Teach your dog basic obedience skills (see *Resources*). Your dog should, at minimum, learn sit, down, stay, come, and leave it. These skills will not only help to enforce leadership (remember, strong leadership makes for a more secure dog), but can make a huge difference in the control you have over your dog's actions. Let's say your two-year-old child drops a fuzzy stuffed toy on the floor. Your dog's fear of your child is temporarily pushed aside by her desire to investigate the toy. Calmly telling your dog to "leave it" as she begins to cross the room would prevent your child and dog from both grabbing for the toy at once. Otherwise, that close-range grabbing

motion could have frightened your dog and in the worst case, might have resulted in a bite.

Attention (calling your dog's name) followed by a request to come can get your dog to stop in mid-action and return to you quickly. Down-stay is another immensely helpful skill, as it can keep a dog and child at opposite ends of a room if necessary. (Well, it will control the *dog*. Be sure your child doesn't wander over when the dog is in a down-stay, as the dog might feel trapped.)

7. Desensitize your dog to actions she finds frightening, such as having her ears and tail pulled. Of course you don't *want* your child to slap or pull at your dog, but those things are bound to happen with younger children. If your dog has been desensitized to those actions, there is a much greater chance that she will tolerate them without becoming defensive and possibly biting. (For detailed instructions on how to desensitize your dog to being touched and handled, see *Chapter 37*.) Build from simple touches to gentle and then less gentle pulling of the ears and tail (each action should be followed by a treat), gentle pushing/slapping (don't go overboard!), hugging, and whatever else your child is prone to do with your dog.

(See the *Resources* section for further reading on child/dog relations.)

The Man of the House

Salesmen of old traditionally targeted the "man of the house." Many fearful dogs, however, have the opposite goal—they want to stay as far away from the man as possible. Sorry, guys—it's the testosterone. You're bigger, stronger, have deeper voices, and move differently than women or children. The good news is, most dogs who are initially afraid of men warm up to their new dad over time, even without any behavioral assistance. (And very often, the dog ends up being most obedient for the man.) Whether you are a man or woman, if you are the person the dog fears, see the advice that follows.

If your dog's fear is moderate to severe:

Do not attempt to befriend the dog. Naturally you want your dog to like and not fear you, but well-meant, friendly gestures can frighten a dog and short-circuit progress. Ignore her completely. That can be difficult, especially when everyone else is petting and cooing over the new family member—but your lack of attention will put the dog at ease and allow her to approach when she feels ready. Remember the instructions for visitors? They apply to you too: no looking at, talking to, or touching the dog. If she approaches to sniff, let her, but don't make any movements or attempt to pet her. You may eventually be able to do all of those things, but for now the idea is to teach your dog that you are not a scary person, but a nice, predictable guy—even up close. Give it some time. Once your dog seems more comfortable, move on to the techniques that follow.

If your dog's fear is mild to moderate:

You da Man. You should be responsible for feeding, walking, ball-tossing (use a small, underhand motion), and any other activity your dog finds enjoyable—with the exception of petting, for now—if your dog is willing. If your dog is afraid to take food directly from you, let her see you prepare it, even if she is standing across the room. Place the bowl on the floor and leave the room so she can eat.

If your dog is afraid to go for a walk with you, accompany another family member on walks with that person holding the leash. Walk parallel to them a few feet away, on the side of the person, not the dog. The leash-holder may feed treats to create a further good association with your presence. If the person takes your dog for walks without you present, treats should not be present either (unless required for a separate behavior modification exercise).

Even if you cannot participate directly at first, a good association will be created by your being connected with the things your dog finds rewarding. Once she becomes more comfortable in your presence, you should be able to play a more direct role.

If your dog's fear is mild:

Enforced togetherness. If you are sure that your dog's fear is mild, it can be helpful for your dog to be left alone with you for a few days. Hey, this is the rest of your family's chance for a vacation! Many dogs who are thrown into this type of situation take the "any port in a storm" approach and bond with the person of whom they were initially frightened.

Togetherness training. If your dog attends a group obedience class and enjoys it (and does not have fear issues in class), you should be the one to train her there. If your dog is likely to be afraid of you lifting her in and out of your vehicle, have another family member do the honors and attend class with you, but be sure to participate in the exercises. If a private trainer comes to your home, participate in the lesson and practice with your dog between sessions. Even a few short repetitions of "sit" will do. Avoid "down" at first, as it places a dog in a submissive position, which could cause anxiety. (See *Chapter 12* for tips on making your dog feel comfortable when you train together.)

Following are three techniques that use treats to help your dog associate good things with you. If you are not sure about the extent of your dog's fear, begin with the first technique and stick with it for a few weeks or until your dog becomes visibly more relaxed in your presence. Then move on to the second or third method.

1. You are such a treat! Fabulous treats should be fed by other family members—but only in your presence. A setup might look like this: woman sits in chair with dog nearby and treats at the ready. Man enters room from around corner (walking slowly, not making eye contact with dog). Woman treats, treats, treats (along with cheerful chatter if desired) until man disappears; as he does, so do treats (and chatter). Repeat throughout the day. Also, your dog should be given extra-special chew bones or stuffed Kongs®, but only when you are in the room.

2. Treats on da Feets. You might feel a bit silly trying this one, but it often works. Sit on the couch with your feet on the floor. Have someone place treats on each of your shoes, with a trail of treats leading up to them. The Treats on da Feets trick is based on the fact that many dogs fear other body parts less than they do hands. After all, hands are what normally reach for them (and may have even struck them in the past). Once the treats have been placed, sit and stay (see how well trained you are?), remain motionless, and do not make eye contact or talk to your dog. (Older kids can try this one as well, but don't attempt it with younger kids, as they are likely to move their feet and scare the dog.) Allow your dog to follow the trail and take the treats that are resting on your shoes. Be sure to remain motionless!

Your dog will come to associate you with the yummy treats, while learning that you are not scary or unpredictable. Treats on da Feets will help your dog to warm up to you and want to spend more time around you. Just don't jump the gun and reach to pet your dog too soon or move too quickly when she approaches. Once she is more comfortable, you can move on to the "Touching Me, Touching You" trick that follows.

3. Treat tossing. If your dog is wary of you but willing to remain in the room, toss treats to her using a slow, underhand motion. Don't talk or make eye contact. The idea is not to lure your dog close enough to be petted, but to create a good association over time. If she seems afraid when you toss treats (for example, she cowers or runs), try tossing the treats farther away from you, making the tossing motion even smaller, or using better treats. If none of those things helps, abandon treat tossing and stick with one of the two previous techniques for the moment.

Touching Me, Touching You (Transferring Touch)

Touch, or targeting, helps dogs to focus on a task rather than being in an emotional, fearful state. (If you have not already done so, read *Chapter 16* for instructions on how to teach the skill.) Once your dog knows what to do on your verbal cue "Touch," it can be used to transfer the touch to the person with whom the dog is uncomfortable.

Note: The following technique is for getting your dog comfortable around a family member or person to whom the dog is exposed frequently. It should only be used if the dog's fear is mild. Again, do not encourage your dog to approach, touch, or interact with anyone who truly frightens her.

A person with whom your dog is comfortable (the "Safe Person") should sit on the couch next to the person your dog fears (the "Trigger Person"). Your dog should stand or sit to the side of the Safe Person. As illustrated in the photos on the following page, the touch will be transferred gradually from the Safe Person to the Trigger Person. Take your time at each step, proceeding to the next only when your dog is comfortable at the present step. If your dog is unwilling to touch or becomes nervous at any point, go back to a step at which she was comfortable, do a few repetitions, then end the session. Getting through only a step or two in one session is preferable to pushing too far too fast. In the following sequence, Laura is the Safe Person and Cliff is the Trigger Person.

1. With Sherman to Laura's side, she asks him to touch her hand. Sherman touches, Laura treats (see *Figure 1*). The sequence is repeated five times.

2. With Sherman to Laura's side, she asks him to touch her hand with Cliff's beneath. Sherman touches, Laura treats (see *Figure 2*). The sequence is repeated five times.

3. With Sherman to Laura's side, she asks him to touch Cliff's hand with hers beneath. Sherman touches, Laura treats (see *Figure 3*). The sequence is repeated five times.

4. Laura lures Sherman with a treat to position him in front of her (this also moves him closer to Cliff). Laura asks Sherman to touch her hand (see *Figure 4*). The sequence is repeated five times. (If your dog will not switch positions, she is not ready for this step— remain at Step 3, then change her position more gradually.)

5. With Sherman in front of her, Laura asks him to touch her hand with Cliff's beneath. Sherman touches, Laura treats (see *Figure 5*). The sequence is repeated five times.

6. With Sherman in front of her, Laura asks him to touch Cliff's hand with hers beneath. Sherman touches, Laura treats. The sequence is repeated five times (see *Figure 6*).

7. With Sherman in front of her, Laura asks him to touch Cliff's hand. Sherman touches, Laura treats (see *Figure 7*). The sequence is repeated five times.

Figure 1

Figure 2

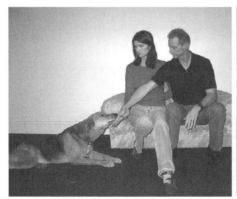

Figure 3

Figure 4

Figure 5

Figure 6

Once your dog is comfortable with Step 7, work through the steps again, but this time with the Trigger Person giving the verbal cue and the treats. The Safe Person can still do the luring to change the dog's position at Step 4 if necessary.

Figure 7

If you feel your dog is not ready to take treats directly from the Trigger Person, add the intermediary step of working through the protocol with the Trigger Person giving the verbal cue, and the Safe Person giving the treats; then have the Trigger Person do both.

Once the sequence has been completed (which could be a matter of minutes, days, or weeks), the Trigger Person should continue to ask for touches, positioning his hand so that your dog gradually ends up doing touches while standing directly in front of him. As long as your dog is comfortable, the Safe Person should move begin to move slightly farther away from the Trigger Person with each repetition, resulting in your dog doing touches with the Trigger Person alone.

Tricks to Try:

- See *Chapter 28* for the "Glove of Love" technique; it might be just the thing to get your dog interacting with the Trigger Person.

- If you have taught your dog to target an object such as a coffee can lid, place the lid on the floor and give your dog the signal to touch it. Do a few repetitions, rewarding each success. Gradually move the target closer and closer to where the Trigger Person is seated. The person should remain motionless. Eventually, the person may be able to hold the target as the dog touches it. This approach works well because, as always, it puts the power in the dog's paws by allowing her to make the decision to approach.

Above all, be patient. It might take your dog weeks or even months to bond with the family member or person she fears. In most cases, bonding *will* eventually take place and family life will begin to resemble everyone's original vision. If there has been no progress at all after a few weeks, or if things have worsened, consult a professional. A behavior specialist can point out body language (yours or your dog's) that you might not have noticed, and can design a behavior modification protocol based on your specific needs. As long as you are willing to make the effort, there is always hope.

Tail End Wrap-Up

Use management and supervision to ensure everyone's safety.

Teach your children and visiting kids how to behave around your dog.

Associate good things with your child's presence.

Give your dog a designated "safe spot."

Teach your child how to interact with your dog properly.

Teach your dog basic obedience skills.

Desensitize your dog to child-type actions (such as pulling ears and tail) in a gentle, gradual manner.

The person your dog fears should initially ignore the dog.

If your dog's fear is mild to moderate, the feared person should be involved in everything the dog perceives as positive such as feeding, walks, play, and training.

If your dog's fear is mild, try these:
- other family members present treats in the presence of the feared person
- "Treats on da Feets"
- treat tossing
- "enforced togetherness" may result in faster bonding.

The "Touching Me, Touching You" trick can help to transfer touch from a family member the dog trusts to one she fears.

Other tricks to try: the Glove of Love, and targeting with a coffee can lid.

30

Veterinary Visits

One of my favorite *The Far Side*™ cartoons features a dog hanging his head out of a car window, boasting to his canine friend in the next yard, "Ha, ha, ha, Biff. Guess what? After we go to the drugstore and the post office, *I'm* going to the vet's to get tutored." Sure, it's hilarious to us, but probably not so much to the dog, once he realizes that he's going to be *neutered!*

Some dogs do absolutely fine on veterinary visits, wagging their tails at the receptionists, greeting other dogs, working the room like social butterflies. But others practically have to be dragged through the front door. It's unfortunate that we cannot explain to dogs the way we do to children that everything will be okay and the visit is actually for their own benefit.

Even when a veterinarian and his/her staff are skilled, experienced, and handle animals gently, a veterinary clinic can still be a frightening place for dogs. There are bright lights; strange, medicinal odors; slippery floors; unfamiliar people; and a room filled with other animals—some of whom are obviously distressed. In the waiting room, a dog may hear dogs whimpering or barking fearfully from other areas of the clinic. Then there is the exam itself: a dog is usually lifted on to a cold steel table, and may then be restrained, prodded, manipulated, pierced with a needle, and be subjected to other things that dogs understandably find unpleasant and even frightening.

Being able to be examined by a veterinarian is vital to your dog's health. It is all too easy to postpone or avoid vet visits when you have a dog who feels about them the way you do about visiting your dentist for a root canal. But rest assured that there are steps you can take to make vet visits easier for both of you.

Friendly Visits

The goal is for your dog to regard trips to the vet's office in a positive light. To that end, ask your vet's permission to bring your dog in for "friendly visits." Ask which days and hours the clinic is normally less busy, so as to make your visits convenient for the staff. During a friendly visit, walk your dog inside (or carry him if he is a young puppy), keeping your manner light and nonchalant. Since your dog will pick up on your emotional state, it is important that you do not seem worried or concerned. Act as though you are happy to be there! Ask a front desk staff member to feed your dog a few super-yummy treats that you have brought along. If the staff appears busy, feed the treats yourself. Stay for just a few moments, feeding treats the entire time, then leave. Drop in for friendly visits frequently. If vet techs or assistants happen to be available to feed treats, ask them to do so as well.

If your dog is so fearful that he will not accept treats inside the clinic, start at a distance at which he will accept them, even if that means standing in the parking lot twenty feet from the entrance. You will be able to close the distance gradually and eventually be able to work inside the clinic.

If your dog growls or shows other signs of reactivity during friendly visits, do not correct him; just walk him out of the clinic as quickly and calmly as possible. Next time, start at a distance from the entrance and work closer in gradual steps, or do even briefer in-clinic visits at first.

> Remember: It is never appropriate to punish growling under any circumstances. Doing so can lead to biting with no warning. It is best to diffuse the situation at the time (for example, by walking slowly away) and then figure out how to address the underlying cause of the distress.

Once your dog is comfortable, spend a few minutes sitting in the waiting room feeding treats, then leave. You could also place your dog on the scale (lure him with treats if he's large), feed treats, then leave. If there is an open exam room, once your dog is comfortable with the waiting room, ask whether it would be permissible to allow him inside. If so, walk him in, feed a few rapid treats, then leave. If it is okay with the staff, build up to placing him on the table, feeding a few treats, them removing him from the table and leaving. Practice friendly visits a few times a week.

Of course, your dog will eventually have to have an actual veterinary exam. But when you are making frequent friendly visits, any perceived unpleasantness from an actual exam will happen, say, one time out of ten rather than on every visit, so your dog's positive association with the vet's office will be maintained. You can help by feeding super-yummy treats during actual exams as well (clear it with your vet first) and by keeping your own manner light. If you are a nervous type or are apprehensive about your dog's reactions, wait in the waiting room; many dogs do better without their owners present. Continue friendly visits periodically, even after your dog is comfortable with vet visits.

Playing Doctor

Examination

If your dog has issues with being handled, read Chapter 37 first and work through those exercises before attempting these. If you are starting with an adult dog, proceed very slowly and use extra caution.

You can help your dog to become accustomed to various aspects of a veterinary exam by recreating them at home. Choose a time when your dog is relaxed. Sit on the floor with him, with a supply of yummy treats close by. Your dog may sit, lie down, or even stand if he is not likely to wander off. (If your dog is likely to wander you may tether him, so long as he is already accustomed to the tether and is not likely to become overly stressed by the "exam.")

Stroke your dog calmly to get him accustomed to your touch and to help him relax. Next, you will examine different parts of his body. Your touches should be gentle yet firm, last only a few seconds, and should each be followed by a treat. Keep the mood light and playful. If you would like to speak during the exam, keep your tone happy. Feel free to use silly phrases such as "Peekaboo, there's your ear!" or "Here I go, touching your toes!" in a singsong voice. You might feel a bit foolish, but this approach will help to keep both of you relaxed. Once your dog begins to look at you with happy anticipation when touched (after all, he's learned that touches predict treats), you may progress to longer and slightly firmer (never rough) handling, continuing to treat after each touch. You may also intersperse examining touches with whatever other type of petting your dog enjoys, such as ear scratches or tummy rubs.

- Look briefly inside each ear.
- Lift the upper and lower lips to inspect the gums.
- Open and close your dog's mouth: Place one hand gently palm-down on his muzzle with your thumb on the upper lip, just behind a canine tooth; the other hand should cradle his jaw (see photo). As you say, "Open!" in a soft, pleasant voice, gently open the upper jaw. Hold for one second, then release and feed a treat. Or, pop a treat into your dog's mouth as you hold it open for one second, then release. (This will also prepare your dog for taking pills if needed.)
- Lift the tail and release.
- Manipulate joints, bending and flexing each leg gently as your dog lies on his side.
- Feel gently around your dog's belly.
- Handle each paw, briefly spreading and looking between the toes.

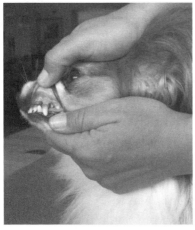

Inspecting upper gums

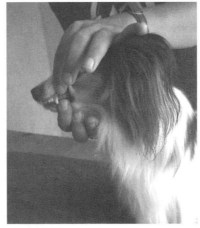

Hands positioned to open mouth

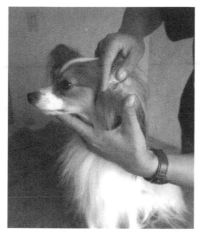 

Peeking in ear   *Spreading paw pads*

Paw handling tips: Many dogs are sensitive about having their paws handled, so go slow. With your dog either sitting or lying down, after a few relaxing strokes, gently touch and stroke the top of a front leg, and work your way down gradually to the paw. (For back legs, your dog should be lying on his side.) At first, touch the paw without lifting it, then treat. Once your dog is comfortable with that, lift the paw gently *without squeezing* then release, working up to holding it for longer periods. Treat after each step. Always position your dog's paw in close to his body rather than pulling it outward. Practice gently spreading toes to look in between, as well as examining the undersides of the paws, spreading the paw pads.

Mouth handling tips: If your dog is sensitive about having his mouth touched, put a bit of peanut butter, cream cheese, or flavored doggy toothpaste on your finger and allow your dog to lick at it. As he does, push the finger gently into his mouth, working in brief sessions towards the ultimate goal of massaging his gums and running your finger over his teeth. Do daily practice sessions until you see a look of happy anticipation as you prepare for the exercise, or at least until your dog remains relaxed throughout. For the actual brushing, purchase a "doggy toothbrush;" it resembles a nub-covered, rubber thimble that slips over the finger. (There is also toothpaste made specifically for dogs—be sure to use it rather than "people toothpaste.") With the brush over your finger, repeat the motions you previously made with your finger alone.

If your dog seems very stressed or fearful at any point during any of these exercises, back off. You are moving too fast. Return to a level of handling with which your dog is comfortable, then introduce firmer and more invasive touches in a more gradual manner. If your dog attempts to bite at any point, stop immediately and consult a behavior specialist for assistance. (Also, see the following section on muzzles.) Follow practice sessions with rousing games of chase or fetch, walks, meals, or whatever else your dog finds enjoyable, so that yet another good association with being handled is created.

Exercise Restraint!

For many dogs, restraint is the most difficult part of a veterinary exam to tolerate. However, it is crucial to restrict movement of a dog's body and head during an exam for the protection of both the dog and the veterinary staff. Although vets and technicians at different clinics may employ different restraint techniques, practicing the following exercise at home will help to teach your dog that restraint is nothing to fear. If at any point during the exercise your dog bites or attempts to bite, enlist the assistance of a professional—do not attempt to continue on your own.

As with most things, it is best to accustom dogs to being restrained when they are young pups. If your dog is still a young puppy, sit on the ground and hold him gently but firmly in your arms. If he struggles, do not correct him; just continue to hold him firmly. Once he relaxes, say, "Good dog!" then let him climb down. This teaches your dog that relaxing when restrained earns his freedom. Begin to add one second of calm restraint before saying, "Good dog!" before allowing your dog down, then two seconds and so on, so your dog becomes accustomed to remaining calm when restrained for longer periods.

If your dog is small to medium-sized, he will probably be examined on a table at the vet's office. To accustom your dog to the sensation of being up high, practice the restraint exercise that follows with your dog on a table. Add a thin, rubber-bottomed mat if necessary for traction. (Although an actual examining table is made of metal and does not offer traction, it is best to keep your dog sure-footed and safe for this exercise.)

If your dog is not comfortable being up on a table, take the time to accustom him to it first, before attempting the restraint exercise. Place him on the table, praise and treat, then remove him from the table. If he enjoys petting, pet while he is on the table as well. Repeat, adding a few seconds with each repetition, until he is comfortable remaining on the table for one minute. This could take some time over repeated sessions, so be patient.

Large dogs are normally examined on the floor. Whether your dog is on a table or on the floor, he should be standing for this exercise. If he is on the floor, kneel or crouch facing his side. If he is on a table, stand with your belly against the table facing his side. Place the arm that is closer to your dog's rear over his back. Bend the arm so you are cradling his side securely against your chest. Place your other arm under his neck and hold it firmly against you. Hold your dog to your body in this position gently but firmly for one second, say, "Yes!" then release and feed a treat. As long as your dog does not show any signs of discomfort, do five repetitions. Watch for those subtle lip licks and yawns! Do the exercise in front of a mirror if necessary so you can see your dog's face. Next, increase the restraint time to two seconds. After two seconds of restraint, say, "Yes!" then release and feed a treat. After another five repetitions, increase the restraint time to three seconds, and so on. Break the exercise up into a few sessions, especially if your dog is nervous. You should eventually be able to restrain your dog for a slow count of ten.

Note: Regardless of your dog's size, if he is having difficulty with being restrained for longer periods, try having an assistant feed treats every second or two *during* the restraint, rather than giving the treat afterward.

A vet tech supports this geriatric patient's hindquarters as she restrains her, as the dog is unable to support herself.

The following should only be attempted if your dog is fairly relaxed with people other than yourself, and has never attempted to threaten or bite anyone. Once your dog is obviously relaxed when being handled and restrained by you, employ family members and friends to practice the same techniques, starting with a one-second restraint followed by a "Yes!" and treat. Begin with people your dog knows and is comfortable with, and then move on to friends he does not know. If there is a certain type of person your dog fears—for example, men—avoid having those people restrain him until he becomes much more comfortable with them. Supervise all interactions and monitor your dog for signs of stress. Coach your helpers through it, letting them know when to slow down or touch more firmly or gently. The greater the number of pleasant experiences your dog has being handled by others, the easier veterinary visits will become.

Introducing a Muzzle

Unfortunately, some dogs fear being examined to the point that they will attempt to bite the vet or staff. If your dog is likely to bite, do yourself, your dog, and your veterinary staff a favor and get your dog acclimated to wearing a muzzle. That way you can calmly place the muzzle on your dog before an exam. Muzzling your dog yourself will allow your dog to avoid the stress of having the vet staff place it on him, which might cause even more apprehension at future visits. Another positive benefit of muzzles is that for some dogs, wearing one appears to have a calming influence. (Having worked for a vet, I can tell you that it certainly has a calming influence on the staff!)

As previously mentioned, there are two main types of muzzles: *basket muzzles*, which are made of open-weave sturdy wire or plastic formed into a basket; and *nylon muzzles*, which are sometimes made of other fabrics as well. In *Chapter 19*, instructions were given for acclimating a dog to a basket muzzle. While basket muzzles can be extremely helpful during behavior modification programs, the better choice for vet exams is a nylon muzzle, as it is lightweight, easy to take along, and will keep your dog's mouth in a closed position. Besides, a dog wearing a hard basket muzzle can still deliver quite a "muzzle-punch" if he attempts to bite, which can cause pain and bruising.

Because dogs must pant in order to keep cool, nylon muzzles should not be used on hot days unless you are in an indoor, air-conditioned area, and should not be left on your dog for long periods. (Muzzle your dog just before the vet exam, not in the car!) Choose a muzzle that is the correct size for your dog. If you are purchasing the muzzle in a store, the box should list which sizes fit which breeds. If you are ordering online, measure around the circumference of your dog's muzzle, approximately one-half inch below the eyes. Correct fit is important. Although the muzzle should restrict your dog's ability to open his mouth, he should be able to open it slightly in order to take a treat. With the muzzle straps firmly in place, the muzzle should not ride up too close to your dog's eyes.

Acclimating your Dog to the Nylon Muzzle

Introduction: Sit on the floor with your dog in front of you. The muzzle should be lying on the ground to the side of you, where your dog can see it. Your dog will not be able to chew large or hard treats once muzzled, so use tiny, soft treats, peanut butter, cream cheese, or squeeze cheese. Lift the muzzle an inch off the floor, give your dog a treat, then lay the muzzle down. With each repetition, bring the muzzle slightly higher off the ground and slightly closer to your dog. Repeat each step as many times as necessary, proceeding to the next tiny incremental step only when your dog shows no stress at the current step. Once you can pick up the muzzle and hold it near your dog's face, proceed to the steps below.

Application: Remain sitting on the floor with your dog. Hold the muzzle in one hand and, with the other, poke a treat through the smaller end so your dog can take it by placing his nose into the large end. (If your dog has learned touch—see *Chapter 16*—you can also ask him to touch your fingers through the muzzle.) Gradually, with each repetition, poke the treat through less and less so that your dog has to push his muzzle in deeper to get the treat. He will eventually have his muzzle fully inside the nylon muzzle. But don't touch the straps yet! Just feed three treats in rapid succession, then immediately remove the muzzle. Repeat a few times, making sure your dog is completely comfortable. If at any point he tries to pull away, go back to the step at which he was comfortable and proceed in tiny increments from there. If your dog shows a strong fear reaction at any point, put the muzzle away and try again another day, starting with a much easier step and proceeding more gradually. Remember too that attitude is key; if you become worried, so will your dog. Breathe, and be happy and unconcerned. This is a great game!

Once your dog is comfortable taking treats with his face in the muzzle, it is time to fasten the straps. Begin as before, and once your dog's face is in the muzzle, feed a treat. While your dog is chewing it, bring the straps together behind his head and touch them together momentarily; release them and remove the muzzle. After a few repetitions, as long as your dog remains calm, feed a treat, then, as your dog chews it, fasten the straps; feed three treats in rapid succession, then undo the straps and remove the muzzle. Build by three-second increments to leaving the muzzle on for longer periods.

Figure 1

Figure 2

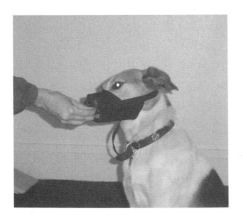

Figure 3

In this sequence, Sammy has already reached the point where he will poke his nose and mouth through the muzzle to take treats. Between Figures 2 and 3, his owner practiced attaching the straps as Sammy chewed the treats. Finally, in Figure 3, she is able to feed treats as Sammy wears the muzzle.

Feed treats every three to five seconds as your dog wears the muzzle, and feel free to use cheerful chatter as well. Gradually extend the time between treats until your dog is comfortable wearing the muzzle for longer periods. Practice a few times daily, and take your time. It may take a few weeks for your dog to become acclimated to the muzzle, but it will be worth the effort. Once he can wear the muzzle comfortably for five minutes at a time, muzzle him and give a brief massage or petting. (Remember, this type of muzzle should not be used in hot weather.) Practice muzzling your dog periodically, always associating it with pleasant things. The muzzle will become associated primarily with things your dog enjoys, rather than being associated only with the vet's office.

Tricks to Try:

- At home, pet and massage your dog while he lies on a mat, dog bed, or towel. Then take this "comfort mat" with you to the vet and, with permission, let your dog lie on it to be examined. (Wash it afterward.)

- Some dogs make negative associations with the white lab coats worn by vets, or the "scrubs" worn by vet techs. Purchase a facsimile at a uniform store or use the closest approximation that you have, and wear it whenever you "play doctor" at home.

- If your dog is especially sensitive about being touched on certain parts of his body, let the vet and staff know before the examination begins. Work on the issue at home as well.

- If your dog is nervous in the waiting room, ask beforehand whether you can leave him in the car until you are called into an examination room. (Do not do this in hot weather.)

- An alternate solution for dogs who are nervous but not totally panicked in the waiting room is to bring along treats, and have your dog practice touches and other tricks as you wait. Engaging your dog in this manner will keep him in a cognitive, focused state of mind, rather than slipping into an emotional/fearful state.

- Try a Calming Cap™ for exams, as described in *Chapter 48*.

- If your dog knows touch and/or tricks, it can be helpful to use them during the actual exam. Have your dog do touches with you as your vet administers a vaccination or examines him. Touch can also be used to move your dog's head into position as needed. If your dog knows sit, down, settle, or "play dead," those cues can be used to position him as needed for examination.

- Doing Ttouches (see *Chapter 45*) while in the waiting room can relax your dog as well.

- If your dog must have surgery (for example, being neutered), find out what time the procedure will be done. Many vet's offices have owners drop their dogs off early in the morning, but do not perform routine surgeries until mid-day when the clinic is closed. If your dog is likely to have an extreme fear reaction if caged for hours, ask your vet whether an alternate arrangement such as bringing your dog in later in the morning would be possible; or perhaps they could sedate him earlier in the day. Crate training your dog will also help to make him more comfortable in confined areas (see *Chapter 32*).

- For twelve hours before visiting the vet, do not administer herbs or other calming agents that are taken internally, as they could interfere with blood work or other tests. Instead, spray DAP on a bandana and have your dog wear it to the vet's office. Expose your dog to DAP beforehand to guard against the unlikely possibility that he might have an adverse reaction to it. Be sure your dog has worn the sprayed bandana in other calm, happy situations such as when being massaged or romping in the park, so it does not become associated only with the vet's office. DAP may also be sprayed on your dog's "comfort mat." (For more on DAP, see *Chapter 47*.)

- Although veterinarians are normally very busy, yours should still take a moment to greet your dog in a friendly manner to put him at ease before an exam. And while a certain amount of firm handling is necessary to ensure everyone's safety, being overly rough with or mistreating your dog is not acceptable. If at any point you are uncomfortable with the way your dog is being handled, speak up. If your concerns are not addressed, find another vet.

Tail End Wrap-Up

🐾 Practice "friendly visits" to your veterinarian's office.

🐾 Practice handling exercises at home.

🐾 Practice restraint exercises at home.

🐾 If necessary, acclimate your dog to wearing a nylon muzzle.

🐾 Try some "Tricks and Tips" to make your dog even more comfortable.

On the Road Again: Fear of the Car

"Wanna go for a ride?" For most dogs, that magical phrase conjures images of fun, adventure, and a moving smorgasbord of scintillating scents. But to some, the car is an unpleasant, frightening place to be. Vehicle-phobic dogs may drool or whine with fear at the very sight of an open car door. Some protest being lifted inside to the point of biting their owners. Once inside, the dog may pace, whine, drool, and be unable to settle down and relax.

Hondas, Toyotas, and Fords—Oh, My!

A dog's fear of the family car, van, truck, or SUV may consist of a single component or a combination of factors. The sound, vibration, or movement of the vehicle can each be frightening in and of itself. Inside the vehicle, a dog experiences all of those things at close range in a small space from which there is no apparent escape. To some dogs, those ingredients constitute a recipe for intense fear.

Some dogs have learned by association that a car ride can only mean one thing—a visit to the vet's office or some other destination they perceive as unpleasant—since those are the only places they are ever driven. Who could blame a dog for not wanting to climb on board? Other dogs' fears are due to having experienced a traumatic incident such as a car accident.

If your dog's fear is due to learned associations (having associated the vehicle with unpleasant destinations), it can be fairly easy to fix: simply drive your dog to lots of places she enjoys. Destinations might include the park to chase a ball, a friend's house to play with his dogs, or the local pet supply store to pick out a new toy or treats. Go wherever your dog loves to go. Of course, there will still be times when your dog must visit a destination she'd prefer to skip, but because a car ride results in something wonderful the majority of the time, the pleasant association will remain. If you must visit a place that your dog would consider unpleasant, do something positive on the way home. Let your dog pick out a new toy or treat at the pet supply store, or drive through a fast food spot and give her a special treat, such as a bit of plain hamburger.

Some dogs are averse to riding in the car because they have associated it with feelings of physical illness. If your dog is prone to carsickness, try one of these:

- Powdered ginger root in capsule form, given 30-45 minutes before the car ride (ginger root is available at health food stores). Check with your veterinarian for the correct dosage and to rule out any potentially harmful interactions with medications your dog is currently taking.
- Dramamine™. Yes, dogs can take it too! Check with your vet for the correct dosage.
- Try a homeopathic remedy made specifically for canine carsickness.
- Crate your dog (assuming she is crate trained and likes her crate). Use a plastic crate rather than a metal one, to limit vision. Face the crate toward the front or back of the vehicle and secure it.
- Many dogs do better if they are not fed right before a car ride. Try withholding food for at least two hours beforehand. There are, however, some dogs who become less queasy if there is a small amount of food in the stomach. Try it both ways to see which helps your dog.

Driveway Play

So what should you do if your dog would love to ride down the Yellow Brick Road but fears the Wicked Wagoneer of the West? Rather than working through a step-by-step desensitization protocol to get your dog comfortable with approaching the vehicle, try using *play*. Think of the emotions that accompany play: Joy! Freedom! Delight! Those wild, wonderful feelings are in direction opposition to fear. To get your dog comfortable in the vicinity of your vehicle, play with her there. If you normally park in the garage, make sure the garage door is closed or your dog is on a long-line—an extra-long leash held by you or tethered to something—for safety. A long-line should be used for safety if you are working in your driveway as well.

Start playing with your dog at a distance from your vehicle at which she seems comfortable; as she relaxes, move gradually closer. What type of play you engage in should be dictated by what your dog enjoys. Does your dog light up when she practices tricks? Grab a bag of treats and ask for shakes, spins, touches, or whatever tricks your dog knows. Or maybe your dog lives for a game of tug; bring along a tug toy and have a rousing game. If your dog prefers retrieving, toss a toy (use a toy rather than a ball to prevent the item rolling into the street) as far as the long-line will allow. Avoid tossing the toy too close to the vehicle at first.

You could also associate the area around the vehicle with special treats. Pull up a lawn chair and relax with a good book while your dog lies nearby with a special stuffed chew toy. If your dog enjoys her meals, you could feed her near the vehicle. By doing those things, you will be helping your dog to create pleasant associations with being in the vicinity of the vehicle. Once she seems happy and relaxed, it's time to move even closer.

Targeting can also be helpful in getting your dog close to the vehicle. See *Chapter 39* to learn how to transfer touch to an object. Transfer the touch to the vehicle itself, so that your dog voluntarily touches her nose to it.

Gotta be Inside to Ride

Look...up in the sky! It's a bird! It's a plane! No, wait! It's the Dynamic Duo! Yes, it's our old friends desensitization and counterconditioning to the rescue. They'll help to introduce your dog to your vehicle in a gradual manner so that she will feel comfortable every step of the way.

In regard to the protocol that follows, keep the following in mind:

- If you drive an SUV or truck and your dog will not jump in, schedule a vet exam to rule out hip, joint, or other physical issues.

- Practice during a period when you will not need to take your dog anywhere in the car.

- As always, use those extra-special treats! Wherever "treat" is indicated, add cheerful chatter as well if you would like.

- Monitor your dog's stress level. Watch carefully for stress signals such as yawning, lip-licking, freezing, and turning the head and/or body away. Adjust your rate of progress as necessary.

- Keep sessions short and stop *before* your dog has a fearful reaction. That might mean performing only three repetitions of one step in a session. It is better to do brief, successful sessions throughout the day than one long session that pushes your dog over her comfort threshold and elicits a fearful response. Whenever you begin a session, rather than beginning where you left off, back up a few steps to ease your dog back into the process.

- If your dog appears stressed at any point, go back to a step that was comfortable for her, repeat it a few times, then end the session. Begin the next session at the step at which your dog was comfortable, repeat it once or twice, then progress in tiny, incremental steps, splitting the existing steps into even tinier ones if necessary.

- If your dog becomes very stressed or panics at any point, stop immediately. This is gradual desensitization, not flooding. Make a mental note as to which step was overwhelming. Try to get your dog to do something simple such as sit or shake while still near the vehicle, so she thinks that sitting, rather than reacting fearfully, is what made the exercise end. Then go do something fun together. When you begin the next session (resume the following day, or if your dog is very sensitive, wait a few days), start with the car parked in a different spot, begin with a much easier step, and progress even more gradually.

Protocol

Note: If your dog rides in the front passenger seat, she should wear a seat belt. Acclimate her to the device separately, outside the vehicle, in advance of beginning this protocol. Wherever the instructions call for your dog to be in the front seat, belt her in. If you drive an SUV and your dog rides in the back, install a metal barrier between the front and back seats for safety.

Start with your vehicle parked in the driveway with the doors closed. Your dog should be on a long-line for safety purposes; *keep the line slack*. The tension of a tight leash could cause stress. (Alternately, tether the long-line to something sturdy so your dog has enough line to be near the car but not enough to run into the street.)

Do a few relaxed repetitions at each step before proceeding.

Part I – The Doors

If you drive a car, use whichever door your dog would normally use to enter. If you drive an SUV and your dog normally enters through the hatchback, use that door, unless your dog finds a side door less intimidating. Stand with your dog next to your vehicle.

1. Hold the treats and leash in one hand. Place your other hand on the door handle for one second. Treat.

2. Place your hand on the door handle and hold for three seconds. Treat.

3. Place your hand on the door handle; work the handle but do not open the door. Treat.

4. Place your hand on the door handle; open the door slightly. (Do not close it.) Treat.

5. Close the door gently. Treat.

6. Open the door halfway. Treat.

7. Close the door gently. Treat.

8. Open the door halfway, then close it gently. Treat.

9. Open the door fully. Treat.

10. Close the door gently. Treat.

11. Open the door fully, then close it gently. Treat.

12. Open the door fully, treat continually for 3 seconds, then close the door gently. Treat.

13. Open the door fully, treat continually for 5 seconds, then close the door gently. Treat.

Repeat step 13 a few times to be sure your dog is absolutely comfortable before proceeding to Part II. Remember, you do not have to get through the entire protocol in one session! Take your time, and break it down into as many sessions as necessary to keep your dog comfortable.

Part II – Now Boarding

14. If you have an SUV, sit in the cargo area with the hatchback door open. If you have a car, open the door to the seat your dog would normally occupy and sit in the seat next to it. If your dog normally rides in the front passenger seat of your car, have someone hold the long-line (if it is not tethered) as you get into position. *Allow your dog to remain outside the vehicle.* Be sure not to put any tension on the long-line. Toss a few treats to your dog, then step out of the vehicle. Even if your dog started a few feet away from the vehicle, with enough repetition she should approach closely enough to take the treats from your hand. Do not move on to the next step until your dog will stand directly outside the door in a relaxed manner to take treats.

15. Sit in the same place in your vehicle as in Step 14, with the door open and your dog outside. Assuming your dog is physically able to jump in on her own, scatter some yummy treats inside (some close to your dog), and appear very interested in them. Pick one up; ooh and aah over it. Pretend to eat a piece, smacking your lips, saying, "Mmmmm!" If your dog jumps in, allow her to take the

treats. Feed a few extra treats from your hands, then allow her to jump out whenever she is ready. Even if she just puts a paw or two up at first, allow her to take the treats, then feed a few more. After a few repetitions, move the treats back a bit so she will have to climb further inside.

Once your dog has eaten the scattered treats, feed a treat every three seconds. (Use cheerful chatter as well if you'd like.) It is important to keep to a regular treat rhythm at first, because knowing what to expect will help your dog to relax. If your dog wants to leave the vehicle at any point, allow her to do so. Once your dog will stay in the vehicle while being fed treats every three seconds, switch to feeding treats every five seconds. When your dog appears more relaxed, switch to feeding treats at random: for example, treat, wait three seconds, treat; wait five seconds, treat; wait two seconds, treat; and so on. In time, your dog will become more and more comfortable spending time inside the vehicle. (Keep in mind that any of these steps could take minutes, days, or weeks depending on your dog.)

Note: For dogs who are physically unable to jump into a vehicle, use a ramp (available through pet supply stores and mail order). If your dog is not accustomed to a ramp, have her practice in a non-vehicle-related situation first, such as leading up to your porch, or inside the house, even if it must be laid flat. Once your dog is comfortable with the ramp and not afraid to get inside the vehicle, leash your dog and help to guide her up the ramp into your vehicle.

16. Once your dog is comfortable spending a full minute inside the vehicle with the doors open: Stand outside the vehicle. Open the dog-loading door, coax your dog inside, then close the door and move quickly to the driver's seat. Once seated, toss a few treats to your dog, close the driver's side door, feed a few more treats, then let your dog out. Gradually increase the time your dog spends inside with the doors closed and you in the driver's seat, tossing treats to her sporadically (more often at first and then gradually less often), until your dog can remain calmly in the vehicle for five minutes. (Alternately, have a quick game of tug, pet your dog calmly, or give her a brief but relaxing massage.)

17. Once your dog can calmly spend five minutes inside with the doors closed, it is time to add the sound and vibration of the engine. First, get your dog settled. If she is riding in the back of your SUV, ask her to lie down. If she is riding in the passenger seat of your car or truck, make sure she is belted in and calm. Then turn on the engine, feed a treat, and turn off the engine. With each repetition, increase the time the engine is left on, by a few seconds at a time. Your timing is important: remember to start all treats (and cheerful chatter if you'd like) immediately after turning on the engine, and stop immediately after the engine is turned off.

Note: If your dog absolutely panics at the sound of the engine, desensitize her to it by standing with her at a comfortable distance from the vehicle. Have a friend turn the engine on, then play with your dog, have her do tricks or whatever else she enjoys. Gradually work closer and closer to the vehicle. (For more specific instructions on addressing fear of sounds, see *Chapter 35.*)

Part III – Driving Miss Daisy

You should begin Part III only when your dog is absolutely comfortable spending time in the vehicle with the engine running. "Absolutely comfortable" means that not only do you not see signs of stress, but that your dog actually looks happy to be there.

18. With you and your dog inside and the doors closed, get her settled as you did in Step 17. Turn on the engine. Feed one treat and then, as long as your dog has remained calm (if not, get her settled again), as smoothly as possible, move the car just twenty feet or so. Stop the car and turn off the engine.

19. Repeat Step 18, but this time move the car a bit further. Turn off the engine. With each repetition, move the car a bit further, so long as your dog is relaxed. As you drive along, reach your hand over (without turning your head—keep your eyes on the road!) every ten seconds or so and hand your dog a single treat. Use cheerful chatter between treats if you would like. Remember, this is for a short drive to get your dog accustomed to the vehicle's movement; if the entire exercise takes you once around the block, that's plenty. Gradually extend the time between treats. Very soon you will not need to toss treats at all.

If there is a park nearby, drive there, have a game of chase or toss a favorite toy, then drive home. Or drive to a friend's house for a doggy play date, or to a pet store for a special new chew bone. (Offer the bone in the vehicle, immediately after leaving the store.) The more frequently you can practice short sessions with positive outcomes, the sooner your dog will not only come to accept, but will actually look forward to, riding in the car.

Tricks to Try:

- Some dogs may fear the vehicle because they receive static electricity shocks when riding inside. Try wiping your dog and the inside of your vehicle down with anti-static laundry sheets before your next ride.

- Some dogs do better when they cannot see outside movement. Try having your dog ride in a secured, covered crate.

- Spray DAP (see *Chapter 47*) inside your vehicle before your dog enters.

- Try these complementary therapies: body wrap (see *Chapter 46*), Ttouch ear slides (see *Chapter 45*), and Calming Cap™ (see *Chapter 48*).

 # Tail End Wrap-Up

🐾 Consider whether carsickness plays a role in your dog's reluctance to ride. If so, use appropriate remedies.

🐾 Use play to get your dog more comfortable around your vehicle.

🐾 Proceed through the suggested protocol at a pace that is comfortable for your dog.

🐾 Drive your dog to fun destinations!

🐾 Try some of the suggested "Tricks to Try."

Fear of the Crate

Crate training—teaching your dog to feel comfortable in a crate—is valuable for many reasons. A crate offers one of the easiest ways to housebreak your dog, and is a safe way to transport him. A dog who is comfortable being crated will have an easier time if he must be caged at the groomer's shop or veterinarian's office, or confined at home after surgery. Crates are extremely valuable to fearful dogs, as they provide a safe, den-like sanctuary. A dog who is afraid of visitors or feeling overwhelmed by rowdy kids can take refuge in his crate. A dog who fears thunder can ride out the storm in a place he feels safe. Regardless of what is scaring a dog, a crate offers a safe way to remove himself from the situation and feel more secure. But despite the many advantages of crate training, some dogs, unfortunately, fear the crate itself.

Why Cautious of Crates?

Dogs fear crates for different reasons. Some have developed an early negative association with being crated. For example, a pup who was flown from a breeder in one state to an owner in another might have been frightened by the sound, vibration, and overall experience of being in an airplane, and associated that trauma with the crate. Others dogs fear crates simply because they were never properly introduced to one.

> There are some dogs—for example, those with extreme separation anxiety—who absolutely panic and may even mutilate themselves if left in a small, enclosed space. *Those dogs should not be crated.* (If you have a dog with extreme separation anxiety, consult a professional.)

Over the years, I have helped many rescued dogs overcome their fear of being crated. Whether your dog is an adult or a pup, chances are excellent that you can successfully do the same for him.

Choosing the Right Crate

There are two main types of crates: those with a plastic snap-together top and bottom and a metal grille door (the type required for airline travel), and the metal-barred type that resembles a cage. I prefer the first type because it offers more of a den-like, enclosed feeling. If you already have the latter type, be sure your dog cannot get his paws stuck in the narrow horizontal spaces between the lower bars. (Place bedding inside if necessary to block those spaces.) You can give a metal crate more of an enclosed feel by draping a sheet or towel over the top and sides.

When it comes to crates, size matters! If you are using the crate for housebreaking, it should be large enough for your dog to stand up, lie down, and turn around in, but no bigger. If your dog is already housebroken the crate can be a bit larger, but don't purchase the equivalent of a canine condo—you still want the crate to engender a safe, enclosed, den-like feeling.

Introducing the Crate

The first rule of introducing your dog to the crate is *never force him inside*. Instead, place the crate in a high-traffic area such as the living room, and prop the door open so it cannot swing shut by accident and frighten your dog. Place a sweatshirt you have been wearing or a towel or blanket with your scent on it (rub it on your body or place it in your laundry hamper for a while) in the bottom of the crate. Then "forget" the crate is there. Do not try to lure your dog into the crate or call his attention to it—give him a few days to get used to the new object in his environment on his own. You may, however, place treats and other enticements inside when your dog is not watching, so he can discover the goodies and begin to associate the crate with good things.

After a few days of leaving the crate in a central area:

- Place your dog's meal just inside the crate door. If he eats it, on the following day place the dish a bit further inside. Over the course of a few days, the dish should end up in the back of the crate with your dog's entire body inside the crate while eating. (Very cautious dogs may manage to stretch their necks to get the food while their back legs remain outside the crate—that's fine.) You could also attach a treasured chew item to the inside back wall of the crate so that your dog must remain inside to chew it. (There is a version of the Kong™ that comes with a rope already attached—stuff it and then tie it to the crate's metal bars.) Whether you place a meal or a chew toy inside, *leave the door propped open*. Both approaches will not only get your dog inside the crate, but will help to create a good association between the crate and things your dog likes.

- Lay out a line of mixed treats spaced a short distance apart, starting a few feet from the crate and ending inside it. The best treats should be placed closest to the crate and inside. The final treat should be placed at the back of the crate. Stand a distance away and ignore your dog (or leave the room altogether) so he can approach and take the treats in his own time. Practice a few times daily.

- If your dog will not enter the crate using either of the previous methods, remove the bedding and sit by the side of the crate with the door propped open. Toss a few treats in or near the crate (depending on your dog's comfort level) and allow him to eat them. (If you have a wire crate, block the back so the treats don't fall through.) Then wait. Any time your dog even glances at the crate say, "Yes!" and immediately give him a treat. Repeat until your dog is consistently glancing at the crate. Then raise the bar; wait for him to do a bit more. (You are *shaping* the behavior of entering the crate by rewarding small, incremental bits.) The "bit more" might be moving his head to glance further inside, or taking one step toward the crate. When he makes his move say, "Yes!" and treat. By continuing in this fashion, you will eventually shape your dog's movement until he is venturing inside the crate. Once he has his head or a paw inside, instead of feeding him the reward treat directly, toss it inside the crate to encourage further progress. When you toss, make sure the treat hits the back of the crate. The sound will alert your dog to the treat's presence.

Continue to reward small bits of progress until your dog is standing completely inside the crate, looking at you expectantly as if to say, "Where's my treat?" At that point, reward rapidly a few times. Then close the door, feed a treat through the door, open it immediately, and let your dog out. Gradually increase the time your dog spends inside the crate by feeding two treats the next time the door is closed (roughly one treat per second) and so on, until he can remain calmly inside with you feeding treats through the closed door for ten seconds. Then begin to increase the time between treats by feeding a treat, saying, "What a good dog!" then feeding another. Continue to build duration in this treat-praise-treat manner, and space the treats further and further apart (treat, give a few more seconds of praise, treat). (To see this method in action, see *Resources* for the DVD *Train Your Dog: The Positive Gentle Method.*)

Don't feel that you have to get your dog completely inside the crate with the door closed in one session! Doing only a few repetitions of a step or two is fine for one lesson. Try to end each session on a successful note. If at any point your dog shows signs of stress or fear, go back to a step at which he was comfortable, do a few repetitions, and call it a day. Pick up the next day at a step at which he was comfortable and build small steps from there.

- If your dog will absolutely not go anywhere near the crate no matter what you have tried: Place an out-of-this-world-yummy treat deep inside the crate. Choose something that your dog would not normally get, such as a bunch of pieces of boiled (boneless) chicken, or a handful of hot dog pieces or cheese. I can't emphasize enough that this should be a jackpot of a treat; you want your dog salivating just looking at it. Now for the sneaky part: shut the treat inside the crate and leave the room. Chances are, your dog will become very frustrated, wishing he could get at the food. After a few minutes, return and open the crate door, then leave the room again. There is a very good chance that your dog will dash inside to get the goodies.

With daily practice sessions, your dog will soon be lounging happily in his crate. If necessary for housebreaking or management, your dog may be crated overnight in a spot where you can hear him vocalize if he needs to go out to eliminate, but he should not be crated for more than four hours at a time during the day.

Tricks to Try:

- If your dog is more than mildly frightened of your current crate, start with the opposite type.

- Remove your dog's collar before crating him to avoid the potential danger of the collar getting caught on the crate bars.

- Avoid using the crate as a time-out or punishment area. For time-outs, use a small, enclosed area such as a laundry room with a baby gate across the entrance. (Your dog should already be comfortable in the area so it is not associated only with punishments.)

- Whenever your dog seeks refuge in his crate, leave him alone; make sure family members and visitors do so as well. Do not attempt to coax him out, and do not reach inside to pet him or pull him out. A crated dog has no means of escape. Thanks to the fight or flight instinct and the fact that a crated dog has no way to flee, reaching in to pet a fearful crated dog is an excellent way to get bitten!

- Make sure the crate is available to your dog when you have visitors and at other potentially frightening times, so your dog always has a safe refuge.

Tail End Wrap-Up

🐾 Choose the right size and type of crate for your dog.

🐾 Go slowly when introducing your dog to the crate. Never force him inside.

🐾 Place the crate in a common room and allow your dog a few days to get used to its presence.

🐾 Use one of the suggested methods to get your dog comfortable with the crate.

🐾 Once your dog is accustomed to the crate, he can be crated overnight, up to four hours during the day, and for car rides.

33

Fear of Stairs

At the age of five months, Ami the Chihuahua was still not reliably potty trained. To prevent her from roaming their two-story house unsupervised, Ami's owners placed a baby gate across the bottom of the staircase. One day, when seven-year-old Freddie moved the gate and forgot to replace it, Ami ventured upstairs to explore. Freddie caught her halfway up the staircase, and yelled, "No, no, no!" as he slapped her over and over on the rear. Months later, potty trained and allowed full run of the house, Ami refuses to go anywhere near the staircase.

Having a traumatic experience while climbing stairs could certainly cause a dog to fear them. Other traumas that could cause a fear of stairs include slipping, falling, or being injured on them. More common reasons for a dog's fear of stairs, however, are a lack of previous exposure, lacking the motor coordination to navigate the stairs successfully, perceiving the staircase as visually overwhelming, or simply having an instinctive fear of heights. Fear of climbing stairs can also be due to joint-related pain; if you suspect this might be the case or your dog is a senior citizen, a vet checkup is in order.

If you live in a split-level home or take your dog to public places, a fear of stairs can be problematic. Fortunately, it is one of the easier canine fears to conquer. Because most dogs' fear involves climbing down, we'll focus on that aspect.

Preparation

Food will be used as a lure and as a reward, so have extra-special treats on hand. Slices of hot dog, cheese, or bits of boneless boiled chicken are all excellent choices.

Be sure there are no objects near the stairs such as statues or potted plants that could be knocked over, or things on or around the stairs (such as kids' or dogs' toys) that could cause your dog to become startled, slip, or fall. Years ago, when working with a client's stair-phobic dog, I did not realize that the upright air purifier, which sat on the lower landing, was not as heavy nor as solid as it appeared. The session had been going well. We had progressed to the point where the dog was enthusiastically climbing down the entire staircase from the top step—until she happened to bump the air purifier, which fell over and startled us all. Fortunately, after moving it aside we were able to convince the dog to continue, but it could have caused a real setback.

Stairs without a Care

Rather than placing your dog on the top step and expecting her to navigate the entire staircase, you will be asking her to climb down a single step at first. As long as she remains comfortable, steps will added one at a time until she is happily climbing up and down the stairs without a care.

Read through the following instructions before you begin. As always, take your time, watch for signs of stress, and proceed at a pace at which your dog is comfortable.

Stand with your dog at ground level, at a distance from the stairs that is comfortable for her. Toss a treat on the floor a foot or two away from you and say, "Get it!" Act and sound happy and enthusiastic, as though this is a fun game. Repeat a few times, moving a few inches closer to the staircase with each repetition, until you are tossing treats on the floor right next to the stairs. Do a few repetitions.

Once your dog is comfortable taking treats at ground level next to the lowest stair, it is time to take the first step—literally. Stand a few feet back from the stairs. After your dog has eaten the last treat from ground level, without pausing, toss a treat on to the lowest step and say, "Get it!" Allow your dog to take the treat. Then call your dog (in a happy voice, of course!) and reward her for coming to you. (Alternately, if your dog knows touch, ask her to return to touch your hand. To teach the skill, see *Chapter 16.*) Repeat a few times. Then, without pausing, toss a treat on to the second step and allow your dog to take it. Again, call her and reward her for coming. Repeat a few times. Depending on the size of your dog, she may not actually have to climb any steps to take the initial treats; that's fine. As you progress, she will have to use one paw, then two, then eventually her entire body in order to reach the treat.

If your first session involves only three steps, that's fine. The goal is not to get your dog to race down the entire staircase in as short a time as possible, but to leave her with a positive feeling about the stairs. Do short, daily practice sessions that end on a good note. Begin the subsequent session a few steps below where you left off. If at any point your dog balks and will not move, go back to a level at which she was comfortable, do a few repetitions, then end the session.

Troubleshooting

If your dog refuses to climb the stairs to take the treats, assuming her fear of stairs is not extreme:

Gently lift your dog on to the bottom step. (If your dog is too heavy to lift yourself, engage the help of a friend with whom your dog is comfortable.) With your dog on the step, stand back and enthusiastically call her to you. Use a high-pitched, happy voice; try crouching down and opening your arms. If necessary (and your dog is food-motivated), try scattering a few treats near your feet. Since navigating the lowest step is not so frightening and you are being so enthusiastic, it is likely that your dog will comply. Repeat until she seems confident and relaxed on the first step, then proceed to placing her on the second step. Stop the session after your dog has conquered just a few steps. Practice in brief, frequent sessions, building up to her confidently navigating the entire staircase.

Tricks to try:

- Are your stairs carpeted? If not, the slippery surface might be contributing to your dog's fear. Lay down a runner (rubber or carpet) temporarily—or permanently, to ensure everybody's safety.

- Do your stairs have risers? If not, that open space between the steps could be frightening your dog. Tape cardboard to the front of each step while working through the exercises. Once your dog is completely comfortable, the pieces can be removed gradually, one at a time.

- If you have two dogs and one is not afraid of the stairs, or you can borrow a friend's non-stair-phobic dog, call that dog up and down the stairs. Your dog may learn through example that the stairs are not so daunting after all.

With practice, your dog will soon be climbing happily up and down the stairs in your home. But do not assume that means she will be fear-free when she encounters stairs in other locations. To help her generalize that *all* staircases are not to be feared, bring along treats and practice at other locations. Take the time to introduce your dog to new staircases gradually as you did at home. You will find that with each new location your dog will show less and less trepidation, until she will ultimately climb any flight of stairs with ease.

Tail End Wrap-Up

 Rule out medical issues.

 Take it one step at a time—literally.

 Do brief, frequent sessions so your dog can master a few steps at a time.

 Once your dog is comfortable with the stairs in your home, practice in other locations.

34

Thunderbolts and Lightning: Very, Very Frightening!

Is the mere hint of a thunderstorm enough to rain on your dog's parade? A single clap of thunder is enough to cause some anxious dogs to pace, drool, tremble, hide, or even soil indoors. Severely thunder-phobic dogs may go into a blind panic and crash through windows, tear through screen doors, or escape from back yards. In their terror, these unfortunate dogs often injure themselves. It is truly heartbreaking to watch a dog who is in a blind panic and be unable to explain that there is nothing to fear. But whether your dog's fear of thunder is mild or severe, there are things you can do to help.

Port in a Storm

One of the kindest things you can do for a dog who is frightened by thunderstorms is to provide a safe refuge. If your dog is comfortable in his crate, make sure it is accessible. Many dogs choose the bathtub as their favorite "port in a storm," and my dog Soko is no exception. Whenever I see the telltale signs that she is becoming nervous—one ear laid back, repetitive lip-licking—I make sure the bathroom door is open so that her safe spot is available. Your dog's subtle stress signals may be different. Watch for pacing, drooling, trembling, rapid blinking, hypervigilance, repetitive behaviors such as paw-licking, and being overly clingy. Be sure your dog's preferred sanctuary is available whenever a storm is predicted, or when you see signs of anxiety—dogs are often more reliable weather forecasters than your local news!

When a storm rolls in, there is an increase in static electricity in the atmosphere. According to one theory, the charged air can cause painful shocks to dogs, especially those with long or thick coats. Some researchers believe that dogs take refuge in bathtubs, shower stalls, and behind toilets because the plumbing in those areas provides grounding. To find out whether static electricity plays a part in your dog's fear, rub him down with an anti-static laundry sheet before the next storm hits; it just might make a difference.

Zone in on Melatonin

Many of those whose dogs suffer from thunder-phobia resort to drugging their dogs whenever a storm is expected. But assess the situation carefully before choosing to medicate; all drugs have potential side effects. Some quiet the body but not the mind, which can result in an extremely frightening experience for the dog as he experiences the fear but is unable to react physically. Recent studies have suggested a potentially better solution, and it's been right there under our noses—well, actually in our pineal glands—all along.

Melatonin is a natural hormone that regulates the human biological clock, and has been shown, in double-blind studies with young adults, to facilitate sleep.[1] Melatonin is not a sedative; it will not leave your dog glassy-eyed or obviously "drugged." What it can do is leave your dog feeling more relaxed and less concerned with what is going on in the environment.

Drs. Linda Aronson and Nicholas Dodman, after reviewing research describing how melatonin reduced the stress-related behavior of flank-licking in dogs, wondered whether it could help dogs with thunderstorm phobias. Dr. Aronson tried melatonin with her own seven-year-old Bearded Collie and described the dramatic results: "Instead of tearing through the house, urinating, and digging at carpets with a wild look in her eye, she simply stopped being afraid."[2]

Doctors Aronson and Dodman administered melatonin to other thunder-phobic dogs, with good results. In fact, Dr. Aronson estimated that melatonin was helpful in roughly 80 percent of the cases. I also experienced good results using melatonin with Soko. Since she is a large girl (although she swears most of that 90 pounds is fur!) I gave her a three-milligram dose, two hours before a storm was due to hit. (Standard dosage is one milligram for dogs up to 15 lbs., 1.5 milligrams for dogs 15-30 pounds, 3 milligrams for dogs 30-90 pounds, and sometimes more for larger dogs.) *Be sure to check with your vet to confirm the proper dosage for your dog and that melatonin is safe for your particular dog, especially if he has other health issues.* While Soko still took refuge in the bathroom at the first thunderclap, she soon became more relaxed. There was none of the usual trembling, which was a big improvement for her and a relief to me. During subsequent storms, with the assistance of melatonin, Soko simply lay calmly on the carpet.

According to Dr. Aronson, melatonin can be administered up to three times a day. The effects last a few hours, and dogs do not habituate to the effects. It is best to have the hormone in your dog's system before the storm hits, although some dogs will respond to melatonin even after the storm has arrived and they have become fearful. (If your dog is in a blind panic, however, the hormone is not as likely to have an effect.) Administer the melatonin an hour or so before a storm is expected to hit, or before you leave for work that morning.

Melatonin is available in capsules and tablets and can be found in supermarkets, drug stores, and health food stores. Dr. Aronson suggests using tablets only, avoiding formulations that contain other ingredients as well, and avoiding time-release or sublingual formulas. For faster absorption, tablets may be crushed and sprinkled over your dog's food.

Statistics of Interest

"70 percent of dogs who react profoundly to miscellaneous noises also have storm phobias, and 90 percent of dogs with storm phobias react badly to other noises." Also, "70 percent of dogs seen in a clinical setting with noise or storm phobias also have often undiagnosed separation anxiety."[3]

The Sound and the Fury

Because thunderstorms involve multiple components—booming sound, a change in barometric pressure, wind, rain, and lightning—unless you happen to be a Hollywood special effects wizard, it is very difficult to approximate an actual storm. Since sound is the main component that frightens dogs and is the easiest to recreate, desensitizing your dog to the sound of thunder should be your first step.

Pre-recorded CDs of thunderstorms are available by mail order (see *Resources*). Begin with your dog at a distance from your stereo speakers. Start with the volume completely off, then turn it up in tiny increments until you see a sign (a glance, an ear flick) that your dog hears the sound. Keep the volume at that level, and leave the player on endless replay mode for 24 hours. The next day, increase the volume a tiny bit and leave it playing for 24 hours. Continue in this manner, always making sure your dog does not startle at the increase in volume (if he does, go back to a lower volume for an additional 24 hours), until you have built up to a volume that approximates that of actual thunder. *Note:* It is best if, during the desensitization process, your dog does not experience an actual thunderstorm; check your local forecast and plan ahead.

Once your dog is comfortable with a volume that approximates real thunder, it's time to create a good association with the sound. Turn the CD on and then play a game of tug, feed fabulous treats, give a relaxing massage, or do whatever else your dog enjoys. Stop the activity and the sound at the same time. Repeating this often will eventually result in your dog becoming happy and excited whenever he hears the CD.

Of course, actual thunder will not be coming from your stereo speakers. Practice with a portable CD player in different rooms to ensure that your dog hears the sound coming from various places. If you have a two-story home, leave the CD playing on the upper level while your dog is downstairs; if you have an attic, even better. Play the CD outside with your dog in the house, and also with your dog outdoors. You could even go so far as to place the player in a tree so that your dog hears the sound coming from overhead in the great outdoors.

Block the Shock

In his book *Dogs Behaving Badly: An A-Z Guide to Understanding & Curing Behavioral Problems in Dogs* (see *Resources*), Dr. Nicholas Dodman suggests the following measures to address the buildup of static electricity:

- Wipe your dog down with anti-static laundry sheets.
- Mist your dog with water from a spray bottle.
- Spray the undersides of your dog's paws with anti-static spray.
- Make sure your dog is on a tile or linoleum floor.
- Put your dog in the car and take her for a ride. Dr. Dodman notes that "Many dogs are happy as bugs in a rug when put in a car and driven around during a storm."

Helping your dog to acclimate to the sound of thunder, taking anti-static measures, and using melatonin can all be helpful. So can the therapies that follow.

Complementary Therapies

Part VI of this book describes complementary therapies that can be helpful when used in conjunction with behavior modification. Here are a few that are applicable to sound and thunder phobias:

Flower Essences The Bach™ essence Rock Rose specifically addresses extreme fear and panic. It is available as an individual essence or as a part of Rescue Remedy®, a combination of five essences. The liquid can be added to your dog's drinking water (the normal dose is four drops per bowl), rubbed on the gums, or in the case of a dog who is already in a panic and potentially dangerous if approached too closely, sprayed on the coat.

An article in the *Whole Dog Journal* describes the use of a combination of equal parts Rock Rose, Mimulus, and Aspen to treat a two-year-old, thunder-phobic German Shepherd. Within two weeks the dog was no longer afraid of thunder. Also discussed was a three-year-old Belgian Tervuren who was extremely frightened by thunder and other loud noises.

The dog was given six drops of the Rose/Mimulus/Aspen combination by mouth three to four times a day. According to the article, "the transformation was amazing."[4]

The nice thing about flower essences is that although they are not guaranteed to help they certainly will not hurt, so experimentation is possible. In a crisis, the essences should be administered every three to five minutes until improvement is shown. (For more on flower essences, see *Chapter 43*.)

Ttouch Ear slides, tail work, and touches around the hindquarters can be especially beneficial. The touches should be started before the storm hits, administered during the storm if your dog allows it, and continued after it ends. A Ttouch wrap or other other type of body wrap may also be helpful. (See *Chapters 45* and *46* for information and instructions.)

Herbs Valerian root has a relaxing effect on dogs, and may help your dog to remain calm during a storm. Over-the-counter formulas made specifically for dogs often combine valerian with other herbs. Although the formulas are normally sold in pill or capsule form, the liquid form (known as a tincture) has more potency. Dosage information can be found on product labels. *Note:* Although valerian has a calming effect on most dogs (and people), a small percentage react by becoming agitated. Give valerian to your dog before it is actually needed, in order to gauge his reaction.

Other herbs that may be useful include vervain, skullcap (which may help dogs who are sensitive to electrical fields), and St. John's wort. Tinctures may be squirted directly into a dog's mouth. Consult your veterinarian for proper dosage and to be sure the herb you plan to try is safe for your particular dog, especially if he is taking medication. (See *Chapter 50* for more information on herbs, and the *Resources* section for books and products.)

DAP Spray DAP on your dog's bedding and place the bedding in your dog's "safe area." Alternately, leave a plug-in diffuser in that room (see *Chapter 47*).

Acupressure See *Chapter 51* for descriptions of how acupressure treatments—manually stimulating points along the body's energy pathways—helped two thunder-phobic dogs.

Pharmacological Intervention

If your dog is severely thunder-phobic, melatonin and the suggested complementary therapies might not provide adequate relief. In that case, pharmacological intervention may be the kindest course. Talk to your veterinarian about prescribing a drug that can be administered whenever a thunderstorm is expected. Be sure to ask how and when to administer the drug, and what potential side effects to watch for. Try the medication initially when your dog is not agitated, to rule out any adverse reactions.

Acepromazine: Think Twice

Acepromazine is a drug that is often prescribed by veterinarians for short-term fear situations. But as Dr. Karen Overall states, "Acepromazine is a dissociative anesthetic meaning that it scrambles perceptions. Ask yourself if a scrambling of perceptions will make an anxious dog or uncertain dog worse or better. It's always worse, and we make many if not most dogs more sensitive to storms by using this drug. In part this is also because sensitivity to noise is heightened."[5]

Patricia McConnell, Ph.D. took brain wave recordings of dogs on acepromazine and says, "Their brains were going a mile a minute."[6] So although a dog might appear sedated and calm, her state of mind might be something else entirely. Acepromazine can also cause blood pressure to lower and aggressive behavior to intensify. And there is anecdotal evidence that in Boxers, acepromazine can cause an arrhythmia of the heart, which can be fatal. Whatever your dog's breed, use caution with this particular medication.

If your dog is severely thunder-phobic but storms are a rare occurrence in your area, a short-acting drug may be your best bet. But if you live in an area that has frequent thunderstorms, rather than continually medicating your dog, practice sound desensitization in conjunction with the medication so that your dog can eventually be weaned off the drug.

1 Zhadanova IV, Wurtman RJ, Lynch HJ, et al. (1995). Sleep-inducing effects of low doses of melatonin ingested in the evening. *Clinical Pharmacology Ther* 57:552–58.

2 Puotinen, CJ (2000) Bring In Da Noise. *Whole Dog Journal*. May: pp.3-7.

3 Karen Overall, *Storm Phobias*, September 2004 <http://www.dvmnewsmagazine.com/dvm/article/articleDetail.jsp?id=136493> DVM News Magazine.

4 Puotinen, CJ (2000) When the Thunder Rolls. *Whole Dog Journal*. April: pp.9-13

5 Karen Overall, *Storm Phobias*, September 2004 <http://www.dvmnewsmagazine.com/dvm/article/articleDetail.jsp?id=136493> DVM News Magazine

6 McConnell, P. *I'll be Home Soon!* Wisconsin: Dog's Best Friend, Ltd., 2000

Tail End Wrap-Up

- Provide a safe place for your dog to take refuge during storms.

- Try melatonin!

- See whether reducing static electricity makes a difference.

- Use a sound CD to desensitize your dog to the sound of thunder.

- Try the suggested complementary therapies.

- If necessary, consult your veterinarian regarding pharmacological intervention.

Sound Sensitivity

Dogs can hear frequencies just under and twice above those that humans can, and at a much greater distance. In fact, canine hearing is so sensitive that sounds that are loud or jarring to humans could constitute a virtual assault on a dog's ears. While volume alone can be frightening, some sound-sensitive dogs fear sounds of a certain pitch, such as high-pitched beeping. They may fear sharp sounds, such as a car backfiring or a door slamming; shrill sounds, such as a phone ringing; or motor-driven sounds, such as those made by vacuum cleaners.

Some sound sensitivities are genetic. According to author Steve Lindsay, "An innate dread of loud sounds (e.g., gunshots or thunder) and abrupt movement is sometimes evident in such dogs from a very early age or may appear spontaneously as such dogs mature. Fears and phobias associated with an innate predisposition may be controlled to some extent with behavioral and environmental management, but cure is not likely in these cases."[1] So even if your dog's fear of noises is genetic, there is some room for improvement. In cases where a dog's fear of certain sounds is the product of experience, rather than genetics, the prognosis is even better. Remember, if a fear can be learned, it can usually be unlearned.

While one sound-sensitive dog might only flinch at the sound of a car backfiring, another might fly into a blind panic. Very mild sound sensitivities can sometimes be treated by habituation—repeated, frequent exposures to the sound. However, the exposures must not result in an intense fear reaction or the dog could become sensitized, becoming even more afraid of that particular sound, and possibly other sounds as well. Learned sound sensitivities that are mild to moderate have a good prognosis when treated with behavior modification. A solid management program must also be in place, to avoid exposing the dog to the sounds she fears as the program progresses. If a dog's sound sensitivity is extreme, pharmacological intervention may be necessary as an adjunct to behavior modification (see *Chapter 52*).

Name that Trigger

The first step in helping your dog is to identify which specific sounds or types of sounds trigger a reaction. Make a list of every sound you can think of that startles your dog or elicits a fearful reaction. (If you have not already identified your dog's individual triggers, turn to *Chapter 21*.) Here are some examples of sound triggers, including the most common:

Indoor Sounds: vacuum cleaner; air conditioner; fan; heater; blow dryer; electric grooming tools (such as shaver, toothbrush); microwave; teapot whistle; doorbell, knock at door; doors or drawers closing; chairs scraping on hard surface; phone ringing; cell phone ring tone; stereo; sounds on television; electronic sounds (such as computer, pager); raised and/or angry voices; kids screaming; baby crying.

Outdoor Sounds: garbage bins being rolled; garbage trucks; cars; trucks; delivery trucks beeping a backup warning; motorcycles; sirens; planes; weed whackers; lawn mowers; leaf blowers; people yelling; children laughing; shouting or crying; wind; fireworks; thunder (for fear of thunder, see *Chapter 34*).

Types of Sounds: low-pitched; high-pitched; loud; sharp; whirring; shuffling; scraping; sounds that ascend or descend in pitch (like fireworks) or volume (like sirens).

If there is a component of motion—for example, a vacuum cleaner moving back and forth, a garbage bin rolling—and your dog fears the sound *and* the motion, each aspect of the fear must be addressed individually, and then together. (For fear of motion, see *Chapter 36*.)

Controlling Exposure

Once you have identified your dog's triggers, you can begin to address them. The easiest triggers to work with are those you can control. For example, it is much easier to desensitize your dog to the sound of a blow dryer than to the sound of a car backfiring, since the latter happens infrequently and unpredictably. (If the sound occurs very infrequently, such as fireworks on the 4th of July, consider the use of melatonin instead. See *Chapter 34* for more on melatonin.)

Some triggers allow for manipulation of volume. For example, a stereo has a volume control; most blow dryers have low and high settings; air conditioning units normally have a range of settings to adjust the strength of the fan. If the trigger you are working with has such variability, begin on the lowest setting. If the volume cannot be manipulated, use distance to control your dog's exposure to the sound.

Sample Protocol

In the protocol that follows, the trigger is the sound made by an air-conditioning unit. This protocol is similar to one I used with a client whose young terrier mix was extremely fearful of the air conditioner. Because the unit made the most noise at the top of the stairs, the dog refused to go upstairs. That created a problem, as her family wanted the dog to sleep upstairs with them due to a medical condition that needed monitoring. The dog's fear of the sound was compounded by the automatic thermostat, which caused the unit's starting and stopping to seem unpredictable. From the dog's point of view, it just wasn't worth going upstairs when that *thing* could roar to life at any moment!

If your dog experiences sleep disturbances, or paces or appears anxious at specific times, consider whether the air conditioner or heater are running during those times.

A protocol of this type, where volume control is limited, should begin with the dog at enough of a distance from the trigger that she shows no startle or stress response. In Widget the terrier's case, I set the stage by positioning my client at the top of the stairs, where she could turn the unit on and off. I stood on the ground level approximately ten feet from the stairs with Widget, and held a bag filled with her favorite treats.

Widget's owner was instructed that on my signal she was to turn the unit on, then immediately off. I fed a treat at the exact moment the unit was turned on. Because the unit was turned off immediately, the treat coincided with the unit being on, and when the unit was turned off the treat was gone. We then increased the time the unit was left on by one-second increments. I fed treats as long as the unit was on, and stopped immediately when it was turned off. In this way we were able to help Widget associate the sound of the air conditioner with a pleasant feeling. Once he looked positively happy to hear the sound, we moved closer to the stairs in small increments. Had this approach not worked, I could have either started farther away, or started to feed the treats before the unit was turned on, to ease Widget into the process.

By learning how to manipulate variables, you will be able to design your own protocol based on your dog's specific needs. In the protocol that follows, you will notice that whenever one variable becomes more challenging, another is made easier. For example, when the distance from the stairs is decreased (potentially more frightening), the duration of the sound is also decreased (less frightening). Treats are fed in rapid succession while the unit is on, and cease immediately when it stops. Cheerful chatter may accompany the treats if you wish, so long as it stops when the treats stop. Take your time and watch your dog for signs of stress. When necessary, go back to a step that was comfortable and build smaller steps from there.

This portion of the protocol starts with the dog on the ground floor three feet from the bottom of the staircase (where the dog is comfortable) and ends at the bottom of the staircase with the air conditioner turned on for five seconds. In practice, you might build the duration of the sound to ten or twenty seconds to give your dog a chance to get more comfortable with it.

Distance from Stairs	Duration of Sound
3 feet	1 second
3 feet	2 seconds
3 feet	3 seconds
3 feet	5 seconds
2 feet	1 second
2 feet	2 seconds
2 feet	3 seconds
2 feet	5 seconds
1 foot	1 second
1 foot	2 seconds
1 foot	3 seconds
1 foot	5 seconds
At bottom of stairs	1 second
At bottom of stairs	2 seconds
At bottom of stairs	3 seconds
At bottom of stairs	5 seconds

The protocol continues, with the assumption that duration at the bottom of the stairs has been gradually increased to ten seconds, with the dog remaining relaxed. We will now progress gradually up the stairs. (Widget does not have a fear of stairs—if he did, that would have had to be addressed separately.) "Step 1" refers to the lowest step, "Step 2" the next step up, and so on.

Position	Duration of Sound
Bottom of stairs	10 seconds
Step 1	5 seconds
Step 1	8 seconds
Step 1	10 seconds
Step 2	5 seconds
Step 2	8 seconds
Step 2	10 seconds
Step 3	4 seconds
Step 3	6 seconds
Step 3	8 seconds
Step 3	10 seconds

The closer you get to the trigger, the greater the chances are that your dog will become frightened. To prevent setbacks, as you progressed up the stairs, you would drop the initial time the sound was heard to one or two seconds, and build duration more gradually than on the lower steps. Assuming the staircase has 15 steps, the final steps of the protocol might look like this:

Position	Duration of Sound
Step 15	1 second
Step 15	2 seconds
Step 15	3 seconds

...and so on, until you achieved 10 seconds.

Then:

Top of stairs	1 second
Top of stairs	2 seconds
Top of stairs	3 seconds

...and so on.

Once your dog was comfortable at and around the top of the staircase with the unit turned on, you could begin to play games, feed treats, and engage in other activities your dog enjoys.

Without the staircase, this protocol would have been simpler. But even this protocol, although it might appear complicated on paper, is actually simple in practice. Just remember to work in short sessions and monitor your dog for signs of stress. It does not matter how long progress takes, so long as it is steady.

Remember:

- Resist the urge to push too far too fast, no matter how well your dog is doing. If you only accomplish one small step in a session, that's plenty.
- Do a few brief sessions daily.
- If you or your dog are not feeling well or are overly stressed, skip that session.

Further Progress

Back to Widget—although he now felt comfortable with the air conditioner on while he was on the second floor, he would not always be at the top of the steps when the thermostat turned the unit on. We needed him to be comfortable wherever he happened to be when the unit engaged. So we progressed to turning the air conditioner on randomly when Widget was in various areas of the house, paying him immediately (with treats that had been kept hidden) when it started, stopping when the unit turned off. We also took him to various rooms and began to play with him when the unit came on, stopping when it turned off. Widget soon tolerated the air conditioner from anywhere in the house without the treats, as the good association that had been created remained.

Whatever your dog's trigger, once you have completed your protocol, be sure to help her generalize by practicing with her and/or the trigger in different places and at random times.

Alternate Solution: The Endless Loop

Because some sounds have no volume control, or are unpredictable or difficult to manipulate, it can be difficult to address them with the type of protocol described. A useful solution in those cases is the Endless Loop technique. It involves playing a sound continually, first at a low enough volume that the dog shows no startle response, then gradually increasing it until the dog can tolerate the sound at full volume. (The chapter on fear of thunderstorms describes this technique, using a sound desensitization CD.)

The first step is to create or purchase a recording of the sound. If the sound your dog is afraid of is fairly common, you're in luck. There are companies that create and sell recordings for just this purpose. They include sounds made by dogs and children, kitchen noises, street traffic, and more (see *Resources*).

If the sound you need is not available in pre-manufactured form, you can create an endless loop yourself using one of the following techniques. Try the first one if you are technically inclined; if not, use the second.

Compact Disc (CD):

You will need a computer that can accept an analog signal, a plug-in microphone, and the software and hardware to record sound and burn it onto a CD. This method is useful as long as the sound you need to record can be produced in the vicinity of your computer. If it cannot, use a portable digital recorder and then transfer the sound to your computer.

Record the sound, varying between repeating it continually, and with pauses of random length in between. Burn the recording on to one track of an audio CD. Play the CD on a CD player set on endless repeat.

Audio Cassette:

1. If the sound can be easily manipulated (such as a vacuum cleaner or blow dryer), use an audio cassette recorder to make a recording, with continual repetitions and random pauses. Fill the shortest length tape you can find. Play it back on endless repeat. (Many tape players have the feature.) Or…

2. If the sound is more difficult to reproduce at will (such as a delivery truck beeping a backup warning in your driveway), use two audio tape decks (or a double deck) and a microphone. Use the shortest length tape available.

    a.   Record the sound on to tape A, even if you can only get one sample.
    b.   Play tape A and record it on to tape B.
    c.   Stop both decks, rewind tape A only, then record the sound on tape A on to tape B again.
    d.   Repeat step "c" until tape B has five segments (three recorded back to back and two with random pauses).
    e.   Rewind tape B, then play it and record back onto tape A.
    f.   Repeat step "e" until Tape A is full, then play it on endless loop.

It is important to play the tape or CD at a volume that does not produce a fearful response. The initial volume may be so low that only canine ears can detect it. Begin with the volume off, then turn it up gradually until you see a subtle sign that your dog hears it, such as a glance or an ear flick. Play the recording at that volume for 24 hours, then increase it by a tiny increment. If your dog is comfortable with the new volume (if not, go back to a lower level and increase more gradually), leave it playing for the next 24 hours, then increase it again slightly. Continue to increase it a bit each day until your dog shows no signs of stress when the sound is played at the volume at which it would normally be heard.

Once your dog is comfortable with the sound played at full volume, pair it with things your dog enjoys. For example, leave the sound playing as you play with your dog, massage her, or let her chew on a special chew toy. When the sound stops, so does the "good stuff."

Outdoor Sounds

If the sound your dog fears is outdoors, begin at a distance from the source at which your dog is comfortable, then move gradually closer. Let's say your dog fears the sound of passing trucks. The first day, you stand twenty feet from the street and play with her (on-leash), or practice obedience and tricks. As long as she remains comfortable, you move a bit closer to the street each day. You watch for signs of stress and proceed accordingly. Once your dog is comfortable with trucks passing at close range, you pair their passing by with treats, to create a pleasant association.

Tricks to Try:

- Be sure to address any fears that your dog might have generalized from the original trigger. For example, Soko's fear of the microwave beep generalized to a fear of the freezer door opening and closing, because she knew that frozen food went into the microwave. So in addition to treating her fear of the beeping, I had to treat her fear of the freezer door opening and closing.

- Try complementary therapies. Check the end of *Chapter 34* for suggestions, as the same therapies that work for thunder-phobic dogs can be used for other sound sensitivities.

Be patient. Your dog has probably been afraid of the sound for some time, so don't expect it to become music to her ears overnight.

1 Lindsay, S. *Handbook of Applied Dog Behavior and Training, Volume Three* Iowa: Blackwell Publishing, 2005

 # Tail End Wrap-Up

🐾 Consider your dog's trigger. If it has a component of movement, and that aspect frightens your dog as well, address it separately.

🐾 Use management so that your dog is only exposed to the sound under controlled circumstances.

🐾 Adapt the sample protocol to your dog's situation and environment.

🐾 Alternately, try the Endless Loop technique.

🐾 Try the complementary therapies listed in *Chapter 34*.

36

Motion Sensitivity

Lights…Camera…Action! Although some dogs are perfectly comfortable around lights and cameras, the third part of that famous trio can be troublesome. Motion sensitivity is sometimes limited to a specific object or type of object. For example, a dog might fear the motion of a mop swishing back and forth across a floor, or vehicles zooming past on a busy street. Some dogs appear to be globally motion-sensitive, fearing almost any fast or sudden movement. A person standing up or making a sharp gesture, a chair being pushed from a table, a child running, or any of a variety of everyday occurrences could elicit a fearful response from the globally motion-sensitive dog. (These dogs are often described as "skittish.")

There is a range of reactivity levels and ways that motion-sensitive dogs react when startled. Where one dog might flinch or cower, another might take the offensive and nip at the source of the motion—which, unfortunately, might be another animal or a person.

Addressing Individual Triggers

If your dog's fear of motion is limited to one specific trigger, or a few triggers, the best choice is a treatment plan that involves desensitization and counterconditioning. For example, if your dog feared vehicles passing on the street, you could start at a comfortable distance, treat each time a vehicle appeared, then stop the treats as soon as the vehicle was out of sight. You could gradually work closer to the street as your dog's comfort level allowed. (Since vehicles also involve sound, if your dog were afraid of not only the movement but the sound as well, desensitization to the sound would also be necessary. See *Chapter 35* for sound sensitivity.)

When implementing a protocol for fears such as that of the motion of a mop, instead of working with the variables of distance and sound, you would work with distance, range of motion, and duration. In the following sample protocol, an assistant is holding the mop as though he or she is about to mop the floor. You are standing with your dog six feet from the person. (In practice, you would start at a distance at which your dog was comfortable.) Your job is to give treats in rapid succession each time the person moves the mop, and stop giving treats when the mop stops moving.

Distance	Motion	Duration
6 feet	Slight motion	2 seconds
6 feet	Slight motion	4 seconds
6 feet	Slight motion	6 seconds
6 feet	Moderate motion	2 seconds
6 feet	Moderate motion	4 seconds
6 feet	Moderate motion	6 seconds
4 feet	Slight motion	2 seconds
4 feet	Slight motion	4 seconds
4 feet	Slight motion	6 seconds
4 feet	Moderate motion	2 seconds
4 feet	Moderate motion	4 seconds
4 feet	Moderate motion	6 seconds
6 feet	Larger motion	2 seconds
6 feet	Larger motion	4 seconds
6 feet	Larger motion	6 seconds
4 feet	Moderate motion	4 seconds
4 feet	Larger motion	2 seconds
4 feet	Larger motion	4 seconds
4 feet	Larger motion	6 seconds

After building up to six seconds at the six-foot mark, the distance was decreased to four feet. There, the movement increased gradually to moderate movement for six seconds. But then, because the larger movement might have been too frightening at a four-foot distance, you and your dog returned to standing six feet away. The large motion began briefly at that distance, building in two-second increments until you both could stand six feet away during six seconds of larger movement. Then, going back to the four-foot distance, a moderate motion was made for four seconds to ease you back into it, then the larger motion built gradually, from two to six seconds.

Again, this is just one example of a slice of a protocol. In reality, your rate of progress would depend on your dog's reactions; you would proceed to the next step only when he appeared relaxed at the current step. (For more information on creating a protocol of this type, see *Chapter 24*.)

Play it Up

An alternate approach for treating motion sensitivity is to encourage play in the vicinity of the feared motion. For example, if your dog feared motorized scooters, you could start by playing a game of fetch or tug with your dog at the park, with a scooter leaning against a nearby tree. After a few sessions, as long as your dog remained relaxed, you would engage him in play while a child stood nearby holding the scooter upright. The next step would be to continue play as the child walked the scooter around slowly. Gradual progress would continue over the course of as many sessions as necessary, and would consist of the child mounting the scooter, riding it slowly and eventually more quickly as your dog continued to play.

Global Motion Sensitivity

Global motion sensitivity often has a genetic component. If your dog seems to be fearful of just about anything that moves, or has a multitude of motion-related triggers, it would be a full-time job to pinpoint and work through each trigger individually. Because so many variables exist and dogs' responses are so individualized, it would be best to work with a professional who can analyze the situation, determine which techniques would best address your dog's particular issues, and determine whether medication would be useful during the process. In the meantime, get your dog on a Firm Foundation Program (see Part II) and read the upcoming section on complementary therapies. Good nutrition, adequate exercise, training, and strong leadership will go a long way toward making your dog feel more secure. And many of the complementary remedies and therapies can help him to feel calmer in general.

 # Tail End Wrap-Up

🐾 Determine whether your dog has a few specific motion triggers or is globally motion-sensitive.

🐾 If there is a specific trigger, use desensitization and counterconditioning to address the fear.

🐾 Alternately, encourage play in the vicinity of the feared object, gradually building to the object being in full motion as your dog plays happily nearby.

🐾 If your dog is globally motion-sensitive, employ the assistance of a professional, implement a Firm Foundation program, and read Part VI, *Complementary Therapies*.

37

Touch Sensitivity

Humans crave touch. From the time we are babies, we take pleasure in hugging and being hugged. Most of us continue to enjoy the closeness that hugging and physical contact provide throughout our adult lives. We sometimes even share touch with those we don't know intimately; when another needs comfort, we place a gentle hand on their shoulder. We may lightly touch the arm of another during conversation, even if we don't know the person well. Given our fondness for communicating and showing affection through physical contact, it can be hard for us to accept that dogs—affectionate, loving creatures in their own right—might not always appreciate our gestures.

C'mere, Let me Give you a Big Hug...

Part of the problem with hugging dogs stems from the fact that dogs and humans are separate species. Primates, which include humans and apes, enjoy the close chest-to-chest contact that hugging provides; we understand that it communicates affection, and take comfort from it. Canines, on the other hand, have no frame of reference for "hugging." If a dog is "hugging" another, the over-the-back "hug" is normally motivated by sexual drive or the desire to demonstrate dominance—it is certainly not a warm, affectionate hug in the way humans mean it. (For a fascinating book on the subject of body language and interspecies communication, see *The Other End of the Leash* by Patricia McConnell in *Resources*.)

A high percentage of dog bites each year involve children. One reason for that unfortunate statistic is that dogs perceive hugging as restraint, and restraint is frightening to them. Little girls, on the other hand, love to hug! But when a little girl attempts to hug her canine companion the way she would a favorite stuffed animal, bad things can happen. Veterinary technicians are another group at risk of being bitten, usually while restraining dogs for medical procedures. Although many dogs learn to tolerate hugging and some actually enjoy it, the majority of dogs are not the cuddly hug-bugs many of us wish they were.

Other Forms of Touch

Many dogs revel in being petted, patted, scratched, stroked, or massaged. My boy Mojo (whose aliases include, among other things, The Cuddlebug of Love) is instantly transported to pooch paradise by a mere tummy rub. Plenty of dogs enjoy a good scratch around the rump or behind the ears. But while the majority of dogs find physical contact pleasurable, there are those who fear it. Some dogs enjoy being petted but cannot tolerate being touched on certain body parts, such as the hindquarters or the top of the head. Others are fearful of physical contact in any form.

Why so Touchy about Touch?

There are a variety of reasons why a dog might be touch-sensitive. A dog who fears being handled in certain ways or on specific body parts might never have been exposed to that type of handling as a pup. Her owners might not have touched her paws, looked inside her mouth, handled her ears, or brushed her. A dog who cringes at being touched on a specific body part may be experiencing pain in that area, and might even snap or bite when touched there. *Any sudden onset of aggression or fear of being touched in a specific area should be addressed with a vet visit, as it could signify a medical problem.* Lastly, some dogs fear being touched because of having been physically abused. Those poor dogs have learned to associate touch with pain rather than pleasure.

Dogs who fear touch may display subtle stress signals such as lip-licking, yawning, or turning away when people try to pet them. Watch your dog the next time your child hugs her—your dog might not enjoy it as much as you thought. A dog who is extremely fearful of touch might tremble, drool, attempt to flee, or urinate or defecate when someone tries to pet or hug her. On the other side of the coin, a dog who fears touch might try to cut the interaction short by growling, snarling, air-snapping, or even biting.

A dog's fear of touch can make life difficult, not only for groomers and veterinarians, but for owners. In addition to feeling badly about the stress experienced by the dog, it can also be embarrassing to have to muzzle a dog for routine grooming or medical care. At home, it can be terribly dismaying to want to share physical affection with a dog who wants no part of it, especially if your vision of life with a dog included warm, affectionate cuddling sessions. But take heart. With love, patience, and the following exercises, you *can* help your dog. While she might never turn into a total hug-bug, she can learn to accept being handled when necessary, and might even come to enjoy physical contact.

Touch Protocol Considerations and Preparations

- If you have recently adopted your dog, allow at least three to four weeks for her to settle in and bond with you before attempting behavior modification exercises.

- If your dog has developed a sudden fear of being handled, or is particularly sensitive about being handled on a specific body part, rule out physical or medical causes first. Medical issues such as hypthyroidism can cause a dog to be touch-sensitive.

- A muzzle may be used if your dog is likely to bite, as long as you have taken the time to acclimate her to the muzzle first (see *Chapter 19*). If your dog's reaction is severe enough to require a muzzle, it would be best to carry out the protocol under the supervision of a professional behavior specialist.

- Choose a time of day when your dog is apt to be relaxed, such as her normal daily naptime (for many dogs this is late morning/midday).

- The person with whom your dog is most comfortable should work through the protocol first. The person with whom the dog is next most comfortable should go next, and so on. Whenever a new person begins, he should start at the beginning of the protocol. Regardless of who the dog is most comfortable with, adults should always go first and, once successful, supervise children through all steps. Very young children should not be involved at all in these exercises.

- If you want to talk to your dog during the exercises, keep it happy and light-hearted.

- Breathe normally and keep your muscles relaxed. It can be very helpful to take a few deep breaths before you begin. (The book and DVD *The Dog Whisperer: A Compassionate, Non-Violent Approach to Dog Training* by Paul Owens include instructions for relaxation breathing—see *Resources*.)

- Monitor your dog's body language. If she is uncomfortable at any point, go back to the step at which she was comfortable and build smaller steps from there.

- Don't expect to work through all the steps in one session. It is perfectly fine if you only get through Step 1 at the first session.

- A session might last thirty seconds or ten minutes, depending on your dog's comfort level. End each session on a good note, without pushing your dog too far too fast.

- Aim for two to three daily sessions.

- Whenever you begin a new session, rather than picking up where you left off, ease your dog into it by starting a few steps back.

- If there is a part of your dog's body that is most sensitive, begin touches at the opposite end of her body. For example, many touch-sensitive dogs do not like to be handled around the hindquarters. In that case, begin at the sides of the shoulders. (Do *not* begin on top of the head or over the back, or reach over your dog at any time; many dogs find approaches from above threatening.)

- If your dog reacts at any point by growling, barking, or air-snapping, you have pushed too far too fast. If you cannot easily modify your program so as not to elicit the behavior—or if your dog actually bites you—stop immediately and enlist the help of a professional.

Touch Protocol

Don't let the length of the following protocol throw you. In practice, it moves along fairly quickly. Along with gradually desensitizing your dog to touch, you will be using counterconditioning. In this case, you will help to create a positive association between being handled and the pleasurable sensation of eating treats. Take your time and let your dog's reactions dictate your progress. Be sure to read through the entire protocol before you begin.

1. Grab a bag of your dog's favorite treats and have a seat on the floor. Sit close enough to your dog so you will not have to extend your arm to touch her, as the reaching motion might frighten her. Your dog may sit, lie in a relaxed position, or rest comfortably on her side in front of you. Hold a treat so it is partially concealed in your hand. Slowly extend the hand toward your dog's mouth, hold it still, and allow your dog to nibble at the treat (see *Figure 1*). Do not release the treat; as your dog nibbles at it, slowly extend your other hand to touch her gently on a non-sensitive spot, such as the side of the shoulder (see *Figure 2*). This is the *treat-then-touch* method. Be sure to move your arm horizontally toward your dog, rather than coming down at her from above. The touch should be gentle yet firm, delivered with a flat palm. Don't stroke or pet—simply place your hand on your dog. Leave the hand there for one second as your dog nibbles at the treat, then remove the hand and release the treat from the other hand *at the same time*. If your dog grabs the treat from your hand, do not continue; simply start over. You will know you have kept your hand on your dog too long if she turns her head towards the hand that is touching her or attempts to nip at it.

    Do at least ten one-second touches, incorporating various body parts. For the moment, avoid touching those areas on which your dog is particularly sensitive. As long as your dog is comfortable with the touches, leave the contact hand on your dog for two seconds before simultaneously removing the hand and releasing the treat. Repeat two-second touches on various body parts, then increase to three seconds. Once you have built up to five-second touches, proceed to Step 2.

Figure 1   *Figure 2*

2. Still using the treat-then-touch method, touch the side of your dog's shoulder, but this time stroke instead of simply touching. So now the sequence is: offer the treat, stroke as your dog nibbles at it, then simultaneously stop touching and release the treat. The strokes should last approximately two seconds, and be gentle yet firm. Stroke various body parts using this method (one stroke per treat), continuing to avoid sensitive spots. Increase duration in one-second increments until your dog remains relaxed during five-second strokes.

Note: Some dogs find being stroked with the back of the hand less frightening than the front. It may help to start that way and then transition to using the front of your hand.

(If you have reached this point in one session, stop here so as not to overwhelm your dog. Begin the next session with Step 1 and work through Step 2 as well—you should be able to progress more quickly this time— then continue directly to Step 3 without pausing.)

After each session, take your dog for a walk or play a favorite game like fetch. Your dog will soon associate touch sessions with fun, and will develop a positive feeling about them.

---

3. Revert to one-second touches using the treat-then-touch method, this time touching mild-to-moderately sensitive spots (see *Figure 3*). For example, if your dog is somewhat sensitive about having her paws touched, do one-second touches that start at the chest and work gradually down each leg to the paw. Monitor your dog's body language carefully for signs of stress, and remember to breathe and stay relaxed yourself! Build by one-second

Figure 3

increments until you can do five-second touches on mild-to-moderately sensitive spots. If your dog reacts when you touch a particular area, avoid that spot for the moment and go back to touching where she was comfortable. Build more gradually toward the sensitive area over the course of several sessions.

4. Touch the same areas worked in Step 3, this time using strokes instead of touches. Begin with two-second strokes. Increase by one-second increments until you can stroke mild-to-moderately sensitive spots for five seconds.

(If your dog has remained relaxed during the preceding steps, continue. If she has become at all uncomfortable, stop here. Begin the next session at Step 2 and continue straight through to Step 5, as long as your dog remains relaxed.)

5. Repeat Steps 3 and 4, but now work toward the spots on which your dog is most sensitive (see *Figure 4*). Be extra vigilant about monitoring body language, and proceed more slowly than you did with other body parts. Even one or two touches at first is fine. (Again, if at any point your dog reacts by snapping, biting, or becoming extremely frightened, stop and consult a professional.)

Figure 4

(This is another good stopping point. At the next session, begin with Step 4 and continue through to Step 5 or, if possible, straight through to Step 6.)

6. Now it is time to switch things around a bit. Remain sitting close to your dog. Repeat steps 1-5, but this time touch first. So now the sequence is: touch (leave your hand on your dog), immediately offer a treat from the other hand (allow your dog to nibble at it but not take it), then simultaneously remove the touching hand and release the treat (see *Figures 5* and *6*). The original treat-then-touch has now progressed to *touch-first-then-treat*. To increase the time to two-second touches, you would leave your hand on your dog for two seconds, then feed the treat. Whenever you reach a sensitive spot, go back to the original treat-then-touch method for the first few touches, then switch to touch-first-then-treat. By the end of Step 4 you will have built up to touch-first-then-treat strokes for five seconds. Remember to use caution on Step 5 when touching the most sensitive body parts. If your dog suddenly turns her head toward your hand or moves away, she is not yet ready for this step.

         Figure 5   *Figure 6*

(If you have not taken a break, do so at this point. Pick up the next session with a few touches from Step 6 and proceed from there.)

7. Now it's time to add the element of reaching. Sit far enough from your dog so you must stretch your arm a bit to touch her. Repeat

Steps 1-6. At this point you should be able to progress fairly quickly, with fewer repetitions at each step.

8. Next, you'll add speed. Sit at the same distance from your dog as in Step 7. Do a few touches, beginning with the original treat-then-touch technique. Now begin to increase the speed at which the petting arm moves toward your dog: stretch the treat hand toward her at the normal speed, allow her to nibble the treat, then move your other arm rapidly toward her to touch. Release the treat and remove the petting hand at the same time. Do a few repetitions. As long as your dog is comfortable, switch to the touch-first-then-treat approach. Do a few repetitions. As long as she remains relaxed, work gradually toward more sensitive areas.

9. Now you will vary your angle of approach, because most people who pet your dog will be sitting on furniture or standing up, rather than sitting on the floor with her. Sit on a chair and do a few treat-then-touch pats and strokes, then change to touch-first-then-treat. Begin with less sensitive spots and work gradually toward more sensitive ones. Being approached from above can be frightening for dogs, so be vigilant about monitoring your dog's body language. Next, stand facing your dog. Do a few treat-then-touch pats and strokes, then touch-first-then-treat, beginning with less sensitive spots and working gradually toward more sensitive ones.

10. Begin to add distance in small increments until you are walking up from a few feet away to touch your dog.

Nice job! Your dog should now be looking forward to the types of touch you have practiced. Because your dog will need to tolerate other kinds of touches as well, take the time to address them using the same step-by-step process. Practice rougher petting, firmer patting, and scratching-type petting. Gradually introduce more invasive forms of touch such as gently pulling your dog's tail, grabbing her fur, and hugging. These latter types of touch are especially important for your dog to learn to tolerate if you have children. Once you are certain that your dog is completely comfortable with you touching her, it is time to teach her to accept the touch of others.

Hand-Over-Hand Touch Transfer

As previously stated, the family member or person with whom your dog is most comfortable should practice the touch protocol first, under your supervision. Once that person has completed the entire protocol with your dog remaining relaxed, the person with whom your dog is next most comfortable should begin. Work your way gradually toward those people with whom your dog is less comfortable.

If there is one family member your dog fears, it might be impossible for that person to get through even the first step of the protocol, even if other family members have completed it first. In that case, have that person try targeting (as explained in *Chapter 16*), since it allows the dog to touch an offered hand of her own volition, thereby giving her more control. Once your dog is comfortable targeting the person's hand, try the transference technique that follows.

Note: As a helpful adjunct, a person with whom the dog is comfortable could apply a body wrap to the dog (see *Chapter 46*) before the exercise begins. Your dog should be comfortable wearing the wrap before using it for this exercise (pair wearing it with chewing on a great stuffed chew toy for brief periods first). Assuming your dog has worn and is comfortable with bandanas, DAP can be sprayed on a bandana and placed around your dog's neck before the exercise begins. Just be sure to use wraps and bandanas at other times as well so they do not become associated only with being handled by the person your dog fears. (For more on DAP, see *Chapter 47*.)

Sit on the floor with your dog in front of you and the feared person to your side. You will use the same protocol as before, but this time the person's hand will rest on top of yours for the actual touches. Do a few warmup touches first with your hand alone (see *Figure 7*). Hold a treat in your hand, and extend that hand to allow your dog to nibble at the treat as before. As your dog chews, your other hand—now with other the person's over it—will touch your dog (see *Figures 8* and *9*). You will then release the treat and withdraw your hand, with the person's over it, at the same time.

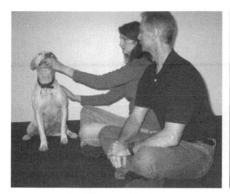

Figure 7

Figure 8

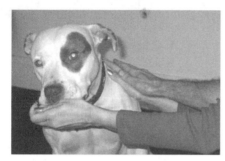

Figure 9

(detail of correct
hand position)

You might only be able to get through a step or two of the protocol in this manner at first. Take your time, and make sure the person is not leaning over your dog as you touch her together. Once you have worked through all the steps, it is time to switch—your hand will now rest on top of the other person's. You will continue to extend the hand with the treat, but when you pet the dog, the person's hand will be under yours so that it is actually touching the dog (see *Figure 10*). Be sure that you both remove your hands at the same time after petting! Work through the entire protocol in this manner.

Once you have gone through the protocol with your hand on top of the other person's, it is time to have that person do the petting solo. Remain seated and continue to offer the treat, but let the other person do all the actual touching on his/her own (see *Figure 11*). Once the person has completed the entire protocol with you, he/she can do the protocol alone, offering the treats as well as doing the touches. You will be able to move gradually farther and farther away from the person, until your dog is completely comfortable with the person doing the touches without you being present.

Figure 10

Figure 11

These exercises will help your dog to build a strong association between treats and being touched so that eventually, even without treats, she will regard being touched as pleasurable rather than frightening. Continue to have familiar people practice the exercise in different environments. So as to avoid setbacks, do not allow strangers to pet your dog.

Alternate Method: "Slide on By"

If your dog is extremely fearful of being touched, stick with the previous handling protocol. If her fear is only mild to moderate, you may begin with the Slide on By technique instead, and later incorporate steps from the original protocol to address especially sensitive areas. The Slide on By technique is effective because it puts the dog in control of whether to participate, allowing her to proceed as she feels comfortable.

Repeat each of the following steps a few times, proceeding to the next only when your dog is absolutely relaxed at the current one.

1. Sit on the ground with your dog standing in front of you. Hold a treat approximately six inches in front of her muzzle. Position your other hand right next to the treat hand, on the side closest to your dog, with palm facing up, fingers curved. To get the treat, your dog will have to place her chin in your empty hand (see *Figure 12*). Allow her to take the treat immediately. Do a few repetitions.

2. Repeat Step 1, but this time the non-treat hand, rather than being cupped, should be flat, open, and at a right angle to the ground. To get the treat, your dog will have to brush her face against your palm (see *Figure 13*). When her mouth reaches the treat, let her take it immediately. Do a few repetitions.

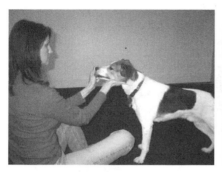 

Figure 12   *Figure 13*

3. Now, sitting facing your dog's side, move the hand with the treat a bit further from your dog, but leave the other hand where it is. This will cause your dog to have to brush more of her body against your hand in order to reach the treat (see *Figure 14*). Do a few repetitions.

4. Continue to move the hand with the treat further away, leaving the other hand in place, until your dog must brush her entire body against your hand to get the treat (see *Figure 15*). Do a few repetitions.

Figure 14   *Figure 15*

5. Keep your hands close together as in Step 1, but position the non-treat-holding hand so it is flat, palm facing the ground; hold the hand just above your dog's head level. Now your dog will have to rub the

top of her head against your hand in order to get to the treat (see *Figure 16*). Let her have the treat immediately. Do a few repetitions.

Figure 16

6.   Repeat Steps 3 and 4 with your hands in this position.

Once your dog is comfortable with the sequence, practice Steps 3-6, but now begin to pet your dog a bit as she brushes by. As long as she remains comfortable, gradually extend the time you spend petting before releasing the treat. Over time, your dog should become comfortable being petted on the areas of the body you have been working on, even without a treat.

Tail End Wrap-Up

- Be cautious about children and others hugging and touching your dog; monitor your dog's reactions.

- Notice whether your dog seems especially sensitive about being touched on certain areas of her body. Rule out medical causes.

- Work through the touch protocol, beginning with the person with whom your dog is most comfortable, then the person with whom she is next most comfortable, and so on.

- If necessary, work on transferring touch to the person your dog fears.

- Alternately, try the "Slide on By" method.

- Go slow! Fear of being touched can take time to overcome, and your dog might not ever become a hug-bug. Every dog is different. Your goal is simply to get your dog more comfortable with being touched, which will make affectionate displays more enjoyable for everyone.

Brushing and Nail Clipping

Just as some people enjoy being pampered—having their hair or nails done, or getting a soothing massage—some dogs enjoy being groomed. But while Princess Fifi might revel in the experience, to some dogs, being groomed is nothing short of a hair-raising experience.

Brushing, bathing, and nail clipping not only keep Fido looking fabulous, but they are necessary for keeping dogs healthy. A coat that is not brushed regularly can develop tangles and mats (clumps of densely compressed hair), which can be painful and cause skin infections. Nails that are allowed to grow so long that they begin to curve under can get caught in carpeting or fences, and can even get pulled out. If nails become overgrown to the extent that they curve around they may grow into the feet, causing pain and infection. You will know your dog's nails are too long if you hear them tapping on hard surfaces as he walks.

If your dog detests brushing or nail clipping, you could take the easy way out and have a vet or groomer perform the tasks, with the assistance of a muzzle if necessary. But why put your dog through the stress? Instead, teach your dog that brushing and nail clipping are nothing to fear. Then, even if you choose to have a professional handle the chores, your dog will be more comfortable with the experience.

> If your dog is afraid of being bathed: smear a light coat of peanut butter on the inside of the bathtub before you even run the water. Your dog will be happily absorbed in licking away at the gooey treat as you run the warm water and bathe him. Not only will you be giving your dog something to do as you wash him, but you will be helping to create a pleasant association with being bathed.

Brushing

If your dog is not comfortable with being petted or handled, go back to the previous chapter and work through those exercises first. Do not attempt to brush your dog until he is completely at ease with petting and touch. Make sure, too, that his aversion to touch is not due to a medical condition.

There are a variety of brushes made specifically for use on dogs. Some have natural bristles, while others have metal or rubber bristles. Slicker brushes, which consist of multiple rows of small, angled metal bristles, are a good choice for sensitive dogs. The sheer number of bristles, combined with the way they are angled and packed together, make for a softer touch than some other brush types. If your dog has an undercoat or a very thick coat, you might eventually need to use a stronger type of brush, such as an undercoat rake. For now, to get your dog accustomed to being brushed, choose a gentler type.

Another type of gentle brush is the rubber brush. Some of these resemble a rectangular sponge with thick rubber prongs on one side. The most popular, sold under the brand name Zoom Groom™ (available at pet supply stores), is designed to stimulate and remove stray hairs, rather than provide a thorough brushing. Another version resembles a thin, flat rubber oval with small rubber nubs and a strap to slide your hand through. If your dog is extremely sensitive you can use a rubber brush to introduce him to brushing, and then make the transition to a slicker or other brush.

slicker brush   *Zoom Groom*™

Touch the Brush

A handy trick to use with dogs who are fearful of being brushed is to teach them to target—to touch—the brush. (If you haven't already taught targeting, see *Chapter 16.*) Targeting puts the dog in charge, as opposed to something being done *to* the dog. That gives the dog a feeling of being in control, which lessens the fear.

First you will get your dog comfortable with the brush. Begin with your dog sitting or lying next to you. Have your dog touch your hand with his nose; reward him with a treat. Repeat a few times. Next, place the brush in your hand so it is almost completely concealed, with the handle pointing away from the dog (see *Figure 1*). Keeping your hand two inches or so below your dog's nose and slightly to the side, ask for a touch. Do a few repetitions, moving your hand to a slightly different position each time, always keeping it under your dog's nose level. Gradually expose the brush so that more of it is showing (see *Figure 2*), and your dog is touching the back of the brush with his nose. Keep the mood light and happy throughout, so your dog thinks this is a great game!

| Figure 1 | Figure 2 |

Next, it's time to get your dog comfortable with the feel of the brush. If there is an area where your dog is especially sensitive, begin at the opposite end of his body. For example, if your dog is fearful of having his hindquarters brushed, begin at his chest. Stroke him on the chest a few times with your hands to get him relaxed. Then hold the brush *with the bristles facing your palm.* With your palm facing your dog, stroke him so that the back of the brush is touching his fur. The touch should be gentle yet firm. Treat. Repeat a few times, treating after each stroke.

If your dog runs at the mere sight of the brush, any type of brush-to-fur contact would be too frightening. Instead, leave the brush near your dog's food dish for a week. Pairing its presence with food will help to create a more positive feeling about the brush. Then, when you begin the protocol, start by picking the brush up at a distance from your dog, tossing a treat from the other hand, then putting the brush down. Work gradually toward bringing the brush closer, holding it for longer periods, and eventually touching it to your dog's fur, always treating after each action.

Monitor your dog for signs of stress, and keep the mood light. As long as your dog remains relaxed, continue to hold the brush in the same manner but progress gradually to longer strokes on other non-sensitive parts of his body. Treat after each stroke. Then turn the brush over so the bristled side is facing your dog's fur. Do one stroke, brushing the fur lightly, then treat. If you find it too unwieldy to handle both the brush and the treats, spread a thin layer of peanut butter on a plate and allow your dog to lick it as you brush. Remember to breathe and stay relaxed! Keep the mood light, but continue to watch your dog for signs of stress. Keep sessions brief. Your dog will eventually become comfortable with longer sessions and firmer pressure, and might eventually come to enjoy being brushed.

Manicure, Please!

Nail clipping is probably the task that dog owners dread most. I can relate. When Mojo was just a pup (I would love to have said "a wee pup," but Mojo was never "wee"), I tried to clip his nails—and succeeded in making him bleed all over the kitchen floor. All it took was one cut into the "quick," the blood supply that runs down the middle of the nail. While it was an honest mistake (and a common one at that), I still felt terrible. And naturally, Mojo developed a fear of those mean, scary nail clippers. I did not attempt to cut his nails again for years, letting vets and groomers handle the chore instead. Then one day I woke up and thought, *This is ridiculous! I should be doing this!* And I did. I can't say that Mojo now adores having his nails trimmed, but he does remain still and tolerate it. I will share what I did with him—but first, some important information.

In white nails, the quick is visible; it appears as a vertical pink line down the center of the nail, which makes it easier to avoid cutting into. In black nails, because the quick is not visible from the outside, the tip of the nail must be checked after each tiny clip. (Look directly down into the nail from the tip.) When you see the quick, which resembles a tiny dot, stop trimming! Cutting into the quick causes profuse bleeding and is painful for the dog—it would be like cutting into your nail close enough to the finger to cause bleeding. The good news is that the more often you cut your dog's nails (once a week is recommended), the more the quick will recede, making it easier to avoid in subsequent sessions.

There are two common types of nail clippers. The guillotine style resembles—well, a guillotine. The dog's nail is placed into a slot and then, as the clippers are squeezed, a blade comes down and cuts it. Many professional groomers and veterinarians prefer this style. The second type resembles a small pair of scissors. The nice thing about the scissors type is that many have a safety plate, a flat oval of metal that lies behind the two cutting blades. The dog's nail is placed at a right angle so the tip rests against the safety plate; when the handle is squeezed, the blades come together to cut the nail. The safety plate ensures that only a tiny bit of the nail is trimmed at a time, which is especially helpful for dark nails.

scissors-style  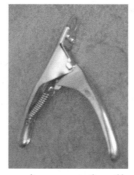 *guillotine-style*

Since the blade is not replaceable, scissors-style clippers should be replaced yearly—the sharper the blade, the less the nail will be pinched and the cleaner the cut will be. I use and recommend scissors-style clippers, especially if you are at all nervous about cutting your dog's nails. (And what owner of a nail-trim-phobic dog isn't?) The other essential piece of equipment to have on hand is styptic powder (sold at pet supply stores), in case you do cut into the quick. Pressing a bit of the powder on the nail tip will stop the bleeding immediately.

Preparation

If your dog fears the clippers but is comfortable with having his paws handled, ask him to sit and shake (give his paw) in order to clip his nails. (We'll get to the back paws in a bit.) As always, putting the power in your dog's paws rather than doing something *to* him will lessen his fear.

Teaching "Shake" is Easy!

With your dog in a sitting position, say, "Shake." Lift one of his front legs by grasping it gently just above the paw. Quickly offer a treat from the other hand, then allow the paw to return to normal position. With repetition, when you give the verbal cue and put your hand out palm-up, your dog will offer his paw.

Practice shake in a fun atmosphere that has nothing to do with nail clipping for at least a week before (and after) you apply it to clipping nails, so it does not become associated only with having nails clipped. Just as with the brush, you may leave the clippers near your dog's food dish for a week so a good association is created before any actual clipping occurs.

If your dog fears the clippers and is *not* comfortable with his paws being handled, desensitization is in order before attempting any actual clipping. First, with your dog sitting or lying down, touch his knee; treat. Do a few repetitions, then touch his leg a bit further down; treat. After a few repetitions, touch the paw; treat. Work as you have with the other desensitization and counterconditioning programs, doing very brief touches and moving incrementally at a pace your dog will accept, treating after each touch. Work toward touching one of your dog's front paws, holding it gently in your hand for a second, giving a treat, then releasing the paw. Be sure to hold the paw close to your dog's body, rather than pulling it outward. Begin to hold the paw for slightly longer periods, giving a treat as the paw is being held, then releasing the paw. Work toward holding the paw more firmly, but *don't squeeze!* A common reason some dogs fear having nails trimmed is because the person holding the paw in position is squeezing it too hard. Manipulate the variables so that when one becomes more difficult—touching the paw more firmly, for example—another becomes easier (for example, holding the paw for less time). Work up to being able to hold each of your dog's front paws individually for ten seconds with a gentle but firm grip.

It will be easiest to trim the back toenails with your dog lying on his side. Do not attempt to clip nails until your dog is comfortable with having his back paws touched in this position. If he knows settle, ask him to do so. If not, once your dog is lying down, gently ease him onto his side. Relax him with soothing words and gentle strokes. If necessary, proceed as you did with the front paws until he is relaxed with your holding each back paw firmly for ten seconds. Whether it is the front or back paws that you are desensitizing to touch, do a few sessions so that your dog is completely comfortable before you attempt any nail clipping.

Trim Time!

Place treats within reach. With your dog sitting, hold a front paw in one hand (ask him to shake if he knows how). (For an alternate position, see the photo on *p. 376*.) Touch the clippers to the nail for one second, then release the paw. Treat. Do a few repetitions, always monitoring your dog's comfort level and never pushing past it. Next, hold your dog's paw with one hand and, with the other, open and close the clippers directly in front of the nail without actually touching it. Treat. Doing this will help your dog to get used to the sound of the clippers. Repeat five to ten times, and end the session there. Do the same thing at separate sessions for the back paws, with your dog lying on his side.

Now it's time to clip a nail. Take a deep breath and relax! If you are nervous, sing a happy tune. (The Beatles' "I Wanna Hold Your Hand" comes to mind.) Warm your dog up by doing a few repetitions of the touch-treat and open-close-but-don't-clip exercises. Then, without pausing, hold your dog's paw firmly but not too tightly. Clip one nail and treat, then immediately do a few touches and treats without actually clipping any other nails. End the session. Begin the next session (later that day or the next) by warming your dog up, then clipping a nail. At each session, do touch-treats without actual clipping before and after each clip.

Over time, by interspersing actual clipping with practice touches, you will be able to build up gradually to cutting all of your dog's nails at one session. I cannot stress strongly enough the importance of proceeding slowly. Ignore people who advise you to restrain your dog and "just get it over with!" Each time your dog has a frightening experience, it will make follow-up attempts more difficult and stressful for both of you. What's the harm if it initially takes two to three weeks of daily sessions to get all of your dog's nails clipped? In the future it will take less and less time, until your dog no longer objects to a timely trim.

Clipping Tricks

1. Now I will share what worked with Mojo. Mojo is extremely food-motivated, and knew "Leave it" (meaning "That thing you were about to touch? Don't even *think* about it!"). So I combined the two. I placed a treat on a countertop, just out of his reach but where it was still visible. I told him to leave it. After a few seconds, I let him have the treat. We did a few repetitions, then I made my move. I placed another treat on the counter and told him to leave it. While he was focused intently on the treat, saliva dripping onto the kitchen floor, I picked up a front paw and clipped a nail, then released the paw and gave him the treat. Mojo was so focused on the treat that he barely noticed I had clipped the nail. I did a few more repetitions without touching his paws, and ended the session. At subsequent sessions, I was able to clip more nails (back paws were done while he was standing as well), always interspersing non-clipping "leave its" between actual clips. Of course, this technique will only work if your dog's fear of having his nails clipped is overridden by his desire for treats. (For instructions on how to teach "Leave it," see *Chapter 9.*)

2. British behaviorist John Rogerson gets credit for this next trick. You will need a wooden matchstick, nail clippers, and treats. Hold your dog's paw with the matchstick beneath the paw, the match head protruding forward. Hold the clippers in the other hand. Clip the end of the matchstick, then give your dog a treat. The sound made by clipping the wooden matchstick closely simulates the sound made by cutting an actual nail. Doing this close to the paw approximates the experience of having the nails cut (sans pressure on the nail), making it a useful way to ease dogs into the process. Practice in short, frequent sessions.

3. Targeting the clippers is another useful precursor to actual clipping. Have your dog target the nail clippers as described in the brush section. I have used targeting with many clients' dogs who were fearful of the clippers, yet none seemed to mind nose-targeting them. You could also have your dog touch the clippers with his paw. (To teach this type of targeting, see *Right on Target* in *Resources*.)

4. See *Chapter 48* for information on the Calming Cap™, which eases anxiety in specific situations by limiting the dog's visual input.

5. Some modern dog owners dispense with clippers altogether and use a mini-dremel tool to grind their dogs' nails. Grinding nails with a motorized, rotating head covered in fine sandpaper results in smooth nail edges and less chance of quicking the dog (cutting into the quick). And some dogs find the dremel much less frightening than clippers. Specific instructions *must* be followed as to equipment and technique, as friction can cause burns if the tool is not used properly. (For links to web sites with explicit instructions, see *Resources*.)

Whether addressing brushing or nail clipping, whichever method you use, proceed slowly and be patient. Your reward will be a well-groomed dog who doesn't mind a little pooch pampering now and then.

 # Tail End Wrap-Up

- Choose the right brush. Slicker brushes are a good choice for sensitive dogs, and rubber-pronged brushes can ease your dog into the process.

- Get your dog comfortable with the presence of the brush by asking him to target it, or by using desensitization and counterconditioning.

- If your dog is sensitive in certain areas, begin brushing at the opposite end of his body.

- Get your dog comfortable with the feel of the brush in a gradual manner. Do brief sessions at first, then build gradually to longer ones.

- Use scissors-style clippers and have styptic powder on hand.

- If your dog is afraid of having his paws handled, desensitization to paw handling must be done before attempting to clip nails.

- Hold your dog's paw firmly, close to his body, without squeezing.

- Intersperse other touches with treats between actual clips.

- Take your time. Aim to trim one nail at the first session, and build from there.

- Try the "Clipping Tricks."

39

Fear of Objects

The first time I walked Soko into the veterinarian's office, she froze. She stood there staring, head lowered, fur standing on end from shoulders to tail. Following her gaze, I realized it was fixed upon a pair of statues that stood against the wall on either side of an exam room. The tall, slender, black statues were fashioned after Bast, the Egyptian cat goddess. Perhaps the notion of cats as deity was too much for poor Soko. More likely, the statues just seemed *odd* to her somehow, perhaps because they resembled animals, but they sure weren't acting like them!

In Soko's case, a combination of my acting nonchalant and allowing her to decide that the cats were not going to spring to life and turn her into a Chihuahua worked well. But for some dogs, novel objects in the environment cause a fear response that does not resolve so quickly. A dog's fear of certain objects can frustrate owners, especially when the objects are in the home. Some dogs react only to large, odd-looking, unfamiliar objects (such as a Christmas tree), while others seem to be uncomfortable with just about anything new that is brought in—a piece of furniture, a statue, or even a dog crate.

Some objects are feared not because they are unfamiliar, but because the dog has formed an unpleasant association with them. For example, many dogs fear nail clippers. Of course, the clippers themselves are not scary until a dog has had an unpleasant experience with nail clipping. If a dog has been jerked roughly on a metal training collar, the collar itself can become a source of fear.

Sound can play a part in a dog's fear of an object. If a dog becomes frightened by a door slamming at close range, she might be unwilling to approach that door in the future. Some dogs fear vacuum cleaners to the point that they are not willing to be in the same room with the appliance—after all, who knows when it might start that scary growling?

If multiple components (sound, touch, and/or movement) are involved, each must be treated separately and then the fear must be addressed as a whole. For example, a dog who fears the vacuum cleaner could be desensitized to the sound first (see *Chapter 35*) and then the movement; eventually the two would be combined. Remember the rules about raising and lowering criteria. When you finally combined the components (moving the vacuum cleaner while it was running), you would make it easier for your dog at first by increasing her distance from the vacuum.

> Never drag your dog up to an object or move an object toward her to "show her it's okay." Your dog obviously feels the object is *not* okay, so let her accept it in her own time.

Regardless of what object your dog fears, it is possible that she will habituate to its presence over time. If that does not happen, try one of the following techniques.

Trail O' Treats

One of the easiest ways to get a food-motivated dog to brave approaching a new object is to lay out a trail of treats leading up to it. Gather a variety of tasty treats. Include some special ones that your dog does not get on a regular basis, such as cheese or hot dog pieces. Start the trail a few feet back from the feared object—the bigger the fear, the farther away you should start. Space treats approximately three to six inches apart, leading right up to the object. Increase the value and quantity of the treats as you get closer to the object. Place the last bunch of super-yummy treats directly on the object. (To stack the odds even further in your favor, have your dog skip the meal that precedes this exercise.)

Do not try to coax your dog toward the object. In fact, if you tend to get anxious when your dog is nervous, it would be best if you left the room altogether, as your coaching could unintentionally make your dog more afraid. Give your dog some time to work it out. Most dogs will readily snatch the first few treats, then hesitate as they get closer to the object. Some will show approach-avoidance behavior, moving tentatively toward the object and then darting back. If your dog snatches a treat and then runs, that's fine; she is not yet convinced that the scary thing won't suddenly grab her when she gets close enough!

If your dog does not take all the treats on the first try, don't worry. Assuming they won't spoil, leave them out for the rest of the day. Then put them away and try again the next day, using another type of treat that your dog might find even more tempting. As long as your dog is making progress, keep laying out the trail of treats each day until she is comfortable with the object. Not only will your dog become assured that the object won't bite, but by having treats on and around the object, a positive association is being created.

If the object is one that will be moved from room to room (such as a fan), once your dog is comfortable with the object in one room, practice the Trail O' Treats with the object in different rooms and in various positions.

> Many dogs are afraid of cameras and video cameras—to a dog, that one-eyed monster staring directly at them can be pretty frightening! A standard desensitization and counterconditioning program, beginning with picking the camera up an inch off the floor and ending with it held to the person's face, can help. Be aware too that some dogs fear the beeping and other sounds made by these devices, so you might have to implement a separate protocol to address the sounds.

Just a Touch

If your dog knows how to target—to touch her nose to something at the verbal cue, "Touch"—you can use the skill to help her overcome her fear of a specific object. (If you have not yet taught the skill, see *Chapter 16*.)

For large, heavy, or stationary objects (such as vehicles, refrigerators):

Stand with your dog at a comfortable distance from the object. Hold a self-stick note paper (a Post-it® type note) or plastic lid (place double-stick tape on one side) in one hand as a target. The other hand should be behind your back, holding treats. Present the target hand and ask your dog to touch the target. As her nose touches it, say, "Yes!" and treat. Withdraw the hand, then present it again for the next repetition. With each repetition, move a bit closer to the feared object.

Once you are standing right next to the object, move your target hand closer and closer to the object with each repetition, so that the hand with the target in it is eventually resting on the object. Do five rapid repetitions (always saying, "Yes!" at the moment your dog's nose touches the target and then treating), withdrawing the target hand after each repetition. After the fifth repetition, without pausing, stick the target to the object, remove your hand (move it behind your back), and ask your dog to touch. Because she has just repeated the motion five times, chances are good that she will touch the target. If she does, say, "Yes!" and treat. If she hesitates, or looks at you as if to say, "You want me to do *what*?" just wait. Stare at the target and don't say a word. Many dogs will, given time, figure it out. If your dog does not touch the target after 30 seconds, go back to the previous step, do a few successful repetitions, then end the session. Pick up the next session where you left off and try again.

Once your dog is touching the target on the object, do a few repetitions, then without pausing, use the object's name as a cue instead of "Touch" (for example, "Fan"). Because your dog is now conditioned to touching the object when a word is uttered, she should respond to the new cue by touching the object. With each subsequent repetition, remove a small piece of the target (tear the paper or cut off a piece of the lid) until it is gone completely and your dog is touching the actual object on your verbal cue. By adding new verbal cues, you can teach your dog to touch various objects by name. You can even teach her to seek the objects out in order touch them—very handy if you are prone to misplacing your house keys!

Another trick to try: Get another dog to play or interact with the feared object in the presence of your dog. Your dog will see that it's not such a scary thing after all.

For small, hand-held objects (such as television remotes, cell phones):

The "large objects" approach may be used for small objects as well. Alternately, have your dog do a few touches to the back of your empty hand in the normal fashion. Then hold the object in your hand so it is mostly concealed. Ask for a few touches to the back of your hand. As you continue, with each repetition move the object so that more and more of it is revealed. Your dog will eventually be touching the object itself. After a few repetitions, change the verbal cue to the name of the object.

 Tail End Wrap-Up

- Consider whether the feared object has a component of sound or movement; if so, desensitize your dog to each separately, and then combine them.

- Never force your dog to confront an object she fears.

- Let your dog follow the Trail O' Treats!

- For large objects, teach your dog to target the object.

- For small objects, have your dog touch your hand with the object concealed in it. Gradually reveal more of the object.

40

Fear of the Leash

The jingle of a leash is cause for butt-wiggling, tail-wagging joy in Dogville. After all, that jingle is an invitation to experience that scintillating smorgasbord of scents and sights—a walk! But to some dogs, even the prospect of a fabulous outdoor funfest is not enough to override the fear of being leashed.

Why would a dog fear a leash any more than, say, a tug toy or a sock? Surely dogs do not have an inborn fear of long nylon strips with metal clips! For some, fear of the leash is a matter of experience. Maybe the dog received harsh leash corrections while wearing a choke chain or other equipment that caused pain. Or perhaps the dog had a frightening experience while on leash such as being traumatized by another dog, and associated the experience with the leash.

Fear of the leash is often due to a simple lack of previous exposure. Some dogs almost never go anywhere on leash because their owners feel that the back yard offers adequate exercise, or because no one has the time or inclination to walk them. Some dogs are leashed to leave the premises only when absolutely necessary, which usually means a trip to the vet or groomer—not fun associations for most dogs. The owner of a leash-phobic dog is likely to have to chase and even manhandle the dog to get the leash attached. Of course, that makes the process even less appealing to the dog the next time around.

It is easy to understand how being tugged by something around the neck can be frightening. Strangely enough, the result of attempting to pull a dog along is at odds with the goal. Dogs have an "opposition reflex," meaning that if they are pulled in one direction, their instinct is to pull in the opposite direction. (If pushed, they will push against the force. This instinct helps to maintain equilibrium.) This reflex is why, when an owner attempts to put a leash on a young pup and pull him along, the pup digs in and "puts on the brakes." A leash is not meant to pull a dog. In fact, when a dog is walking correctly, the leash should be slack, resembling the letter "J." (See *Resources* for obedience training guides.)

Afraid of the Great Outdoors? If your dog "shuts down" and will not walk outdoors on a leash, it may be the outdoor environment that your dog fears, rather than the leash itself. If that is the case and your dog is small enough, carry him outdoors with the leash attached and place him on the ground, ten feet or so from your house. Then encourage him, using a high-pitched, happy voice, to walk with you back to the house. Keep the leash slack—there should be no tension whatsoever. If necessary, use treats to coax your dog along. Gradually start a bit further from the house each time as he grows more comfortable with exploring the great outdoors.

Equipment

In the best of all worlds, leashes would not be necessary; dogs would be perfectly obedient and want to remain near their owners at all times. But even if that were so, due to safety concerns and leash laws, it would still be necessary for your dog to accept being leashed. Before we discuss how to accomplish that goal, a few words about equipment. In order for your dog to wear a leash, he must be wearing a collar. Be sure the collar's D-ring—the metal ring the leash attaches to—is large enough so that you won't have to fumble to get the leash clip attached. As to the leash itself, a four- to six-foot, lightweight nylon or cotton leash is best for our purposes. (Do *not* use a chain leash or other heavyweight leash.) Even if you already have a lightweight leash, if your dog has a negative association with it, start fresh by purchasing a new one.

There are two basic types of leash clips: The key chain-style is easy to snap on and remove with a minimum of fuss. The scissors clip is not as fast or easy to attach and detach. If you don't already have one, take the time to purchase a lightweight leash with a light, key chain-style clip before beginning the protocol.

scissors-style  *key chain-style*

Walk with Me

The easiest way to introduce any dog to a leash is to teach him to walk beside you off-leash first. For a fearful dog, providing a task to concentrate on as he walks along will help him to stay focused once the leash is attached, rather than slipping into an emotional, fearful state. To that end, you will use the "touch" skill. (If your dog does not yet know the skill, turn to *Chapter 16* and teach it before proceeding.)

Practice in a safe, enclosed area such as a back yard or large room. Refer to the instructions in *Chapter 16* for walking with your dog by your side, doing touches as you go. Practice walking in a large circle toward the left, with your dog on your left side. (If you prefer that your dog be on your right for walks, reverse the directions.)

If your dog is very short, you can use a long-handled wooden spoon with a bit of peanut butter on it to reward him. First, get your dog accustomed to the spoon by allowing him to lick some peanut butter from it. Then hold the spoon at waist level as you walk along with your dog; reward him for touches by swinging the coated end of the spoon down toward his mouth. Allow him one lick, then swing the spoon back up to waist level. With practice you will be able to reward your dog and continue to walk along without pausing.

Once your dog has the idea, vary your movements so that you are walking unpredictably: turn to the left, take a few steps, then turn to the right, asking for touches as you go. Your dog will have to be vigilant and focused in order to keep up with you. After you have done a few sessions in this manner, it's time to add the leash.

If you have a helper available, have the person feed treats as you clip the leash to your dog's collar. It is crucial that you do not restrain your dog or act nervous in any way; try to attach the leash to the metal ring without even touching the collar itself if possible. Breathe, and keep the mood light. If you're nervous, sing a silly song to relax. If you don't have a helper, hold a large treat in your left hand. Allow your dog to nibble at the treat (don't release it) while your right hand gently clips the leash to the ring. (If you are left-handed, reverse the directions.) This is one more reason to use a key chain-style clip; this maneuver would be very difficult with a scissors clip. With the leash attached, place the loop over four fingers of your right hand so that it crosses your palm. Hold all the treats in your right hand as well. With your dog to your left, the leash should cross in front of your body (see photos *p.124*). Now, *keeping the leash slack*, practice walking as you did in the off-leash exercise. Keep paying your dog for being in the proper position, and don't forget the verbal encouragement! Practice in your enclosed space first and then take it on the road. Very soon you and your dog will forget that the leash was ever an issue.

Meet the Leash

If your dog is so frightened by the very sight of the leash that the previous method will not work, use the following leash introduction protocol instead. Work through the steps at a rate at which your dog is comfortable, and keep your physical movements slow and deliberate. Watch for signs of stress and adjust your approach accordingly, going back a step or two if necessary. As always, the goal is slow and steady progress. Repeat each step as many times as necessary to ensure that your dog is comfortable. It is also important that once the leash is attached, there is absolutely no tension on it. Keep the leash loose and remain relaxed—remember to breathe! Read through the entire protocol before you begin.

Liftoff

1. Sit on the floor with your dog in front of you and the leash to your side. Have treats handy. It is best if your dog is sitting, although standing is also acceptable. Lift the leash an inch off the ground where your dog can see it, feed a treat from the other hand, then put the leash down. (Treats should always be fed from the hand that is not picking up the leash.) Repeat five times.
   Note: If your dog runs off at the mere sight of your lifting the leash an inch off the ground, try this instead: using the hand closest to your dog, bring a treat to his mouth. Allow him to nibble at it but not grab it out of your hand. As he nibbles, lift the leash slightly off the ground, put it back down, then release the treat. If necessary, substitute this treat-first method throughout the protocol until your dog becomes more comfortable.
2. Lift the leash three inches off the ground, feed a treat, then put the leash down. Repeat five times.
3. Lift the leash three inches off the ground and hold for a count of three. Feed a treat, then put the leash down. Repeat five times.
4. Lift the leash to the level of your dog's chest-to-neck area, but do not move it toward him. Feed a treat, then put the leash down. Repeat, holding the leash up for two seconds before treating and putting it down. Build to holding the leash up for five seconds before treating.

Approach

5. Lift the leash to your dog's chest-to-neck level and move it two inches toward him. Hold for one second. Feed a treat, then put the leash down. Repeat five times.
6. Lift the leash to your dog's chest-to-neck level and move it four inches toward him. Hold for one second. Feed a treat, then put the leash down. (If your dog looks uncomfortable, you are moving too fast. If necessary, add intermediary steps, such as moving the leash only three inches toward him.) Repeat five times.

(If your dog has shown any hesitation or discomfort, end the session here and resume the next one at a comfortable step. If your dog has remained relaxed throughout Steps 1-6, continue on.)

Contact!

7. Using the hand closest to your dog, hold a treat to his mouth. Allow him to nibble at it but not grab it from your hand. As he chews, pick up the leash, touch it lightly to his collar for one second, then release the treat and put the leash down. Repeat five times. *Do not attempt to attach the leash just yet.* Move on to the next step only when your dog is comfortable with the current one.
8. Now reverse the order. Touch the leash to your dog's collar lightly for one second, feed a treat, then put the leash down. Repeat five times.
9. Hold a treat to your dog's mouth. As he nibbles at it, touch the leash to his collar. Open and shut the clip, without actually attaching the leash. Then release the treat and put the leash down. Repeat five times.
10. This time, touch the leash to your dog's collar, open and shut the clip without attaching it, *then* feed a treat. Put the leash down. Repeat five times.
11. Now you're ready to attach the leash. Because you may need both hands, treating first will no longer be possible. As gently as possible, using small, slow motions (be relaxed; breathe!), attach the leash. (If you can, attach it using only the hand you have been using.) Feed a treat, then immediately detach the leash. Repeat five times.
12. Attach the leash, feed a treat, wait two seconds, feed another treat, then detach the leash. Repeat five times.
13. Attach the leash, feed a treat, wait three seconds (using soothing praise during this waiting period can be helpful), feed a treat, wait another three seconds, feed another treat, then detach the leash. Repeat five times.
14. Stand up. Bend forward and touch the leash to your dog's collar, without attaching it. Feed a treat, then move the leash away. Repeat five times.
15. Remain standing. Touch the leash to your dog's collar. Open and shut the clip without attaching the leash. Feed a treat, then move the leash away. Repeat five times.
16. Attach the leash for one second. Feed a treat, then immediately detach the leash. Repeat five times.
17. Remain standing. Repeat Steps 12 and 13.

Let's Go Exploring

18. Stand facing your dog and attach the leash. Hold the leash in your right hand. Feed a treat with your left. Show your dog that you have another treat, and take one small step backward. Hold the treat out and encourage him, using cheerful chatter, to walk toward you. *Be sure to keep the leash slack.* After you have taken a few small steps with your dog following you, let him have the treat.
19. Continue to walk backward, luring your dog along, treating after every couple of steps. Aim for continuous movement.
20. Take a step or two backward as you have been, then in one smooth motion, turn to the right and walk forward. (This puts your dog on the left.) Be sure the leash remains slack. Don't forget the verbal encouragement! Treat after every few steps.

Practice in the house, then take treats with you and practice outdoors. Once you move outdoors, chances are your dog will be so distracted by things in the environment that he will practically forget about the leash. Just remember to keep the leash slack. Don't worry about whether your dog is walking nicely next to you; there will be plenty of time for that. For now, your goal is to get your dog comfortable walking on leash so you can provide exercise and have fun outings together. During walks you can also ask for sits, downs, touches, and whatever other behaviors your dog knows. Keep the leash slack throughout and reward each success.

Do short on-leash sessions at first, then gradually longer ones as your dog becomes more relaxed. In no time at all, your dog will be running to you whenever he hears that familiar jingle.

 Tail End Wrap-Up

🐾 Choose the proper equipment.

🐾 Unless your dog's fear of the leash is severe, try the "Walk with Me" method first.

🐾 If necessary, use the "Meet the Leash" protocol instead.

🐾 Always keep the leash slack.

🐾 Practice in the house first and then outdoors.

Separation Distress

Greta Garbo: "I want to be alone."
Fido: "Please don't leave me alone!"

When I was a child growing up in New York City, my mother would take me shopping at a popular department store called Alexander's. Our trips were always a special treat. (Thanks to the in-store restaurant, the Apple Tree, these outings were also the origin of my unnaturally high regard for macaroni and cheese.) As my mother flitted happily from one sales rack to the next, I would tag along, anticipating our lunch break. Every now and then, my mother would get so engrossed in shopping that she would forget to check that I was still beside her. Although I never ended up as the subject of an embarrassing loudspeaker announcement— "We have a lost child at the manager's office"—I did often end up separated from my mother for minutes at a time. I will never forget the rising panic I felt as I frantically searched one aisle after another for her familiar silhouette. Perhaps it is due to those early experiences that I so empathize with the panic some dogs feel at being left alone.

What is Separation Distress?

Separation distress refers to a condition whereby a dog who is left alone, or separated from a particular person or persons, becomes distressed. A dog who has separation issues might pace, whine, tremble, bark, howl, drool, urinate, defecate, or chew or destroy things. The behavior might begin as the owner is walking out the door, or even sooner, during the chain of activities that signals departure such as hair drying, dressing, or picking up a purse or briefcase. While a typical dog might be distressed at an owner's exit for a few minutes, for dogs with true "separation anxiety," an extreme form of separation distress, it may be unrelenting as long as the person is gone. Neighbors may complain that the dog barks or howls non-stop. Dogs who are very anxious when left alone may not eat in the owner's absence even if the filet mignon of dog treats is available, as the physiological changes that accompany anxiety suppress appetite. In severe cases, dogs have been known to claw themselves bloody by scraping at doorways and windows (the owner's exit point or the point from which he/she was last seen), or jump through screens or plate glass windows in an attempt to find their humans. Some dogs with severe separation anxiety, if left crated, will mutilate themselves. Because separation issues range from mild worry to clinical-level separation anxiety, we will differentiate by referring to the most common, mild-to-moderate issues as "separation distress."

Possible Causes

Although a dog with separation distress might be easy to spot, the cause is not. In fact, the issue might have originated with the pup's earliest experiences. Anecdotal evidence points toward pups who were weaned too early or separated from their littermates too soon as being likely to develop separation issues. However, because not all pups in those circumstances will develop the issues, the possibility of genetic predisposition to insecurity may play a part as well.

Some dogs who are adopted from shelters or rescue groups have abandonment issues, and understandably so; most have, for one reason or another, lost their human families. It is easy to see how a dog who had been abandoned once might perceive being left alone as a signal that she is being abandoned all over again. The result is often a "velcro dog" who will follow the owner from room to room, acting as though if the owner disappeared from sight, he might disappear forever. It is important to note that separation issues are certainly not limited to dogs adopted from shelters or rescue groups, and that many adopted dogs are confident and well adjusted.

Even a dog who has been in the same home since early puppyhood can develop separation issues. Sometimes these issues are not genetic, but owner-created. Excited owners usually bring their new fur-kid home during a vacation period or long weekend so the family can spend quality time with her. And spend quality time they do—the kids play with the pup, neighbors come and go, and everyone coos and fusses over the new, adorable bundle of fur. It's puppy nirvana! But all too soon, the owners return to work and the kids to school—and the pup is suddenly left all alone. It's easy to see how a separation issue can develop. Starting a pup or newly adopted dog off on the right paw is important in preventing separation distress. The dog should be left alone for very brief periods, working up to longer ones, so she has a chance to become accustomed to separations gradually and learn that she is not being abandoned.

Sometimes, even a dog who has been introduced into family life in the proper manner and is genetically stable develops a separation issue due to a traumatic incident. Perhaps the dog was home alone when a construction worker used a jackhammer just outside the house, a car accident occurred in front of the home, or the ear-piercing burglar alarm sounded. Any frightening experience that occurs when a dog is home alone could lead the dog to associate the event with being left alone, and consequently to develop separation issues.

Separation Distress versus Sock Party

I once had a client who informed me that his ten-month-old beagle, Fred, had separation anxiety. The vet had agreed and put the dog on medication. Upon careful questioning, my client revealed that the diagnosis had been reached solely on the basis of Fred having chewed a shoe. *One shoe—* and a lowly slipper at that! While shoe chewing is no cause for celebration, it is also no reason to jump to a diagnosis of separation anxiety. Many pups and adolescent dogs (and even some adults) chew shoes, socks, and just about anything else they can get their paws on. *Mom and Dad are gone! Woohoo! Sock party!*

Do not jump to the conclusion that a dog who misbehaves when left alone has separation issues. Digging up the yard or having housebreaking accidents when left home alone do not necessarily indicate separation distress. Dogs who are left outdoors will find activities to relieve the boredom, such as digging up flower beds and chewing garden hoses. And although it is true that dogs with separation distress may urinate and defecate in their owners' absence, a dog who has been taught that doing those things in the owner's presence results in being reprimanded might do them only when the owner is away.

It is true that many dogs who have separation distress exhibit destructive behavior. The objects of destruction may include personal items belonging to the owner, such as laundry or bedding, or items the owner has touched, such as the television remote or reading materials. Then again, the dog might be chewing whatever is at hand in order to relieve stress. Destructive behavior must be analyzed in conjunction with other behavior patterns in order to reach an accurate diagnosis.

Most behaviors stemming from distress at being left alone or separated from the owner occur soon after the owner's departure. But so do most boredom-related acts of mayhem. If you are gone for an hour or two here and there, and your dog sometimes destroys things and sometimes not, chances are your dog is simply bored. If your neighbor reports incessant barking while you are gone, it *is* possible that your dog has a separation issue; then again, it is also possible that she is bored and under-stimulated mentally and/or physically. But if you notice that your dog becomes increasingly anxious as you leave or prepare to leave the house, or has any of the aforementioned symptoms to an intense degree, she may have separation distress.

Setting up a video camera to record your dog's actions when you are gone can give you a better idea of the underlying cause of her behavior.

What You Can Do

The good news is that clinical-level separation anxiety is rare. If you feel that your dog might have this condition, consult a behavior specialist immediately. Pharmacological intervention may be necessary as an adjunct to behavior modification, and there is no reason for your dog to suffer needlessly. In the more likely case that your dog's separation issue is mild to moderate, the following suggestions should help.

Management. The protocol used to address separation distress involves a certain time commitment, during which your dog should not be left alone for long periods. If you are working a full-time job and do not have vacation time coming, your best course is management until you can find the time to address the issue. Do you have a neighbor who would like to have your dog spend the day playing with her dog? Assuming the dogs get along well, this can be a great solution. Is there a doggy daycare center in your area? If your dog is Fido-friendly, let her spend the day romping with other dogs. Even taking your dog to daycare every other day can be extremely helpful, as the dogs are usually so pleasantly exhausted after a play-day that the resulting calm lasts well into the next day. Be sure to tell the daycare staff about your dog's separation issues and furnish a phone number where they can reach you in case of emergency.

What about adding a second dog to your home? If you are not sure whether that would solve the problem, borrow a friend's dog for the day. Was your dog any calmer? (To check, leave a video camera running.) If you do not want another dog, there are other options. Perhaps a friend, relative, or pet-sitter could visit with your dog for a while during the day, then leave her with a pre-prepared stuffed chew toy upon departure so she is kept busy. You might even find a student or retired person who would be willing to stay with your dog for part of the day. *Note:* None of these alternatives will solve the problem if your dog has a separation issue from you in particular. But in the majority of cases, dogs are anxious about being left alone, rather than about being separated from one particular person.

Practice relaxation across the board. It is important that your dog be as relaxed and confident in everyday life as possible. To that end, employ a leadership program (see *Chapter 11*). Remember, dogs with strong leaders feel more secure. Teach obedience skills and tricks (see *Resources*), and engage in other confidence-building activities such as dog sports (see *Chapter 9*). Another great way to keep your dog relaxed is with Ttouch sessions (see *Chapter 45*). Ttouch can be of tremendous help to dogs with separation distress and other emotional issues.

Take a walk before you take a hike. People and dogs both react less intensely to stress when they are relaxed. If you are like most people, you're probably rushing around most mornings; but do your dog and yourself a favor and take her for as long a walk as you can manage before you leave for the day. The exercise will leave you both calmer and in a more positive mood, which will reduce your dog's anxiety level and lessen the chances of destructive behavior. (Don't engage your dog in aerobic activities such as ball throwing just before you go, as you don't want her levels of adrenaline and other stress hormones to be elevated when you leave.) Also, be sure your dog is getting the proper amount of daily exercise for her breed and age. If you are not sure of your dog's particular requirements, consult your veterinarian.

Set the stage. The choice of where your dog is kept when you are gone can affect her stress level. If her issues are not severe, she is comfortable in a crate, and your absence is to last four hours or less, a crate is a good choice (assuming she is old enough that she will not need to eliminate during that time). Be sure to crate your dog for short periods when you are home as well, so the crate does not become associated solely with being left alone.

If your dog is likely to destroy things or have housebreaking accidents when left alone, if her issues are severe, or if you will be gone more than four hours at a time, your dog should be left in an enclosed area. Choose a space that offers confinement but is large enough to be comfortable, such as a bathroom, laundry room, or kitchen. Place a baby gate across the doorway rather than closing the door. A dog in a small space with the door closed is likely to feel more anxious than one who can see out. (In a bathroom, that anxious, closed-in feeling often results in the ever-popular pooch pastime, "Redecorating with Toilet Paper.")

Confining your dog in your bedroom can also be an excellent choice. Since your scent is everywhere, the bedroom can be particularly comforting. If you choose this option, or another small confinement area, practice confining your dog in the space during the day with a yummy chew item while you are at home. That way your dog will have already developed good associations with the room by the time she is left there, rather than it becoming associated only with your absences.

If your dog does not have destructive tendencies or housebreaking issues, you could leave her free in the house. Some dogs do better in smaller, confined spaces, while others do better with more freedom. Experiment to see which arrangement makes your dog more comfortable.

Keep it cool. Keep your comings and goings low key. As much as you might miss your pooch while you're gone (*who* has the separation issue?), cooing in a concerned voice or making a big deal of leaving will not help your dog to relax. On the contrary, it might cause her to become nervous or worried that something unpleasant is about to happen. When you leave, utter a parting phrase in an unconcerned, casual tone. *What* you say is not as important as *how* you say it. You could toss out a cheerful, "Be sure to do the dishes and put away all your toys!" for all it matters—just be sure to use a happy, nonchalant tone.

Your greetings upon returning home should be low key as well. I am not suggesting that you ignore your dog completely. Give a casual, "Hey, buddy," perhaps ruffle your dog's fur, then go about your business. Dogs pick up on our emotional states, so if you don't make a big deal of your comings and goings, neither will your dog. With repetition, she will learn that your parting phrase indicates that you will be returning soon, so there is nothing to worry about.

Calming Considerations

- You might have heard that it is a good idea to leave a television or radio playing for your dog while you are gone. If your dog is accustomed to hearing those sounds when you are at home, by all means, leave one playing when you are gone. But if the television or radio is not normally on much when you are home, turning it on for your dog when you leave will only cause it to become associated with your absences, which could have the opposite of the desired effect.

- Speaking of leaving things on when you are gone, there is a new product that is definitely worth trying. Sold under the brand name Comfort Zone™, this unique invention resembles a plug-in air freshener. (No, it doesn't waft the scent of fresh kitty!) Instead, the active ingredient, DAP—Dog Appeasing Pheromone—mimics the pheromones given off by lactating female dogs, which is comforting to dogs of all ages. *You* won't smell a thing. Many of my clients' dogs who have mild separation issues have been helped by this product. (For more information, see *Chapter 47*.)

- Flower essences can help. The most common remedy used is Rescue Remedy®, but Heather—a stand-alone essence—is perfect for dogs who are fearful of being left alone, and can be combined with Rescue Remedy®. (For more on flower essences, see *Chapter 43*.)

- Place something with your scent on it in your dog's resting area. Use a T-shirt or sweatshirt you have just worn, or a towel you have rubbed on your body. Your scent, even without your actual presence, is very comforting to your dog. (If you have to board your dog, give the kennel a scented T-shirt to leave with her. If you're going to be gone more than a week, leave the kennel one shirt for each week in sealed plastic bags.)

- It is important to leave your dog with something to occupy her time, especially since most acts of doggy mayhem are committed soon after the owner's departure. Provide your dog with a well-stuffed Kong®, food-dispensing toy, or chew bone (see *Chapters 9* and *10*). Be sure to offer the fabulous treat when you are home as well so it does not become associated only with your absence. Present the chew item five or ten minutes before your departure so your dog is blissfully engrossed and in a happy state of mind when you depart. Just be sure not to give the chew toy only when you're going to be gone for *long* periods, as chew toys would then come to predict long absences. There is also a new product called Kong Time® that will automatically dispense pre-stuffed Kongs® at random times while you are away. (This product can be ordered through your local pet supply retailer, or located online via a Google search.)

> For in-depth help, see my new book *Don't Leave Me! Step-by-Step Help for Your Dog's Separation Anxiety*. (See *Resources*.) It contains behavior modification protocols, plenty of creative management solutions, stories from experts detailing how they solved this issue, and much more.

If you come home to find that your dog has destroyed something or had a potty accident, don't reprimand her. It is too late for her to associate the act with the reprimand. More importantly, if you appear angry each time you walk in the door, your dog will become even more anxious, fearing your absence *and* your return!

Desensitization to Triggers

If your dog begins to whine, drool, or display other signs of anxiety as you prepare to leave, desensitize her to each anxiety-causing trigger in your departure routine. Common pre-departure triggers include gathering your things, picking up a purse or briefcase, putting on a jacket, picking up keys, arming an alarm, and, of course, heading for the door. Some dogs become anxious earlier in the sequence, as they realize that using a brush or blow dryer, drying dishes, or getting dressed predicts a departure. Dogs are much better at this particular type of associative learning than we give them credit for. For example, many dogs understand that a pair of jogging shoes indicates a short absence, while dress shoes indicate a night out.

Watch your dog carefully and list her triggers. Then desensitize her to each by repeating it many times throughout the day. For example, pick up your keys at random but don't go anywhere—put them back down after carrying them around for five seconds. Turn on your blow dryer for ten seconds, then turn it off. (Just don't point it toward your head—I won't be liable for frizz!) Work towards combinations of activities. For example, pick up your keys and put on your jacket, but don't go anywhere.

It can also be helpful to change the sequence of the individual actions in your departure routine, both in practice and when you must actually leave. Change the order in which you do things: get dressed after you brush your hair instead of before; brush your teeth and then shower; gather your things at random times before you leave, instead of at the last minute. With desensitization and the unpredictability factor, these actions will transform from triggers into boring, everyday activities.

Graduated Departures

While graduated departures are the mainstay of most separation anxiety protocols, for dogs with severe issues, even the briefest out-of-sight absence can be overwhelming. If this describes your dog, begin with brief separations within the home. Begin by separating yourself physically, but remain within visual range. For example, place your dog behind a baby gate in the kitchen (or wherever you plan to leave her when you are gone) with a stuffed chew toy. Give her a few minutes to become absorbed in chewing, then go sit a short distance away. Remain in sight as you engage in an activity such as reading a book or watching television. (An additional incremental step can be added if necessary by limiting your dog's vision with the Calming Cap™—see *Chapter 48*.) Practice physical separations for brief periods and then for longer ones, beginning at a distance at which your dog is comfortable and increasing the distance as long as she remains so. If your dog becomes agitated, you have either moved too far away too soon, or increased the time too quickly. Go back to an easier step and build smaller, incremental steps from there.

When your dog is completely comfortable being physically separated with you at a distance but still in sight, it is time to begin the out-of-sight phase. With your dog happily engaged in chewing, disappear around the corner for a few seconds and then return. Do this at random times, and—you guessed it—gradually increase the time you are gone, until you can spend time in another part of the house without your dog becoming anxious. Alternately, if your dog knows "stay," ease her into the process by giving her the verbal cue to stay, then disappearing for just a few seconds. Praise her when you return. Giving your dog something to focus on can help to prevent her from slipping into an anxious state.

Once your dog is comfortable with you being out of sight for longer periods, it is time to practice very short departures from the house. Prepare to leave, put your dog in a confined area if necessary, then give your casual departure phrase and go. Even though you are only going to stand outside the house, bring your coat, pick up your purse or briefcase, and do whatever you would normally do if you were to be gone longer. How long you should remain outside depends on the intensity of your dog's separation distress. The initial departure could be thirty seconds, or five minutes. Remember to keep your return low key. If you normally drive away, add starting the car and then turning it off to the routine. After a few repetitions (return home after each one), drive around the block once and then return, and gradually work up to being gone for longer periods.

> If you do not have the time to practice gradual departures, perhaps you know someone who does. A friend, relative, neighbor, student, or retired person could be quite effective in getting your dog to accept being alone, by following your directions for brief departures.

Practice multiple outings each day, gradually increasing the time you are gone by five or ten minute increments. Drive around the block; visit a bank machine; put gas in your car; go to the market. Where you go doesn't matter, so long as the duration of your absence is increased gradually. Do not, however, increase the duration in a linear fashion. In other words, the length of your departures should increase gradually but unpredictably. So departures might last two minutes, then five minutes, seven minutes, three minutes, ten minutes, seven minutes, fifteen minutes, and so on. Once your dog feels comfortable being left alone for ninety minutes or so, she should be fine with being left alone for longer periods.

How long it will take your dog to become comfortable with being left alone will depend on the intensity of the distress and on how long it has been going on. Be patient. Once you have worked up to leaving the house entirely, your progress will become much faster. Canine behaviorist Dr. Patricia McConnell, author of *I'll be Home Soon!* (a booklet specifically about separation issues—see *Resources*) believes that mild cases of separation anxiety can be improved in a few weeks, while more serious cases can be cured in roughly six to eight weeks. And, as McConnell points out, "Unlike some other behavioral problems, once you're done, you're done, and all your troubles become part of you and your dog's interesting history, rather than a daily disaster." [1]

Pharmacological Intervention

Most mild-to-moderate cases of separation distress do not require medication. But if your dog's issue is severe, consult a behavior specialist as well as your veterinarian. The behavior specialist can determine whether pharmacological intervention would be appropriate, and can help to create a successful treatment plan. If necessary, your veterinarian can prescribe medication and monitor your dog's reactions.

The most commonly prescribed medication for separation anxiety is clomipramine (sold under the brand name Clomicalm®), although there are other drugs that may be used instead. What these drugs have in common is that they are meant to be used in conjunction with a behavior modification program, rather than being a solution in and of themselves. Once a dog's anxiety has lessened, she can be weaned off the medication.

Be patient; trying to change your dog's feelings about being left alone can take time. Even if you follow every one of the aforementioned suggestions, your dog's behavior will probably not change overnight. But it will change, and your dog will eventually feel calm and confident when left alone. And just think how much more relaxed that will make *you* feel when you're away from home!

1 McConnell, P. *I'll be Home Soon!* Wisconsin: Dog's Best Friend, Ltd., 2000

Tail End Wrap-Up

- Some dogs are anxious when separated from a particular person or persons, while others simply fear being left alone.

- Rule out boredom and other possible causes of your dog's behavior before jumping to the diagnosis of separation distress. A video camera can be helpful.

- Choose an appropriate containment area for your dog or leave her at liberty, depending on her house behavior and what makes her most comfortable.

- Look into dog-sitters, play dates, and other options for daytime fun.

- Encourage a feeling of security by employing a leadership program and regular training sessions.

- Exercise your dog regularly and take her for a long walk before you leave in the morning. Give your dog a stuffed chew toy a few minutes before you depart.

- Keep your comings and goings low key.

- Consider complementary therapies.

- If necessary, desensitize your dog to anxiety-producing triggers in your departure routine.

- Practice departures, building in tiny increments.

- If necessary, consider pharmacological intervention as an adjunct to behavior modification.

Part VI

Complementary Therapies

Complementary Therapies

There are more remedies and therapies available today for dogs than ever before. Some are useful for treating acute fear responses, while others can help to settle a nervous disposition over time. Some have been around for thousands of years, while others are more recent discoveries. Some are taken internally, some applied hands-on. What these treatments have in common is that although they all have a calming effect in and of themselves, when treating ongoing fear issues, they are most effective when administered in conjunction with a behavior modification program.

While the efficacy of some therapies is backed by scientific data, the success of others is anecdotal. You might already be familiar with therapies such as massage, but had not thought to apply them to your dog. Other therapies, such as Ttouch, DAP (Dog Appeasing Pheromone) and body wraps, might be unfamiliar or even seem downright odd at first. But keep an open mind; each is worth your consideration, and might be just the thing to help your dog.

Some healing helpers, such as flower essences, have absolutely no side effects and no chance of overdose, which makes them a safe place to start. Others, such as homeopathy and herbs, are also relatively safe but have some caveats; just because something is "natural" does not mean it is 100% safe for all dogs, or in all doses. And although pharmacological intervention can be extremely effective, each drug carries its own cautions and limitations. Considerations for each remedy are discussed in their respective chapters.

Read through the entire section to get an overview before trying any of the remedies or therapies. Then try the ones that appeal to you one at a time, allowing time for results to manifest so that you have a clear idea of which one is helping your dog. Once he is in a calmer state of mind and is less tense physically, your dog will be more receptive to behavior modification. The two-pronged approach of complementary therapies and behavior modification is safe and effective, and addresses underlying issues rather than simply suppressing symptoms. It also allows for the therapies to be discontinued once the behavior issues have been resolved.

And now, the exciting, effective, and sometimes downright extraordinary complementary therapies!

Flower Power

Plants have been used for healing in diverse cultures throughout history, and the tradition continues. Many of our modern pain-relievers and anti-inflammatory medications are derived from plants. Aspirin, for example, was originally derived from the flowering plant *Spiraea ulmaria*. Morphine and codeine, two extremely potent painkillers, are extracted from the unripe seed capsules of the opium poppy. Although all parts of plants have been used for healing, flowers are considered to embody the essential *character* of the plant, and to have specific healing powers.

If you have been raised in a society that primarily uses allopathic, western medicine, the notion that flower essences can heal may be a difficult one to accept. This unique healing modality is based on the concept that everything in the universe has a specific vibration. When a flower is processed into an essence and that essence is taken into the body, the body begins to vibrate at the same frequency as the flower. As the body's cells and tissues vibrate at that frequency, healing begins on both the physical and emotional planes. In short, the flower essences change the *energy* of the body so that healing can take place.

In 1930, British physician and homeopath Edward Bach developed the first modern therapeutic system using flower essences. Bach believed in treating the cause of an illness rather than simply masking the symptoms, and that the underlying cause of the illness could be traced to a distortion of the body's energy field. He concluded that a positive, healthy state of mind could be restored by utilizing the energies found in plants, trees, bushes, and special waters. Bach identified 38 essences, each with its own specific purpose. The essences were divided into seven groups, each representing fundamental conflicts. Two of the groups are "Uncertainty" and "Fear." The Bach Flower Essences were originally created for humans, but are now commonly used for animals as well. They are widely available at health food stores and via mail order.

Rescue Remedy®

Rescue Remedy®, the Bach Flower Essence that is most often used for dogs, is actually a combination of five essences. It contains Impatiens (for mental stress and tension), Clematis (for disorientation), Rock Rose (for terror and panic), Cherry Plum (for desperation), and Star of Bethlehem (for shock). The five-essence combination is used to ease stress and anxiety, which allows the body to achieve relaxation. The same combination of essences is sold by other manufacturers under the brand names Calming Essence and Five Flower Remedy (see *Resources*).

Years ago, I worked at a doggy daycare center where 30 to 40 dogs romped together off-leash daily. For the most part, it was a fun experience for both the dogs and the staff. But some dogs were anxious because their owners were absent; some were nervous around other dogs; others did not want to be bothered. Fights were inevitable. The staff always kept Rescue Remedy® on hand, and it often helped to calm the dogs—and the staff. The normal dosage is four drops in a dog's drinking water, but if water is not available, it can be dropped directly into the dog's mouth. (Administer carefully, as the dropper is made of glass!)

Rescue Remedy® can be used to help a dog who is in shock or unconscious—for example, as you drive to the veterinarian. (Flower essences are never a substitute for proper veterinary care.) In emergency situations, the liquid may be rubbed into the gums, lips, nostrils, or skin. The recommended emergency dosage is two drops every five minutes.

In their book *Bach Flower Remedies for Animals* (see *Resources*), authors Helen Graham and Gregory Vlamis suggest a myriad of uses for Rescue Remedy®. Listed below are those that apply to nervous, fearful dogs.

Uses for Rescue Remedy®

- A safe alternative to sedatives and tranquilizers.

- For vet visits, to relieve tension and make for easier examination (apply two drops directly to your dog's tongue beforehand).

- To be administered prior to visiting the groomer (the authors state that "groomers report fewer bites and scratches when Rescue Remedy® is given to their charges") or before grooming your dog at home.

- For dogs who are nervous when being transported (place a few drops in drinking water).

- To produce a calming, sedative effect in animals who react adversely to strangers in the home (place a few drops in drinking water or spray the environment with an atomizer).

- For dogs who are stressed because of domestic arguments or upheaval.

- For dogs who fear thunder and lightning.

- For dogs who fear separation from owners or other animals.

If your dog is having an acute fear reaction, the authors recommend administering the remedy every three to five minutes until improvement is shown.

Individual Essences

Rescue Remedy® can be used alongside individual essences. It will not interfere with their healing effects, but rather, will work synergistically to reinforce them. Here are some individual essences and their uses.

Aspen	Inexplicable, vague fear; fear of the unfamiliar; sudden anxiety indicated by trembling, shaking, panting, urination, fearful look in the eyes, ears and tail down, cowering, and avoidance behaviors.
Cerato	General lack of confidence in everyday situations.
Heather	For dogs who cannot bear to be left alone.
Mimulus	For dogs who are timid, insecure, nervous, anxious; fear of specific triggers such as heights, water, the dark, other people, or being left alone.
Red Chestnut	Anticipatory fear (a dog who is seemingly convinced that something bad will soon happen).
Sweet Chestnut	For overstressed dogs who engage in self-destructive behavior.

Flower essences may be administered in a variety of ways. As previously mentioned, the most popular is to add a few drops to the dog's drinking water. In the case of individual essences, however, the Nelson Bach company recommends two drops rather than four. If drinking water is not available, the essence may be dropped directly onto the dog's tongue. (Some dogs dislike the taste, since most tinctures have an alcohol base.) Alternately, the drops may be sprinkled over the dog's food or fed on a small piece of bread. The essence may also be diluted with water and sprayed around the dog or the environment, or rubbed into the dog's gums, ears, nose, or paw pads.

Frequent dosage is key. There is no need for concern regarding overdosing—there *is* no chance of a dog overdosing on flower essences, other than the alcohol base creating a problem if enormous amounts were administered. It is said that if a dog does not need a particular essence, no change will take place. If the essence does help, the effects are usually fairly subtle. In other words, your dog may become calmer, but he will not look dazed or act as though he had been given a tranquilizer.

Although there has not been a great deal of scientific study on the efficacy of flower essences, there is plenty of anecdotal evidence of their usefulness for animals and people. Like everything else, flower essences may or may not work for your dog. But because they are safe to use alone or in conjunction with other treatments (although they should not be given with homeopathic remedies—see *Chapter 49*), and are inexpensive and widely available, they are a good starting point.

If you have questions about flower essences or would like more individualized help, The Flower Essence Society (see *Resources*) can answer questions and refer you to a practitioner in your area.

Massage

For my money, there is nothing more relaxing than a good massage. Strong, gentle hands kneading muscles, tension flowing away—*aaah*. Being massaged is not only enjoyable, but can also be extremely healing on both a physical and emotional level. It is no different for dogs.

Benefits of Canine Massage

Massage has many physical benefits for dogs. It increases circulation, stimulates the lymphatic system so toxins are drained from the tissues, and can serve as a first alert to any lumps or abnormalities. Conditions experienced by older dogs such as arthritis, stiffness, certain spinal disorders, and muscle cramps can be greatly improved by routine massage. Massage can also help your dog to heal more quickly after surgery, by increasing circulation and promoting a relaxed state of mind so the body can better heal itself.

Note: Dogs who have sprains, broken bones, broken skin, fever, or cancer should not be massaged. If you are not sure whether massage is safe for your dog, consult your veterinarian.

As I write this chapter, Mojo is recovering from surgery to repair a torn cruciate ligament. At 11 years of age and 120 pounds, recovery from knee surgery is not rapid. The slow restoration to activity and full strength has been especially tough on Mojo, as he is normally a very playful and rambunctious dog. Since the surgery he has been understandably more sedate, but he has also become needy and anxious, as so many of us do when we are feeling unwell. Massage has helped Mojo immensely. I can always tell when his tension is easing, as he inhales deeply and then exhales a long, shuddering sigh. He often falls asleep during massage. And as Mojo's dedicated and sometimes stressed caretaker, I am happy to report that our massage experiences relax me as well.

> Bonus benefit for owners! Massaging your dog can lower your blood pressure, reduce your risk of heart disease, decrease cholesterol levels, and produce a lovely state of mental, physical, and emotional relaxation.

The link between emotional and physical health is strong in dogs, just as it is in people. Chronic stress and anxiety weaken the immune system in both species. Dogs who are constantly stressed or anxious can develop conditions such as ulcerative colitis, and are generally less resistant to infections and disease. By easing stress, regular massage can help to strengthen the immune system, lighten depression, and keep your dog more relaxed in general. And the caring, attentive touch that forms the basis of massage strengthens the human-canine bond—important to any relationship, but especially crucial for a fearful dog who must regard her human as a trusted leader.

Preparation

You need not be a professional massage therapist to give your dog a thorough, relaxing massage. What you do need is a quiet space where you will not be interrupted, a pad or comfortable surface on which your dog can lie, and a calm state of mind—and I am referring here to *your* state of mind. It is a good practice to take a few deep breaths before you begin any massage. Position your body so you will not have to stretch or lean over your dog in a way that will cause you undue physical stress or make your dog uncomfortable. It is important that you remain physically relaxed and breathe calmly throughout the massage. Playing soft music can help you and your dog to relax.

Although your dog may stand, sit, or lie on her side or stomach for a massage, having her lie on her side will probably be easiest for both of you. If your dog is trained to settle (lie on her side calmly), ask her to do so; if not, gently coax her onto her side. (To learn how to teach settle, see

Chapter 14.) Begin by petting your dog using long, slow, open-palmed strokes, with your hand flat and fingers held loosely together. Avoid any areas on which your dog is touch-sensitive. Don't be concerned about technique just yet, as the goal of these initial touches is simply to encourage relaxation. Breathe deeply and visualize calm, soothing energy flowing down through your arms, out through your hands, and into your dog's body. Even if your dog has experienced massage before, move slowly and watch for signs of discomfort or pain.

Massage Techniques

Effleurage is a light friction meant to relax the body and prepare it for deeper work. Use an open palm and fingers to deliver long, slow, even-pressured strokes. This is a more purposeful, systematic stroke than the initial relaxation petting. Begin by stroking down your dog's side, then from shoulder to front foot, and hip to hind foot. Avoid massaging over bone, and use a lighter touch when moving down the legs. (Legs do not have as much muscle mass and can be sensitive in areas such as the backs of the knees.) Aim for roughly fifteen strokes per minute in the direction of the growth of the fur. At first, the strokes should have just enough pressure to gather any loose fur. If your dog's paws or any other body parts are sensitive to touch, avoid those areas until your dog is more relaxed and comfortable with being massaged. As one hand massages your dog, keep the other resting lightly on her body. Slide the massaging hand from one spot to another, rather than removing it and placing it down again, so your dog will not be surprised by the touch. Gradually increase the pressure of the strokes from light to medium, but continue to use a lighter touch when massaging the legs.

You may be wondering just how much pressure to use. In *Effective Pet Massage for Dogs* (see *Resources*), author Jonathan Rudinger recommends using your fingers to make small circles on your closed eyelids without pressing on the eye itself, to show how little pressure you need to massage your dog.

If your dog stiffens or becomes uncomfortable at any point during the massage, lighten the pressure immediately. Assess whether there was pain or sensitivity in the area, or whether perhaps you were stroking too intensely. If your dog gets up and walks away, allow her to do so. Some dogs take to massage immediately, while others take a while to get accustomed to it. Even if your dog does not object, do not attempt a full massage the first time out. Initial petting strokes, a bit of effleurage, and a few more petting strokes might be all you do at the first session, depending on your dog's reaction. If you'd like, add some of the following techniques as well, but again, keep the first massage brief—five to ten minutes at most.

Fingertip massage. Rest your thumb lightly on your dog's body. Extend two or three fingers (two for smaller dogs, three for larger ones) and, keeping them close together, massage in a circular pattern in a clockwise direction. Don't glide over the surface of your dog's fur, but rather, move the skin in a circle with your fingers. When you work on the hips, thighs, shoulders, or forelegs, use your other hand to hold the body part steady. Monitor your dog's reaction. As you feel her relax, increase gradually to a firmer pressure. How much pressure you should use depends on your dog's physical build and comfort level, but the touch should never be too hard or invasive. This is a nice, relaxing massage, not deep tissue work.

Petrissage (no, not *petmassage!*) is the technique most of us envision when we think of massage. Petrissage lifts the skin, kneading and rolling it between the fingers and thumb. Petrissage can be done along the meaty parts of the back (avoid the spine, which runs straight down the middle of the back), flanks, and chest. Be careful not to pinch! When working on the shoulders and thighs, the deeper muscles can be kneaded between the thumb and fingers of one hand while the other supports the limb. The movement should be slow and rhythmic. Think of constant kneading and rolling, rather than direct pressure. As always, monitor your dog's response and adjust your approach accordingly. Once you have finished on one side, gently turn your dog over to repeat all the strokes on the other side. Then end the massage with a bit of light effleurage from nose to tail. Sweep gently from shoulder to forepaw, rump to hind foot. Make five to ten slow passes.

Tips for Effective Massage

- Set aside a regular time for daily massage.

- Do not engage in massage right after your dog has been fed or when she is overly excited. A better time is after returning from a walk. Make sure your dog has eliminated before you begin.

- For puppies, a massage should last just a few minutes. For dogs six months and older, ten to twenty minutes is fine. Add time and intensity of touch gradually as your dog becomes more comfortable and accepting of it. If your dog walks away at any time during a massage, allow her to go.

- If you want to talk to your dog during massage use a low, soothing voice. Praise your dog for relaxing.

- Be sure to do both sides of your dog's body!

- Once your dog is thoroughly enjoying massage, spray DAP (see *Chapter 47*) on a bandana or rag and place it next to your dog as you massage her. The scent will become associated with a feeling of relaxation. You can then spray the DAP on a bandana and have your dog wear it around her neck in situations that would normally cause stress.

- Another olfactory trick is to use a calming essential oil such as lavender as you massage your dog. Place the oil in a diffuser (these are inexpensive and widely available) and let it work its magic as your dog relaxes. After a few sessions, place a drop of the oil on a bandana or on your dog's collar when she is to be exposed to a potentially stressful situation.

- Massage oil is not necessary when working on a dog; in fact, it would be quite messy!

- If your dog doesn't absolutely love massage at first, don't give up. Ease up on your strokes and shorten the length of the massage. Many dogs learn to enjoy massage even if they didn't care for it at first—some even become downright pesky about demanding it!

This has been a very brief introduction to canine massage. It would, of course, be impossible to offer a comprehensive guide in just a few pages. I encourage you to expand your knowledge further by purchasing books and visual aids (see *Resources*).

Ttouch

Ttouch—or Tellington Ttouch, as it is sometimes called after creator Linda Tellington-Jones—is a hands-on technique that can be used to help animals heal both physically and emotionally. Tellington-Jones, a practitioner of Feldenkrais bodywork and a successful competitive horse rider and trainer, developed the Ttouch method in the 1970s for use on "problem horses." Since then it has been used successfully on dogs, cats, a variety of domestic animals, and exotics including llamas, snow leopards, elephants, and alligators! Surely if Ttouch can help an ornery 'gator it can calm your fearful fur-kid.

Proponents of Ttouch credit it with being able to help with everything from aggression and other behavior issues to speeding post-surgical healing. Of special note for fearful dogs is that the method is said to alleviate extreme fear and shyness, and to reduce anxiety-related behaviors. It is also credited with lessening resistance to grooming and handling, and decreasing nervousness, fear-biting, and the fear of thunderstorms and other noises.

Ttouch uses a combination of specific touches, lifts, and movement exercises to release tension and increase body awareness. Practitioners say Ttouch activates the function of the cells and awakens cellular intelligence. Because the nervous system is affected, patterns of habitual response are interrupted and dogs are given the opportunity to think, rather than simply react to a situation. Once the connection between the dog's body, mind, and emotions is improved, so are coordination, self-confidence, and behavior. And because many physical and behavioral problems stem from and/or are worsened by habitual tension in the body, teaching dogs to notice and release areas of tension begins the healing process. Once a dog relaxes and his body posture changes, his emotional state changes as well. Ttouch sessions have the added benefit of deepening the bond of love and trust between dog and owner.

I have seen the results of Ttouch myself. When I worked with the wolves at the rescue center, I did two types of healing therapy with those who would allow physical contact: regular massage, and Ttouch. Because I am a certified massage therapist (you can imagine the looks I got from other students when I said I wanted to massage dogs and wolves), I knew how to give a proper, thorough massage. The wolves and I enjoyed our massage sessions greatly, but when I began to use Ttouch, there was a deeper, more profound letting go. Those beautiful, furry chests would heave heavy sighs as the wolves relaxed into the connection created by the touches. Those moments were magical.

When administering Ttouch, it is important that you be as relaxed and comfortable as possible. Sit on the floor next to your dog, take a few deep breaths, and check that your body is in a comfortable position. Your dog may be lying down, standing, or sitting.

Because Ttouch is done over the dog's entire body and is not invasive, explicit knowledge of canine anatomy is not necessary. The circular movements of the fingers and hands are meant to make the dog more aware of his own body, rather than aiming for overall relaxation. Experiment with the touches that follow.

Basic Touch

The foundation touch, "The Clouded Leopard," involves a circular movement of the fingers in a clockwise direction. The fingers should be slightly curved, with the pads close together and the thumb approximately two to three inches from the forefinger. The pads of the fingers will create the circle. Your wrist should remain straight yet flexible.

Each "circle" is actually a circle-and-a-quarter. Imagine the face of a clock lying on your dog's fur. Anchoring with your thumb, place your fingers at 6:00. Move the fingers around the dial once, then pass the starting point and end at 9:00. Each circle should take approximately two seconds. It is important that you move your dog's skin, rather than simply sliding your fingers over his fur. Then, maintaining contact with the fur, slide the same hand a bit further down his body and do another one-and-one-quarter circle. You can either slide to a random position, or create parallel lines by sliding in a straight line from one spot to the next, parallel to your dog's spine or down one of his legs. As the circling hand works, the other should rest lightly on the body. When working on the limbs, one hand should support the limb as the other performs the touches.

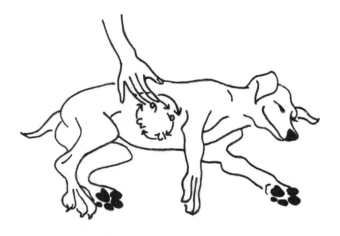

Ttouches, unlike the deeper strokes of massage, use light pressure. Pressures are assigned numbers, depending on their strength. To get an idea of what a Number One pressure feels like, place your thumb on your cheek. Using two fingers, gently move the skin of your closed eyelid in a circular motion using the lightest touch possible. (If you wear contact lenses, make the circle above your eyebrows instead.) Now do the same thing, but use as firm a pressure as is comfortable—that is what a Number Three pressure feels like. Doubling that amount of pressure (do *not* try this on your eyes!) would result in a Number Six pressure. For areas of a dog's body that are not sensitive or painful, a Number Three or Four pressure is normally used. For sensitive areas, the highest recommended pressure is Number Two. In general, more pressure is used with larger animals, but always respect your dog's responses and adjust your approach accordingly. If your dog appears uncomfortable, reduce the pressure of the touch or switch to doing touches on another area of his body.

Ttouches for Fearful Dogs

There are over a dozen Ttouches, with fanciful names such as "The Raccoon Ttouch," "The Lick of the Cow's Tongue," and "Tarantulas Pulling the Plow." Using the appropriate touch or touches on specific body parts can help to alleviate specific fears.

- Performing Ttouch on a dog's mouth can help with fear of veterinary exams, as well as with nervousness and emotional upset.

- Touches around the tail and hindquarters (many fearful dogs hold their tension around the hindquarters) are said to be especially beneficial for nervous dogs and those who have a fear of loud noises, including thunder. These touches can also help those who tend to tuck the tail in fear, fear-biters, and those who are timid in general.

- Ear touches are helpful for relaxation and alleviating stress, and are even said to be able to help a dog who is going into shock.

- Ttouches on the paws are helpful for dogs who are afraid to have their paws handled or nails trimmed, or those who are afraid of stairs or slippery floors.

All of these touches have other physical and emotional benefits as well.

It would be impossible to do the Ttouch system justice in one short chapter. There are many aspects that merit investigation, especially for treating fear issues. In addition to the various touches, Ttouch employs labyrinth-like walks that help dogs to build confidence, and wands that help dogs to focus and balance while working through exercises. (See the *Resources* section for reading suggestions and an organization that can direct you to a Ttouch practitioner in your area.)

46

Body Wrap

Pop quiz! The definition of *swaddle* is:

a. a new dance craze
b. to wrap or restrain
c. what penguins do when drunk

If you guessed "b" you're right! (If you chose "c" put the book down and go take a nap; you've been working too hard.) Mothers have long known that swaddling an infant—wrapping it tightly in a blanket—has a calming effect. In fact, an invention called the Hug Box has successfully calmed autistic children. Some animals can be calmed by restraint as well. For example, nervous cattle can be made less so by a well-designed "squeeze chute," which restricts their movement and thereby reduces anxiety (and injury). The good news for dog owners is that the deep, uniform sensation of pressure created by being encased in a body wrap can help to calm a fearful dog. Note that this type of restraint differs from that of hugging a dog or holding her tightly for a veterinary procedure!

Body wrapping can be used to calm dogs who are anxious around other dogs, people, or new environments, afraid of specific sounds (including thunderstorms), fearful of nail clipping, ear cleaning or grooming, or anxious about being left alone. Body wraps are also beneficial for dogs who are timid in general. They can help anxious dogs settle and, in conjunction with behavior modification, can even help fear-biters. A body wrap can be used when performing Ttouch circles, lifts, and slides, or even with simple ear massage to increase the calming effect.

T-Shirt Wrap

There are various ways to wrap a dog, the easiest of which involves an everyday T-shirt. The T-shirt wrap is fast and easy to apply, and is a good one to start with if your dog has never worn a wrap before. Choose a shirt of the appropriate size for your dog. For small dogs, a child's T-shirt is fine; for medium-sized dogs, use an adult size medium or large; and for large dogs, use an adult size extra large.

Be sure to act happy and relaxed so your dog will be as well. Begin by pulling the neck hole of the T-shirt over your dog's head with the front of the shirt facing up. Yes, you're putting it on backwards—it fits more snugly that way. Gently lift your dog's front paws through the armholes, one at a time. Next, gather the material by pulling both sides up toward your dog's back. The shirt should now fit like a glove, gently encasing your dog's body. The fit should be secure but not so tight that it restricts movement or causes discomfort. Finish by tying a knot or using a large rubber band to secure the gathered material. (Be sure the knot is not directly over your dog's spine.)

Note: Most dogs will accept wraps if applied slowly and gently; however, some will not. If your dog panics or tries to bite when you attempt to apply a wrap, do not force the issue. Desensitize him to it gradually, pairing it with things he likes. There are other complementary therapies that can also help without causing undue stress. (See *Chapter 37* for handling issues.)

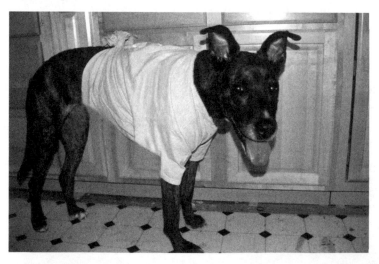

Ttouch Wrap ("Body Bandage")

Practitioners of Ttouch use a body wrap (also referred to as a "body bandage") made of Ace™ bandages held in place with diaper pins. Bandages are available in a variety of widths and lengths. For a small dog, use a two-inch width; for medium dogs, a three-inch width; for large dogs, a four-inch width; and for giant breeds, a four- to six-inch width. The bandages come in lengths of approximately five feet. Once you begin to apply the wrap, the appropriate length for your dog will become obvious.

There are two main types of Ttouch body wraps; the half-body wrap and the full-body wrap. Half wraps are recommended for dogs who have never worn a wrap, or those who are sensitive about their back ends. To apply the half-body wrap, place the middle of the bandage at the center of your dog's upper chest. Bring the ends up and cross them over the shoulder blades, then down behind the front legs. Cross the ends again under the belly, then up to the center of the back. Secure the ends with a safety pin, avoiding pinning directly over the spine. The wrap should be snug but not interfere with movement.

The full body wrap can be done in a variety of ways. A simple one is to pin two bandages together (or use a single, longer one). Begin as you did with the half-wrap, crossing the ends over the shoulder blades and crossing again under the belly. Bring the ends up but instead of pinning them, cross them over the small of the back, then through the inner thighs from front to back, and up on the sides of the tail. Cross at the small of the back and secure the ends with a safety pin. As with the half wrap, be sure the pin is not directly over the dog's spine and that movement is not restricted. Ensure too that the wrap does not obstruct elimination.

For more information on using the Ttouch Body Wrap, see *Getting in Ttouch with Your Dog* in *Resources*.

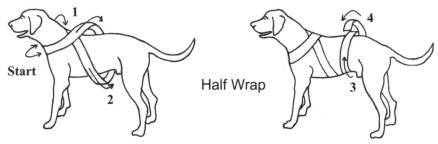

1. *Cross over shoulders*   3. *Cross under belly*
2. *Bring down behind front legs* 4. *Secure ends*

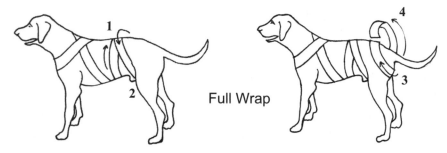

1. *Cross ends over small of back*   3. *Cross and up around tail*
2. *Through inner thighs from front* 4. *Secure ends*

Prefabricated Wraps

If you're not the do-it-yourself type and prefer the ready-made route, you'll be pleased to know about two ready-to-wear products, the Anxiety Wrap™ and the Thundershirt™. Both use constant, gentle, uniform pressure to calm dogs. The Anxiety Wrap™ hugs the body like a dancer's leotard, and uses various elastic bands and "butt straps" to enhance the fit. The Thundershirt™ is made of a one-piece, lightweight, comfortable material with enough stretch to be form fitting. Its velcro closures make it easy to apply, and I have successfully used it with many of my clients' dogs. (See *Resources* for both products).

Both wraps can be used for thunderstorm anxiety, grooming issues, carsickness, and more. Although they are safer to leave on a home-alone dog than Ttouch bandage wraps or T-shirt wraps, I do not recommend leaving *any* wrap on an unsupervised dog for long periods of time.

My newly adopted dog Sierra, a four-time shelter dog who came complete with a sweet personality and a serious case of separation anxiety, models the Thundershirt™. We both appreciate the fast, easy on and off application.

Chase, a 7-year-old Golden, suffered from separation anxiety and severe storm phobia. The Anxiety Wrap™ calmed him within five minutes.

Introducing Your Dog to a Body Wrap

Introduce your dog to your chosen type of wrap when she is relaxed, rather than waiting until a thunderstorm or other fear-inducing event is expected. Create a good association by doing "Happy Wrap" sessions: place the wrap on your dog, then give her a stuffed chew toy or engage in soothing massage, petting, or whatever else she enjoys. Once you have created a good association with the wrap over the course of a few brief sessions, place the wrap on your dog before a stressful situation and remove it afterward. For example, wrap your dog before a thunderstorm is expected, then remove it after the storm has passed. If your dog is anxious in a group training class, place the wrap on her before class, have an enjoyable training session with lots of treats and praise, then remove the wrap afterward. Be sure to do Happy Wrap sessions now and then outside of fear-inducing situations to keep up the good association.

Very soon you'll be saying of your dog's fear issues, "It's a wrap!"

DAP
(Dog Appeasing Pheromone)

DAP is an acronym for Dog Appeasing Pheromone. Sounds like something Fifi the Poodle would dab behind her ears to attract Spike the Doberman, doesn't it? No, it's not pooch perfume, but the reality is just as fascinating. According to the French scientists who first identified it, this type of pheromone is found in all lactating mammals within three to five days after giving birth. Produced in the mammary glands, the pheromones convey a sense of security to the offspring. Dogs detect pheromones of their own species through the vomero-nasal organ located in the nasal cavity. Because the receptors in that organ are neurologically linked to the limbic system—the part of the brain that controls many moods and emotions, among other things—the molecules can affect behavior in times of anxiety.

Products that contain DAP—a synthetic reproduction of the naturally occurring pheromone—have a calming effect on pups and adult dogs alike. The use of DAP to calm anxious dogs is a fairly recent development, and a promising one. The most common form of DAP resembles a plug-in air freshener. A small, electrically heated diffuser releases the scent molecules into the air. (Don't worry, the molecules are odorless to humans.) The product, sold under the brand name Comfort Zone™ (see *Resources*), covers an area of 500 to 650 square feet. With constant use it lasts approximately one month, and refills are available.

The product is also available in spray form, which can be used around a dog's resting area, in the car, and anywhere calm behavior is desired. An especially helpful application is to spray the product on a bandana, which can then be placed around your dog's neck. The treated bandana can be worn to help calm your dog in any environment he finds stressful, such as a group class or a walk around the block. Although no preparation is necessary, you can boost the good associations by having your dog wear the treated bandana a few times while receiving massages or enjoying a special chew toy before wearing it in stressful situations.

At the time of this printing, the product has become available in collar form as well, and is sold under the name "D.A.P. Collar" (see *Resources*). This option would be advantageous for a dog who is nervous in general. A standard nylon collar holds the diffuser, and the effects last up to four weeks.

Preliminary Findings

Here are a few findings from preliminary studies of DAP's effects on dogs:

- A study compared the behavior of adult dogs housed in a public animal shelter before and after DAP was administered. After seven days, there were significant differences in resting, barking, and sniffing frequency in response to a friendly stranger, with the DAP-treated dogs showing less stress.[1]

- In clinical trials coordinated by French scientist Dr. Patrick Pageat, 11 investigators working in four different countries used 26 dogs that displayed problem behaviors when left alone. Twenty displayed destructive behavior; 18, excessive vocalization; and 12 house-soiled. In each case the pheromone was emitted by way of the DAP diffuser, which was placed in the room most often frequented by the dog during the day. By the end of the first week, the destructive behavior was down 27 percent. By the 28th day, the dogs showed an 85 percent level of improvement. Vocalization incidents decreased by almost a quarter in the first week, and after 28 days there was an overall decrease of 72 percent. House-soiling incidents were reduced by half by the second week of the trial, and after 28 days the incidents were down by 66 percent. Overall, at the end of the 28-day trial, 85 percent were confirmed as cured or improved.[2]

- A study presented at the 2004 Annual Symposium of Animal Behavior Research involved veterinarians using a gel form of DAP. Two groups of dogs received physical examinations. Those in the control group were examined without any exposure to DAP, and those in the DAP group were seen by vets who had rubbed the gel on their hands prior to the examination. Previous to the examinations, owners had been asked to rate their dogs' fear levels during a typical medical examination. The vets were asked to use the same rating scale to evaluate each dog's responses during each phase of the exam. The results showed a great difference between the reactions of the two groups in each situation of the medical exam: regardless of the testing phase, there were always more "fearful" dogs in the control group and more "calm" dogs in the DAP group.[3] These preliminary results suggest that the use of DAP during veterinary exams could help some dogs to feel calmer.

Anecdotal Evidence

I have recommended DAP to many of my clients whose dogs were anxious when left alone. These dogs displayed anxiety by whining, pacing, barking, or chewing on themselves or on objects. According to the majority of the owners, after a week or two of constant exposure to DAP (the diffuser must be left plugged in, as opposed to plugging it in only when a stressful situation arises), the dogs seemed significantly calmer. Some trainers I know spray their training rooms with DAP before group classes, and they are convinced it makes for calmer canine students.

DAP can be useful for treating separation issues, generalized anxiety, fear of noises, barking, whining, howling, destructive behavior, stress-related urination or defecation, and compulsive disorders such as incessant paw-licking. It may even help to encourage harmony in homes where there is tension between resident dogs, as it creates a more relaxed atmosphere.

Ways to Use DAP

- If your dog is nervous in general, leave DAP diffusers plugged in around the house.

- Spray DAP on a bandana and place it on your dog (or nearby) while you do massage, Ttouch, or whatever form of touch your dog finds calming. Your dog will get a double benefit: the calming effect of the DAP, and the positive association that is created by pairing exposure to DAP with the relaxation. After a few sessions, have your dog wear the bandana in situations he normally finds stress-inducing.

- If your dog is afraid to ride in the car, spray some DAP in the vehicle before your next trip.

- Spray DAP on your dog's bedding. This can be especially helpful if your dog is anxious about being left alone, or when bringing home a new dog. You can also take the bedding along to a group class or other environments your dog finds stressful.

- If you are taking your dog to an indoor environment in which he normally becomes anxious, ask whether you can bring DAP spray and treat the environment. If your dog fears vet exams, ask your vet whether it would be okay to spray the treatment room; your vet just might find the effects encouraging enough to consider using DAP diffusers in the clinic.

- If your dog is anxious around visitors and you are having overnight guests, plug in a diffuser near your dog's sleeping area.

Note: There are some dogs on whom DAP will have no effect, and a small majority may react in a negative way and become more stressed. Test the product on your dog in a non-stress-producing environment at home first.

As with so many other adjunct therapies, DAP is not meant as a substitute for behavior modification, although some relief may certainly be obtained through the use of DAP alone.

1　　Tod, E., D. Brander and N. Waran. Efficacy of Dog Appeasing Pheromone in Reducing Stress & Fear Related Behavior in Shelter Dogs. In press.

2　　Mills, D. (2002) Veterinary Times Magazine, October

3　　Gaultier, E., L. Bonnafous and P. Pageat. (2004) Interests of the Use of a Synthetic Dog Appeasing Pheromone (DAP) on Behavior During Medical Examination: Preliminary Results. *Proceedings of the Annual Symposium of Animal Behavior Research.* Philadelphia. AVSAB. pp. 33-34.

Calming Cap™

Trish King is the Director of Animal Behavior and Training at the Marin Humane Society in northern California. She is also a popular seminar presenter who teaches creative solutions to behavior problems.

One of Trish's most inspired ideas came when she was working with an excitable dog who couldn't settle down in a car. The standard solution would have been to put the dog in a crate to block out environmental distractions, but the car was too small. Trish joked that they needed to turn off the lights so the dog could calm down—that was when she first thought of using a cap to create that effect. She soon designed a prototype for what is now known as the Calming Cap™.

The Cap is a useful tool for easing canine anxiety in high-stress situations. It is made of a soft fabric that is held in place by elastic and two Velcro® strips that wrap around the dog's collar. The panel that covers the dog's eyes is made of a sheer fabric that filters vision, but still allows the dog to make out shapes. This effectively "dims the lights" on outside stimuli so the dog can settle down. The Cap allows dogs to remain calmer during behavior modification exercises, which leads to greater success. Suzanne Hetts, Ph.D., a Certified Applied Animal Behaviorist, comments, "I've found that the Calming Cap tends to have an overall suppressive effect on behavior," and that it "helped to decrease my Dalmatian's alarm barking in the house in response to outside noises."

Uses for the Calming Cap™

- For nail-clipping, at home or at the groomer's.
- During veterinary visits for vaccinations, blood draws, exams, and other procedures.
- During a desensitization and counterconditioning program, to ease dog-dog and dog-people introductions.
- When riding in cars.
- For dogs who suffer from separation anxiety. The dog wears the Cap in the owner's presence, which helps the dog to become accustomed to the diminished view of the owner while still sensing her presence—an intermediate step to the owner being completely out of sight.
- In any situation that provokes anxiety.

The Cap should be introduced to your dog slowly while creating pleasant associations. The process involves slipping the Cap on while praising continuously, giving a treat while it is on, then slipping it off. See the product brochure for detailed instructions on acclimating your dog to the Calming Cap™, how to ensure a proper fit, and how to use the product correctly. (See *Resources* for purchasing information.)

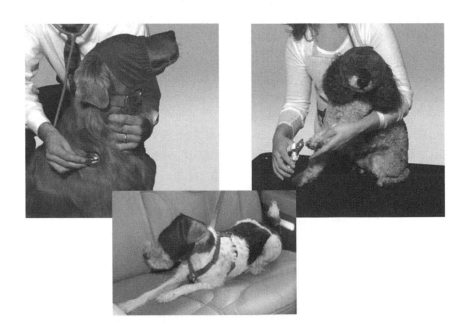

49

Homeopathy

The system of medicine known as homeopathy was developed by Samuel Hahnemann, M.D., in the 18th century. It is based on the "Law of Similars," which states that "like cures like." In other words, the appropriate medicine for an illness is the one that, in larger doses, would create the very symptoms of that illness. Administered in a miniscule amount, the micro-dose of medicine (from a plant, mineral, or animal source) instead stimulates the body's natural defense mechanisms, which helps the body to heal itself. Homeopathy works for both people and animals, and can heal not only physical symptoms, but emotional issues as well.

Strength and Dosage

Homeopathic medicines are diluted many times and are potentized through a system of vigorous shaking called *succussing*. The strength or dilution of the remedy is designated on the label. The designation 1X means the remedy was formulated with one part of the active ingredient to nine parts liquid (1:10), usually distilled water or alcohol. 3X signifies that after making the initial 1:10 dilution, one part of the resulting solution was mixed with nine parts of a dilutant, and then that solution was mixed 1:10 again. 1C signifies that a remedy has been diluted 100 times, and 1M, 1000 times (notice the use of Roman numerals).

In homeopathy, an interesting phenomenon occurs: the more a remedy is diluted, the more powerful it becomes. Although proponents might not be able to explain exactly how and why it works, they agree homeopathy is powerful medicine. For home use, the lower strength X potencies are normally used. But regardless of the potency, remedies should be used under the care of a holistic veterinarian who is trained in homeopathy.

Homeopathy differs from traditional medicine in regard to dosage. With homeopathic remedies, exact dosage is not crucial. Since the medicines work on an energetic level, it is more important that the subject be exposed to the vibrational energy of the remedy, which is what induces the change. Energy is qualitative, not quantitative. The correct remedy will resonate with the body and help the desired change to occur. An incorrect remedy will not resonate no matter how much is given.

A typical dose is 3 to 5 tiny pellets, or half a dropperful of liquid. As to frequency of dosage: higher potencies generally require and tolerate less repetition. Lower potencies may be repeated as needed, or on a schedule. The length of time it takes to treat an issue is directly related to how long the issue has been present.

Administration

Homeopathic remedies are found in both pill and liquid form. Pills are more widely available and less expensive. It is advisable that neither dogs nor owners touch the pills or liquid directly. Because the remedies work at a subtle energetic level, they are easily contaminated. For best results, the remedy is normally placed directly inside the dog's mouth. (Adding it to food could cause neutralization.) A pill is administered by tapping it into the vial cap. The owner then holds one hand palm-down over the dog's muzzle, with the other hand cradling the lower jaw while holding the cap. The top hand is used to open the mouth and tilt the pills inside, toward the back of the throat.

Liquids can be given from a spoon and deposited anywhere in a dog's mouth. Gently pulling the back portion of the lower lip (near the molars) out to the side creates a pocket in which to deposit the liquid. It is not necessary that a dog swallow the pills or the liquid; so long as the remedy comes in contact with the gums, it will be absorbed. If a dog objects to the taste of the liquid, it is probably due to the alcohol base, in which case a few drops can be placed into one-fourth to one-half teaspoon of spring water or filtered water. A few drops of the resulting solution can then be administered in an eyedropper.

After a single dose is given, one waits to see whether there is improvement, as it can take time for the body to respond. Higher potency remedies sometimes need be given only once. Lower potencies are often repeated until the desired result is achieved. If symptoms worsen, either the potency is too high or the particular remedy was not the right choice.

Applicable Remedies

Classical homeopathy takes into account not only physical symptoms, but mental and emotional states as well. A holistic veterinarian who is trained in homeopathy will, after careful questioning, prescribe the correct remedy for your dog. Remedies are highly individualized and homeopathy is somewhat of an art. The following is a list of some of the remedies that are commonly used to treat fear issues.

Aconite	For dogs who seem to be afraid of almost everything, and are generally anxious. These dogs usually have fear reactions that are sudden and strong.
Calcarea carbonica	For dogs who are fearful of new situations and people. Dogs who are candidates for this remedy fear change, and will often avoid a specific room or area.
Passiflora incarnata	This remedy will not stop a fear from recurring, but it can be used for its calming effect.
Stramonium	For dogs who are in such a state of terror that they may bite. (Obviously, this one requires very careful administration!)

Tips

- Administer only one remedy at a time (unless combined for you by a homeopath).

- While using homeopathic remedies, do not give non-homeopathic treatments such as flower essences, herbs, or even acupuncture or acupressure, unless directed to do so by your homeopathic vet. Also, avoid feeding raw garlic during homeopathic treatment.

- Do not feed your dog within 15 minutes of administering a remedy.

- Do not expose remedies to electromagnetic fields, as the potency could be reduced.

- Do not expose remedies to heat or sunlight.

- Remedies last almost indefinitely when stored in a cool, dark place.

A referral to an accredited veterinary homeopath can be found through the Academy of Veterinary Homeopathy (AVH), as well as the American Holistic Veterinary Medical Association (AHVMA). Even if there is no homeopathic vet in your vicinity, consultations can often be done by phone. (For contact information for these organizations, as well as books and homeopathic products, see *Resources*.)

50

Healing with Herbs

When wild animals are sick or in pain, they can't very well visit the local drug store for medicine. They are, however, surrounded by an amazing natural pharmacy—the world of plants. Many of our modern medications are derived from plants. In fact, many experts believe that *phytochemicals*, the active ingredients found in herbs, may offer the best protection against many of today's diseases.

Herbology 101

Humans have a long history of using herbs for healing. The art of Chinese herbal healing dates back to at least 3000-5000 BCE, and herbal healing was taught in ancient Greece and Rome. Every world culture has had its own knowledge of healing with plants. Plants were used as antiseptics, anti-spasmodics, painkillers, and contraceptives, and can be used to address both physical illness and emotional stress. Herbal healing enjoyed a renaissance in the United States in the 1960s and is still going strong today.

Whereas medical drugs are synthesized from a plant's active ingredient (and then patented by a pharmaceutical company), herbs contain the complete, natural plant and so contain the plant's full healing properties. Herbs have a lower concentration of the "active ingredient" than do synthesized drugs, but because the substance is in its natural form, it is much less likely to create side effects in the body.

Herbs are powerful, effective healers. They help the body to eliminate and detoxify, thus addressing the underlying cause of the illness, rather than simply masking or suppressing the symptoms. Herbs are often less expensive than medical drugs and are available over the counter.

Dosage for Dogs

Herbs can be used to heal dogs of physical ailments and to assist in the treatment of emotional issues, fear included. The most common herbal formulations are tablets, capsules, and liquid tinctures. There are no precise doses for animals, but a standard guideline for pills is half of a human dose for medium-to-large-sized dogs, and a quarter of a human dose for small dogs. The dosage is considerably less for tinctures, although recommendations vary from herbalist to herbalist: some recommend four to eight drops twice daily, while others recommend starting with one-third of the recommended human dose; that is, five to fifteen drops for a 50-pound dog. Follow the directions on the label if the product is made specifically for dogs, or consult your holistic veterinarian (or the books listed in *Resources*). Tablets and capsules can be mixed in with your dog's food. Tinctures can be administered by spoon; pour the liquid into a pocket created by pulling the back portion of your dog's lower lip out gently. Start with a single dose and watch for signs of stomach upset; nausea is the most common side effect of herbs.

Some pills or capsules may contain less of the actual herb, depending on the manufacturing process. In the United States, herbs are classified as foods and are therefore not eligible for approval by the Food and Drug Administration (although the FDA has banned certain herbs due to potential health hazards). Because of this lack of regulation, product quality varies from one manufacturer to the next. Do your research and stick with reputable companies (see *Resources*).

Although herbs are widely available, they must be used with care. Some are poisonous, while others might not be appropriate for your dog, depending on her physical, mental, and emotional health. *Check with your veterinarian or a holistic veterinarian (see Resources) to be sure the herb you wish to administer is safe for your particular dog.*

The Calming Herbs

Herbs can be quite effective in calming fearful dogs. Unlike some drugs, herbs will not cause your dog to become sluggish or dazed, and will not affect mental capacity or physical capabilities. But just as with traditional medicines, some herbs work well on certain individuals while they do nothing, or even have an adverse effect, on others. Some herbs that are commonly prescribed for anxious or fearful dogs are extremely effective, although on a small segment of dogs they actually make the condition worse. It is a good practice to administer an herb before it is actually needed, so you can monitor your dog's reaction.

Valerian is the most commonly used herb for calming. It gently soothes the nerves and helps dogs to achieve physical relaxation. Valerian is also an anti-spasmodic, which makes it useful for dogs whose nervousness is accompanied by stomach upset. It can be extremely useful for helping dogs with nervous anxiety, and is a good choice for specific situations such as thunderstorms and visits to the veterinarian or groomer. Because valerian loses potency when dried, it is best used as a tincture. In the case of an anticipated severe anxiety-causing event, begin to administer valerian three days beforehand. Give five drops of a low-alcohol tincture three to four times a day, continuing through the event as needed. *Note:* In a small number of cases valerian can actually have the reverse effect, causing stimulation instead of relaxation. In that case, try *Passionflower*.

Passionflower. Gregory Tilford is a renowned expert on herbs, a consultant to many homeopathic veterinarians, and CEO of Animal's Apawthecary, which develops herbal products for use in animals. Passionflower is Tilford's top herbal choice for dogs who are fear-biters and those who show aggressive behaviors when stressed. It is indicated where valerian has had the opposite of the desired effect, and is a good choice for dogs who could be described as "hot-tempered." Passionflower can help to "take the edge off" dogs who do not want other dogs visiting their homes or have aggression issues associated with jealousy of other dogs. Passionflower is also a good choice for emotional upsets such as separation anxiety.

Skullcap is useful in cases of acute or chronic nervous tension or anxiety. It can help to calm dogs who are nervous in general, especially those who express their anxiety through jumpiness, trembling, or hypersensitivity to movement, sound, or touch. It may also help dogs who are sensitive to electrical fields, and can help to relieve nervousness related to traumatic experience. Squirt 10-15 drops of the tincture into your dog's mouth (for an average-sized dog—dosage should be adjusted according to size, so check with your veterinarian) or onto her food, repeating at 15-20 minute intervals as needed. You could even massage one full dropper of the liquid onto the skin at the back of the neck. The dosages for herbal tinctures to treat fear issues are high; if they weren't, the herb's effects could be overridden by the dog's heightened emotional state.

Vervain is for dogs with a sensitive, "on edge" disposition whose fear reactions tend to escalate out of control. It can be also used to treat thunderstorm phobias. For general nervousness, Robert McDowell, an Australian herbalist, recommends five drops of vervain along with five drops of *St. John's wort* (best known as an anti-depressant) twice daily in the dog's food for at least three months. After three months the dog's reaction pattern should be greatly reduced. St. John's wort is helpful for the nervous system that is so physically sensitive that loud noises cause not only fright, but actual pain. Mixing together three fluid ounces each of vervain and St. John's wort will make a three-month supply for an average-sized dog. McDowell also adds two drops each of the following flower essences: Mimulus (for fear), Walnut (for over-sensitivity), Rock Rose (for panic), Cherry Plum (for loss of control stemming from fear/panic), Honeysuckle (to help break habitual patterns of response), and Larch (to support self-confidence). He advises that the formula be given twice daily at the following dosage: five drops for small dogs, ten for medium-sized dogs, and fifteen for large breeds.

In addition to being useful individually, herbs are also available in ready-made combination formulas. Most calming formulations contain valerian, skullcap, and passionflower. Some also include non-herbal agents such as L-tryptophan, a naturally occurring amino acid. Before administering any herbal formula check with your vet, and investigate any ingredients with which you are not familiar. Always follow the label for the manufacturer's suggested dosage unless your veterinarian advises otherwise.

Tips

- Once you choose an herb that is appropriate for your dog, administer it twenty minutes to an hour before an anxiety-producing event is expected.

- If an herb is having no effect, or the opposite of the desired effect, stop using it.

- Calming herbs should never be used within 48 hours of anesthesia (before or after).

- Calming herbs should never be used in combination with anti-depressants, anti-convulsants, or sedatives.

Although herbs can be immensely helpful, do not expect an instant miracle cure. You may have to do some experimentation to find which herb works best for your dog and at what dosage. And if you are using herbs to address an ongoing anxiety issue, behavior modification should be done in conjunction with the herbal remedy. (To find a holistic veterinarian, see *Resources*.)

51

Acupuncture
and Acupressure

According to Chinese medicine, life force energy—Qi (pronounced *chee*)—flows along energy pathways in the body called meridians. Each meridian is associated with a particular internal organ and physiological system. When there is an imbalance or deficit of energy in the meridians, disease can occur. By stimulating specific points along these energy pathways, blockages can be released and the flow of energy restored. With energy flowing unimpeded, the body can re-balance and heal itself.

Acupuncture uses fine needles to stimulate points along the meridians, while acupressure uses manual pressure. Both modalities are used to relieve physical pain, aid in the removal of toxic wastes, heal illness, relax the body and mind, and increase feelings of overall well-being.

Acupuncture

Acupuncture has been used in China for over 5,000 years to relieve people of various pains and illnesses, and was also practiced on large animals, including elephants and horses. Veterinary acupuncture, developed in Europe, adapted the Chinese techniques for use on smaller animals, including dogs and cats. Today, acupuncture is used to treat many physical ailments in dogs including hip dysplasia, arthritis, lameness, and dermatitis. Soko's arthritis and degenerative myelopathy have been helped immensely by acupuncture. If a dog's fearful behavior has a physiological cause, and acupuncture can address that cause, the fear can be alleviated. There are also specific acupuncture points for nervous tension and mental stress, which can greatly benefit dogs who have a generally nervous disposition.

If you are experiencing a fearful reaction of your own at the thought of needles being inserted into your fur-kid, relax. The needles are extremely fine and rounded at the tips; insertion is virtually painless. Soko and I have both had many acupuncture treatments, and neither of us has had a painful response to the needles.

It *is* important that acupuncture be administered by a professional. Some states require that a practitioner be a licensed veterinarian to perform acupuncture on animals. Some states do not have that regulation, but do require that the acupuncturist perform treatment only under the direct supervision of a veterinarian. Others have less stringent requirements. The International Veterinary Acupuncturist Directory (see *Resources*) can provide information on acupuncture societies and help you to find a qualified veterinary acupuncturist in your area.

Acupressure

The same points that are stimulated in acupuncture can be stimulated manually. Acupressure is applied using the thumb, finger, or hand. While acupuncture must be administered by a professional, acupressure may be done at home.

An article in *The Whole Dog Journal* includes descriptions of two cases where acupressure was successfully used to treat fear issues. In the first case, a Golden Retriever named Stella had been traumatized by a lightning strike. Subsequently, she cowered and trembled whenever she heard thunder, fireworks, or fire engines. This was especially problematic because Stella was meant to be a companion dog in the Canine Companions for Independence program. Nancy Zidonis and Amy Snow, canine acupresssure experts and co-authors of *The Well-Connected Dog: A Guide to Canine Acupressure* (see *Resources*), recommended one acupressure treatment daily, along with a homeopathic calming remedy. Within two weeks, Stella was less affected by the frightening sounds. After another two weeks of treatment every three days, the therapy was completely successful.

The second case involved Sheba, an Irish Setter who was thunderstorm-phobic. Zidonis and Snow administered weekly acupressure treatments, with Sheba's owner giving treatments in between. Within two weeks Sheba's behavior improved. After two months of treatment, she could tolerate thunder and other loud noises.[1]

Zidonis and Snow often combine acupressure with homeopathy, calming herbs, or essential oils. Their book includes detailed treatment plans.

1   Puotinen, CJ. (2000) Bring In Da Noise. *Whole Dog Journal*. May: pp. 3-7

52

Pharmacological Intervention

For most dogs with mild to moderate fear issues, pharmacological intervention is neither appropriate nor necessary. However, for dogs with severe fear issues, or those that do not respond to behavior modification alone, medication can be extremely beneficial.

Considerations

In the majority of cases, long-term-use drugs are recommended as adjuncts to behavior modification, not alternatives to it. It is all too tempting to avoid the work involved in following a behavior protocol for months and instead just "give the dog something." After all, American culture is all about rapid results, the "quick fix." Why eat sensibly to lose weight when you can take a pill that will cause rapid weight loss? Waiting even five seconds for a web page to load leaves us gritting our teeth! But there is no shortcut to solving severe behavior issues. Medicating your dog without practicing the necessary behavior modification exercises would be like slapping a bandage on the problem; it would only mask it. There is no way around it—the underlying cause of the behavior must be treated.

The decision to use drug treatment should be arrived at with the assistance of a professional behavior specialist, applied animal behaviorist, and/or veterinarian. If there is a board-certified veterinary behaviorist in your area, even better (see *Resources*). Drugs must be prescribed by a veterinarian, and should be dispensed only after physical causes for the behavior have been ruled out. The vet should do blood work to determine that your dog is in good physical health and to serve as a baseline, and should inform you of any potential physical and behavioral side effects and potential interactions with other medications your dog is taking. Dogs, like people, tolerate and respond to some drugs better than others. Your vet can help you to decide when and if to switch medications.

> Don't assume that your veterinarian is an expert on canine behavior. Some vets have a great deal of knowledge on the subject, while others have close to none. This unfortunate lack is due to the fact that, traditionally, university veterinary curriculums have not placed much emphasis on behavior issues. Some vets do, however, pursue further knowledge of canine behavior, and some actually specialize in it. (See the *Resources* section for help on locating a veterinary behaviorist and other helpful professionals.)

Which Drugs are Commonly Prescribed?

There are a variety of drugs available to treat canine fear and anxiety issues. Some are prescribed for short-term situations where acute anxiety is involved, such as a thunderstorm or a long car ride. The class of drugs most often prescribed for short-term use is *benzodiazepines*, which include diazepam (Valium) and alprazolam (Xanax). (See *p. 273* for a warning about acepromazine, another commonly prescribed short-term drug.)

Other drugs are meant to be used over a longer period, and can take a few weeks to build up in the system. The two classes of drugs normally prescribed for long-term therapy are SSRIs (Selective Serotonin Reuptake Inhibitors) and TCAs (Tricyclic Antidepressants). SSRIs include fluoxetine (Prozac), paroxetine (Paxil), and sertraline (Zoloft). TCAs include clomipramine (Clomicalm) and amitriptyline (Elavil). Each class of drugs works in its own way to affect the body's neurochemistry, thereby affecting the mental and emotional state.

Will Drugs Turn my Dog into a Dope?

Many owners are afraid that drugs will turn their dogs into little fur-covered zombies. Although TCAs generally have more of a sedative effect than do SSRIs, neither will cause a drug-induced stupor. Anti-anxiety drugs increase levels of specific neurotransmitters. They "take the edge off" so anxiety is lessened, much as they do in humans.

Although the majority of canine behavior issues can be addressed without resorting to pharmacological intervention, there are those cases in which modifying behavior without it would be extremely difficult, if not impossible. If a dog fears other dogs to the point that she flies into a blind panic whenever she encounters one, no matter the distance, employing a standard desensitization and counterconditioning program will be impossible. If a dog is chronically or globally fearful, employing drug therapy can not only be helpful, but it can be a tremendous kindness as well. And if medication can help to lower a dog's anxiety to a workable level, behavior modification becomes possible.

Are We There Yet?

Most anti-anxiety medications are prescribed with instructions to increase the dosage gradually. As Karen Overall, Ph.D., states, "With the newer, more specific drugs, the long-term anti-anxiety effects and the learning effects are dependent on new protein synthesis involved in remodeling receptors. This process takes at least three to five weeks to kick in, so minimum treatment time to evaluate any effect, or any change of dose, is six to eight weeks."[1] Once the drugs have taken effect and the dog has demonstrated calmer behavior, behavior modification can be used to transform the dog's reaction into what would be considered a "normal" response to the trigger. Once that change has taken place (usually over the course of a few months or longer), the dog should be weaned off the medication gradually under the supervision of the veterinarian.

In most cases, although a behavior modification program has been completed and the medication discontinued, the dog should still not be considered "permanently cured." (The exception would be separation anxiety, where the dog gradually learns to tolerate the owner's absence and is very unlikely to backslide.) Take, for example, a dog who is extremely frightened by the mere sight of other dogs. The dog undergoes a treatment program of behavioral and pharmacological therapy, and can finally remain calm in the presence of other dogs. But if the dog is not exposed to other dogs for a long period afterward, or aspects of the behavioral protocol (such as giving treats when the dog sees another dog) are not periodically reinforced, the dog's behavior may regress.

If your dog's fear issues are mild to moderate, try behavior modification first, with the help of a professional if necessary. If your dog's issues are chronic or extreme, speak with a veterinary behaviorist, behavior specialist or your veterinarian about whether pharmacological intervention, along with behavior modification, might be beneficial.

1 Karen Overall, *Treating anxiety is different than "managing" the problem*, January 2003 <http://www.dvmnewsmagazine.com/dvm/article/articleDetail.jsp?id=43492> DVM Newsmagazine.

Tail End Wrap-Up

I sincerely hope that the behavior modification techniques and therapies you have learned will help you to help your dog overcome her fears. For helpful products, information, and a listing of professional organizations that can provide further assistance, continue on to the *Resources* section.

I commend you on your kindness, compassion, and patience in taking the time to help your best friend. And although time limitations prevent me from being able to answer personal requests for advice, if you found this book helpful, please let me know.

Wishing you and your dog a long, happy, relaxed life together.

Nicole Wilde

author@phantompub.com
www.phantompub.com

Nicole Wilde
c/o Phantom Publishing
P.O. Box 2814
Santa Clarita, CA 91386
U.S.A.

Resources

Many of the following books, videos, and DVDs are available through Dogwise (www.dogwise.com), amazon.com, and your local book retailer.

Body Language

Dog Language: An Encyclopedia of Canine Behavior
Roger Abrantes
Wakan Tanka Publishers, dist. by Dogwise Publishing, 1997 ISBN 0-9660484-0-7

How to Speak Dog
Stanley Coren
New York, NY: Fireside, 2000 ISBN 0-684-86534-3

The Other End of the Leash
Patricia B. McConnell, Ph.D.
The Ballantine Publishing Group, 2002 ISBN 034544678X

On Talking Terms with Dogs: Calming Signals
Turid Rugaas
Wenatchee, WA: Dogwise Publishing, 2006 ISBN 1929242360

Child/Dog Relationship

Living with Kids and Dogs...Without Losing Your Mind
Colleen Pelar, CPDT
Woodbridge, VA: C&R Publishing, LLC, 2005 ISBN 1-933562-66-8

Raising Puppies & Kids Together: A Guide for Parents
Pia Silvani and Lynn Eckhardt
Neptune, NJ: T.F.H. Publications, 2005 ISBN 0793805686

Doggone Safe
(Articles, Doggone Safe board game)
www.doggonesafe.com, 877-350-3232

Family Paws
(Articles, educational CD, phone consults, Dogs and Storks™ program)
www.familypaws.com, 919-961-1608

Clicker Training

Click for Joy!
Melissa Alexander
Waltham, MA: Sunshine Books, 2003 ISBN 1-890948-12-8

Right on Target!
Mandy Book and Cheryl Smith
Wenatchee, WA: Dogwise Publishing, 2005 ISBN 1929242328

The How of Bow Wow (DVD/video)
Virginia Broitman and Sherri Lippman
Available through dogwise.com and sitstay.com

Clicker Fun: Dog Tricks and Games using Positive Reinforcement
Deborah Jones
Eliot, ME: Howln Moon Press, 1998 ISBN 1888994088

Clicking with Your Dog
Peggy Tillman
Waltham, MA: Sunshine Books, 2000 ISBN 1-890948-05-5

Fear Issues

Dogs are From Neptune (also discusses aggression)
Jean Donaldson
Canada: Lasar Multimedia Productions, Inc., 1998 ISBN 0-9684207-1-0

The Cautious Canine
Patricia B. McConnell, Ph.D.
Black Earth, WI: Dog's Best Friend, Ltd., 2002 ISBN 1-891767-00-3

Obedience Training

Dog-Friendly Dog Training
Andrea Arden
New York, NY: Howell Books, 1999 ISBN 1-582450099

The Power of Positive Dog Training
Pat Miller
New York, NY: Hungry Minds, Inc., 2001 ISBN 0-7645-3609-5

The Dog Whisperer: A Compassionate, Non-Violent Approach to Dog Training
Paul Owens
Hollbrook, MA: Adams Media Corp., 2006 ISBN

The Dog Whisperer: Beginning & Intermediate Dog Training (DVD)
Paul Owens
Sand Castle Enterprises, LLC, 2004
www.dogwhispererdvd.com, 800-955-5440

Train Your Dog: The Positive, Gentle Method (DVD)
(starring Nicole Wilde and Laura Bourhenne)
The Picture Company, Inc., 2003 UPC 829637 12237 0
www.trainyourdog.tv, 818-981-0252
(also available through dogwise.com and amazon.com)

Separation Anxiety

Dogs Home Alone
Roger Abrantes
Wakan Tanka Publishers, dist. by Dogwise Publishing, 1999 ISBN 0966048423

I'll be Home Soon! How to Prevent and Treat Separation Anxiety
Patricia B. McConnell, Ph.D.
Black Earth, WI: Dog's Best Friend, Ltd. 2000 ISBN 1-891767-05-4

Don't Leave Me! Step-by-Step Help for Your Dog's Separation Anxiety
Nicole Wilde
Santa Clarita, CA: Phantom Publishing, 2010 ISBN 978-0-981722733

Trick Training

Take a Bow Wow I & II (DVD/video)
(trick training using clicker training)
Virginia Broitman and Sherri Lippman
Available through dogwise.com and sitstay.com

The Trick is in the Training
Stephanie J. Taunton and Cheryl S. Smith
Barrons' Educational Series: 1998, ISBN 0764104926

COMPLEMENTARY THERAPIES & HEALTH

Dr. Pitcairn's Complete Guide to Natural Health for Dogs & Cats
Richard H. Pitcairn, DVM, Ph.D. & Susan Hubble Pitcairn
Emmaus, PA: Rodale Press, Inc., 1995 ISBN 0-87596-243-2

Four Paws, Five Directions: A Guide to Chinese Medicine
for Cats and Dogs
Cheryl Schwartz
Berkeley, CA: Celestial Arts, 1996 ISBN 0890977904

Natural Healing for Dogs & Cats
Diane Stein
Freedom, CA: The Crossing Press, Inc., 1993 ISBN 0895946149

Holistic Guide for a Healthy Dog
Wendy Volhard and Kerry Brown
New York, NY: Howell Book House, 2000 ISBN 1582451532

AltVetMed
(Information about complementary and alternative veterinary medicine.)
www.altvetmed.org

Jean Dodds
(Link between vaccinations and fear issues,
and thyroid and behavior issues.)
http://www.itsfortheanimals.com/DODDS-RESUME.HTM

Acupuncture and Acupressure

The Well-Connected Dog: A Guide to Canine Acupressure
Nancy Zidonis and Amy Snow
Larkspur, CO: Tallgrass Publishers, LLC, 1999 ISBN 0964598248

The American Academy of Veterinary Acupuncture
www.aava.org
860-635-6300

International Veterinary Acupuncturist Directory (IVAD)
www.komvet.at/ivadkom/vapsocs.htm
303-682-1167

International Veterinary Acupuncturist Society
www.ivas.org
970-266-0666

Flower Remedies

Bach Flower Remedies for Animals
Helen Graham and Gregory Vlamis
Tallahassee, FL: Findhorn Press, 1999 ISBN 1-899171-72-X

Ellon USA, Inc.
1-800-4 BE-CALM

Flower Essence Society
(research, education, networking)
www.flowersociety.org, 800-736-9222

Nelson Bach USA Ltd.
1-800-314-BACH

Herbs

The Complete Herbal Handbook for the Dog and Cat
Juliette de Bairacli-Levy
UK: Faber & Faber, 1991 ISBN 0571161154

All You Ever Wanted to Know About Herbs for Pets
Mary Wulff-Tilford and Gregory Tilford
Irvine, CA: Bowtie Press, 1999 ISBN 1889540641

Animal's Apawthecary products (created by Gregory Tilford)
Available through some health food and pet supply stores, or
online retailers by doing a Google search for Animal's Apawthecary.

Gaia Herbs and Herb Pharm products
Available in health food stores.

Herbs for Animals (includes "Calm Down" formula)
(liquid herbal extracts, consults)
www.herbsforanimals.com

Robert McDowell (herbal products/advice)
New South Wales, Australia
www.herbal-treatments.com.au

Veterinary Botanical Medicine Association
www.vbma.org
Fax: 770-926-7796

Holistic Veterinarians

American Holistic Veterinary Medical Association (AHVMA)
(find a holistic vet in your area)
www.ahvma.org
410-569-0795

Homeopathy

Homeopathic Care for Cats and Dogs
Don Hamilton, DVM
Berkeley, CA: North Atlantic Books, 1999 ISBN 1-55643-295-X

Academy of Veterinary Homeopathy
www.theavh.org
Phone/fax 866-652-1590

Arrowroot Standard Direct
(homeopathic remedies)
www.arrowroot.com
800-456-7818

Hahnemann Laboratories
www.hahnemannlabs.com
888-427-6422

Massage

The Healing Touch for Dogs
Dr. Michael W. Fox
New York, NY: Newmarket Press, 2004 ISBN 1-55704-576-3

Canine Massage: A Complete Reference Manual
Jean-Pierre Hourdebaigt
Wenatchee, WA: Dogwise Publishing, 2004 ISBN 1929242085

Effective Pet Massage for Dogs
Jonathan Rudinger
Effective Pet Massage Manual, 1998 ISBN 096648262X
www.petmassage.com offers videos, VHS/DVDs and workshops.

The Pet Owner's Massage Guide for Dogs and Cats (DVD)
Janet Marlow Music, LLC, 2005
Available through amazon.com

Miscellaneous Healing Therapies

International Alliance for Animal Therapy and Healing (IAATH)
www.iaath.com
530-795-5040

Nutrition

The BARF Diet
Dr. Ian Billinghurst
Australia: Billinghurst, 2001 ISBN 0958592519

Darwin's Natural Selections
www.darwinspet.com
1-877-738-6325

Food Pets Die For: Shocking Facts about Pet Food
Ann N. Martin
Troutdale, OR: NewSage Press, 2003 ISBN 0939165465

Dr. Pitcairn's Complete Guide to Natural Health for Dogs & Cats
Richard H. Pitcairn, DVM, Ph.D. & Susan Hubble Pitcairn
Emmaus, PA: Rodale Press, Inc., 1995 ISBN 0-87596-243-2

The Ultimate Diet
Kymythy R. Schultze
Carlsbad, CA: Hay House, Inc., 1998 ISBN 1561706361

Home-Prepared Dog & Cat Diets
Donald R. Strombeck, DVM, Ph.D.
Iowa: Iowa State Press, 1999 ISBN 0813821495

TTouch

Getting in Ttouch with your Dog
Linda Tellington-Jones
North Pomfret, VT: Trafalgar Square, 2001 ISBN 1570762066

Tteam & Ttouch
(information, classes, locate a practitioner)
www.ttouch.com
1-800-854-8326

Wraps

Anxiety Wrap
www.anxietywrap.com
1-877-652-1266

Thundershirt
www.thundershirt.com
1-866-892-2078

DOG SPORTS

Agility

Agility Tricks for Improved Attention, Flexibility & Confidence
Donna Duford
Chicopee, MA: Clean Run Productions, 1999 ISBN 1892694026

Do-It-Yourself Agility Equipment
Jim Hutchins
Chicopee, MA: Clean Run Productions, 2002

The Dog Agility Page
(articles, event listings, and information)
www.dogpatch.org/agility

To locate a local agility club:
American Kennel Club (AKC) www.akc.org/clubs/search
United States Dog Agility Association (USDAA) www.usdaa.com

Freestyle

Dancing with Your Dog
Sandra Davis
Book and videos available through caninefreestyle.com or dogwise.com
El Paso, TX: Dancing Dogs Video, 1997

Canine Freestyle Federation
www.canine-freestyle.org

Musical Dog Sport Association
www.musicaldogsport.org

The World Canine Freestyle Organization (WCFO)
www.worldcaninefreestyle.org

Rally O

Rally-O: The Style of Rally Obedience
Charles L. Kramer
Fancee Publications, 2005

AKC style   www.akc.org.clubs/search (type in Rally)
APDT style   www.apdt.com/rallyo

Tracking

Following Ghosts: Developing the Tracking Relationship
Suzanne Clothier and John Rice
Johnsville, NY: Flying Dog Press, 1996 ISBN 0964652986

Fun Nosework for Dogs
Roy Hunter
Eliot, ME: Howln Moon Press, 2003 ISBN 1-888994-03-7

To locate a local tracking club:
www.akc.org/clubs/search

PUBLICATIONS

The Whole Dog Journal
www.whole-dog-journal.com
(articles can be downloaded)
Subscriptions: 1-800-828-9165
Back issues: 1-800-424-7887

FIND A BEHAVIOR SPECIALIST/TRAINER

Association of Pet Dog Trainers (APDT)
www.apdt.com, 1-800-PET-DOGS
(See listings on web site for Certified Pet Dog Trainers—CPDTs)

Certified Applied Animal Behaviorists
www.animalbehavior.org

International Association of Animal Behavior Consultants (IAABC)
www.iaabc.org

Veterinary Behaviorists
www.veterinarybehaviorists.org

Applied Companion Animal Behavior Network
www.acabn.com/canine.html

PRODUCTS

Calming Cap
Premier Pet Products
www.premier.com, 800-933-5595

Comfort Zone (DAP diffuser and spray)
Available at many pet supply stores and online retailers (search Google)

DAP Collar
www.entirelypets.com
800-889-8967
www.petrx.com
888-887-3879

i-click (clicker with soft sound)
www.clickertraining.com
1-800-47-CLICK

K9 Cruiser (bicycle attachment)
www.k9cruiser.com/561-477-4458

K9 Freedom harness (front-clip harness)
www.waynehightower.com
800-246-6336

Kong®, Molecuball™, Buster Cube®
www.jbpet.com 800-526-0388
www.petedge.com 800-738-3343 (and your local pet supply store)

Muzzles
www.morrco.com
800-575-1451

Premier Gentle Leader® Easy Walk™ Harness
Available at pet supply stores and online retailers (search Google).

SENSE-ible™ and SENSE-ation™ Harnesses
(front-clip body harnesses)
www.softouchconcepts.com
866-305-6145

Sound CDs for Desensitization
www.Hanaleipets.com (click on "Training")
www.Legacycanine.com

Springer (bicycle attachment)
www.springerusa.com
801-532-7941

Tethers
www.dogwhispererdvd.com
www.pettethers.com

Waist Leash
www.buddysys.com
888-363-2818

MISCELLANEOUS

Dremeling Nails

Doberdawn.com
http://www.neholistic.com/articles/0098.htm
or go to Google and type in "dremel dog nails"

Index